A CONGRESSIONAL RECORD

THE MEMOIR
OF BERNIE SISK

Bernie and Reta Sisk on their thirty-sixth wedding anniversary.

A CONGRESSIONAL RECORD

THE MEMOIR
OF BERNIE SISK

AN ORAL HISTORY

B. F. SISK

Interviews Conducted By

A. I. DICKMAN

Head, Oral History Office, University of California, Davis

Preface By Bob Bergland, Secretary of Agriculture

Introduction By Associate Justice Kenneth Andreen

PANORAMA WEST
FRESNO, CALIFORNIA

Library of Congress Catalog Card Number 80-84208
International Standard Book Number 0-914330-36-5

Dedicated to my wife, Reta,
with all of my love and thanks for her loyalty
and devotion over the past fifty years.

CONTENTS

HISTORY OF THE SISK
INTERVIEW

The oral history program of the University of California, Davis, has focused on the field of agriculture. Bernie Sisk, U.S. congressman for twenty-four consecutive years (1955-1979), had served on the House Agricultural Committee and had authored, managed and seen enacted into law the legislation authorizing the San Luis Project which is of major significance to agriculture in California.

Later, the Rules Committee, on which Mr. Sisk served, depended upon him to brief it on the merits of water bills affecting many portions of the country, thus bringing within his sphere of influence matters affecting agriculture nationally.

For these reasons, the U.C. Davis oral history office and its faculty advisory committee believed that securing the Sisk memoir was of prime importance to its collection of the experiences of persons whose activities are of unusual significance to agriculture.

The Davis oral history program receives its funds entirely from off-campus sources. A committee of Fresno citizens sought contributions for the memoir of Mr. Sisk, who had retired from the Congress in January 1979.

As interviewer-editor, I met with Mr. Sisk seven times from March 22, 1979 through September 7, 1979 at his home on North Van Ness Boulevard in Fresno. The final two sessions were of marathon proportions, each lasting about seven hours. The Sisks were planning to attend a school and family reunion in Texas in October and he was keen to complete the taping before he left.

In preparation for the interviews which were to be taped, I talked to Fresno area people about the congressman's career. I learned of Mr. Sisk's willingness to serve his constituents. "It didn't matter whether you were rich or poor, though if you were poor, he seemed to work even harder," I was told. The point was repeatedly made that while Mr. Sisk had left his imprint on national policy, and had earned the respect of his colleagues in Congress, the common folk above all loved him for his readiness to act in their behalf.

As the taping progressed, there were many unexpected dividends. Mr. Sisk explained, as simply and clearly as possible, how the House of Representatives functions and practical ways to better communicate with your congressman. Mr. Sisk provided a fascinating sketch of the presidents, vice-presidents and congressional leaders with whom he served.

I feel deeply privileged to have participated in this project.

A. I. Dickman
Interviewer-editor

PREFACE

I was elected to the Congress in November 1970, and served with Bernie Sisk until his retirement. For two terms he and I were colleagues on the Agriculture Committee. Due to a rules change he gave up serving on the Agriculture Committee to serve exclusively on the Committee on Rules, but all during that time he and I were friends and had a fine working relationship.

When I was first elected I went to seek Bernie's advice as one of the more senior Agriculture Committee members, not necessarily on issues, because California and Minnesota had few things in common in terms of commodity policy-making. Bernie was regarded as a conservative by many who didn't know him. It is true that he represented his district well and became a moderate just because that is what his constituents wanted, but his conservative label was due primarily to his oft-stated disrespect for people who have no staying power. Many of our liberal friends could be put in that latter category. The basic advice and reassurances he gave me from time to time were to that question—staying power.

Bernie would always be at hearings. He would always listen and usually took part in the questioning based on evidence, not hearsay. Many of my friends would show up late, if at all, and were not prepared to raise legitimate points but preferred to deal in slogans/cliches. That used to irritate Bernie no end because he knew they couldn't be counted on when the going got rough. Bernie understood that a member's allegiance to his district was second, of course, to national security and other overriding federal questions, but that a member's attention to his or her district was more important than his or her membership in a party or caucus. Those traits tended to make him an influential person because we all knew his judgment was sound and he was willing on request to give advice.

Many of my senior colleagues were of sound judgment but, for their own reasons, didn't share advice with junior members. He, therefore, was a stabilizing influence in the whole House, and while a legislative body needs to have advocates making arguments which are not mainstream, it also needs to have responsible management that brings matters to a head. That is where Bernie excelled.

I am pleased to call him my friend.

Bob Bergland
Secretary
Department of Agriculture

ACKNOWLEDGEMENTS

The oral history interviewer customarily prepares a list of tentative questions which he asks of the person being interviewed. In following this procedure, I was helped by a number of persons. Dr. Alan Paterson, co-author of *The Sacramento-San Joaquin Delta: The Evolution and Implementation of Water Policy*, suggested questions on water and later commented on the first draft of the transcript. Professor Nelson W. Polsby of the department of political science at U.C. Berkeley, the author of many articles and books on the Congress and the presidency, read and remarked on the first draft. He was also consulted during the course of the interview.

Congressman Tony Coelho, who succeeded Mr. Sisk in office and had served as his administrative assistant, discussed the Sisk years in Congress. His observations helped greatly in formulating the material. Mr. Jackson Carle, who managed the initial Sisk campaign in 1954 and became Sisk's first administrative asssistant, provided keen insight into the events of the political campaigns and the workings of the congressional office. He also reviewed the first draft and made useful suggestions.

University of California Cooperative Extension/Fresno County Farm Director William R. Hambleton, and Farm Advisors W. R. Sheesley and R. N. Eide, provided background information and generously made available the facilities of their offices.

Fresno agriculturists, including Russell Giffen, Jack Woolf, Dick Markarian, Bill McFarland, George Ilg, John Weidert and others, encouraged the enterprise and provided background information.

Henry Schacht of California Canners and Growers was the initial contact between the oral history office and Congressman Sisk. Charles Morrissey, who was then engaged in collecting taped profiles of former members of Congress, aided in setting the focus for the interview.

On the U.C. Davis campus, numerous faculty, library and cooperative extension members contributed ideas and instruction, including Karl H. Ingebretsen, Warren Johnston, Gordon King, Alex McCalla, Jerry A. Moles, John Owen and Doyle Reed. Ted Gould improved chapter headings. Professor Elliot Gilbert suggested the title of the memoir.

Betty Cornelius, long-time worker in the Fresno congressional office, provided access to records and gave invaluable information about casework.

A. I. Dickman
Interviewer-editor

INTRODUCTION

*(Justice Andreen's remarks were originally delivered
March 30, 1978 during a testimonial dinner for Congressman Sisk
at the Fresno Townehouse.)*

We all know that Congressman Sisk is too humble to mention his own achievements. The plaques and awards given him tonight are some indication of the scope of his work, but there is much more. Let's recall a few incidents taken from an outstanding record. Some that we mention concern Mr. Sisk's everyday work in the office; others are monumental accomplishments affecting his district and nation.

What would you do if the Friant-Kern Canal were flooding your farm with unwanted water? First, you might try self-help and build a dike so that the water would go elsewhere. But suppose your tractor bogs down in the mud—what would you do? Should you call the sheriff? The Board of Supervisors? The flood control district? The Bureau of Reclamation? You might, but one smart farmer who found himself in this predicament called Congressman B. F. Sisk. At that time Mr. Sisk was in the process of moving into his Washington office after his first election in 1954. In two and one-half hours Mr. Sisk was back on the phone to the farmer. He did not say, "I'm going to get on it," or "I told so-and-so to do something." No, he told the farmer: "The leak is fixed and your tractor is out of the mud." Two and one-half hours! Nothing happens that fast in government—unless it comes to the attention of Bernie Sisk.

That call from the farmer was the first time a constituent asked Mr. Sisk for help. Since then thousands of valley citizens have called him after finding they could not make their way through the labyrinth of governmental machinery. When they called their congressman, they found somebody who would cut red tape and get them the service they deserved.

The name on the ballot has always read "B. F. Sisk." But to the multitude he has helped and to the thousands of people who are his friends, including those in this audience, he is affectionately called "Bernie."

Nobody who has requested assistance has ever been asked if he or she is a Republican or Democrat, or even registered to vote. All are treated alike. This sometimes creates surprises. Recently a lady near Sanger wrote to complain that the place was teeming with illegal aliens, and that she was having difficulty earning a livelihood because of the competition. Congressman Sisk alerted the Border Patrol. Agents took care of the problem and then reported back that his constituent was a "lady of the night." One way of looking at it is that Bernie struck a blow for law and order. At least now, that illegal activity is not done by illegals.

There are many reasons why Bernie is admired. He has left his imprint on national policy; has won the respect of his fellow members in Congress, and has sponsored bills which have created great public works. But the common people in his district will remember and love him most for his readiness to act as their ombudsman in dealing with gigantic government. You know, big government would not be bad if it were made up entirely of people like Bernie Sisk!

But Bernie has done much more than attend to the legitimate needs and aspirations of his constituents.

The San Luis Project is a striking demonstration of the legislative abilities of its key sponsor. There were a thousand hazards and delays that beset every stage of that bill. The State of California unexpectedly sought to share use of the reservoir, the powerful [Los Angeles] Metropolitan Water District had its own agenda, the delta interests had to be placated. There were many more.

To achieve compromise among the diverse interests of federal and state governments, to reconcile Northern and Southern California, to accommodate the delta and satisfy Santa Cruz and Santa Clara and Contra Costa, to stand against the proponents of the Kern County concept, to deal equitably with governors, senators, bureau chiefs and fellow congressmen and at the same time achieve his objective demanded great ability and influence. It would take consummate craftsmanship for any congressman to get such a vast and imaginative project passed over such determined opposition. San Luis is the largest single project in the history of the Bureau of Reclamation. For a third-term congressman to secure it is an achievement that compels admiration.

For his patience and skill in reconciling the various competing interests, the non-partisan, non-profit educational organization "The California Congressional Recognition Plan" singled out Congressman Sisk for "special recognition," its highest accolade. Incidentally, that group has repeatedly designated Bernie as an outstanding congressman who rendered public service of unusual merit.

Bernie's skill was again demonstrated when he acted as a mediator between the interests of the Kings River Water Association and the Bureau of Reclamation. He helped negotiate a contract which started delivery of water while two or three issues were left for the courts to decide. There was no dispute that a million acres of land needed water. Mr. Sisk's pragmatic approach was to start irrigation and then resolve the disputes in a fair way through court processes.

And while we are on the subject of water, it must come as a great relief to those people who live on the flood plains of the Fresno and Chowchilla rivers to know that Bernie was able to get authorized and financed the Hidden and Buchanan dams. There was an article in the *Fresno Bee* last Friday which described the extensive flooding that would have occurred this year had it not been for those flood control projects. Now, instead of causing widespread devastation, the water stored behind those dams will be put to beneficial uses.

But Congressman Sisk's attention has not been restricted to his district. After Russia launched Sputnik and boasted that it was foremost in the conquest of space, the House Committee on Science and Astronautics was born. This was a blue ribbon committee and positions on it were much desired. The leadership selected Bernie to serve on the committee and through that work NASA was born, ultimately placing the first man on the moon.

Bernie's leadership abilities were not lost on Sam Rayburn, who made our congressman his personal choice to serve on the Rules Committee. The importance of this committee cannot be overstated since legislation goes there for presentation to the House after it has been acted upon by the committee which originated the bill. As a member of that committee, Bernie helped to determine which bills reached the floor.

It had long been an informal regulation, respected by both parties, that members of the Committee on Rules could not hold seats on any other major standing committee. Through special dispensation by a vote of the full House, this rule was suspended in Mr. Sisk's case so he could also serve on the Committee on Agriculture, where he acted to protect the agricultural interests of this district. This unprecedented action by his fellow congressmen is an indication of their high esteem for him. He sat on that committee until Congressman Krebs was elected, at which time he stepped aside and enabled Mr. Krebs to take a seat on the panel.

As another indication of the great respect his colleagues had for him, Mr. Sisk was appointed chairman of the Rules Subcommittee on Congressional Reorganization. This was a sensitive subject; his skills of compromise and his attitudes of moderation were sorely taxed on this job. He did not secure all of the reforms he wanted, but he got all that was obtainable. The Legislative Reorganization Act of 1970 did much to substitute modern procedures and technology for the former archaic ways. One of the benefits was a rule permitting the televising of House committee meetings. This resulted in the public being able to watch the hearings on Watergate held by the House Judiciary Committee.

Congressman Sisk also designed and won approval of the Budget Control and Impoundment Act, which freed funds impounded by former President Nixon and at the same time made Congress more responsible for budget preparation.

In order to make the committee more liberal, Congressman Sisk was appointed to the District of Columbia Committee. He was able to get through the House the first home rule bill in seventy-five years. It was an excellent proposal based on the California plan for chartering municipal governments. It failed to pass the Senate, but was an important step towards home rule for the citizens of the District of Columbia. The next year he threw his weight behind President Johnson's successful home rule plan. Why do I mention this here in Fresno, so many thousands of miles from the District of Columbia? It shows two things: Mr. Sisk's abiding belief in according all people democratic processes; and that he could take the most lackluster of committee assignments and fashion it into a position of influence and power.

Bernie has been able to accomplish all this by hard work, integrity, party regularity and close relationships with the other leaders of the House. Adding to his effectiveness is the ability to disagree with his colleagues without alienating them.

Putting a man on the moon or pulling a man's tractor out of the mud, and all of the thousands of other good works that have been accomplished, came only with arduous, tension-ridden days—and nights. We regret his decision not to run for re-election, knowing that he is stronger now than ever before and that he would have an easy victory. But Bernie, we understand your and Reta's desire to retire after a quarter of a century of public service. We wish you happiness in your retirement.

We, your friends, are not in this room because of anything that you can do for us. We are here because we love and respect you.

And finally, Bernie, we want to give you a resounding "thank you" and to let you know that whenever we review your record, we vote "Well Done."

Kenneth Andreen
Associate Justice, Fifth District Court of Appeal

Part 1:

DOWN HOME YEARS

Bernie Sisk in retirement is an exceptionally busy man, working on major civic and community projects within the city and county of Fresno, as well as continuing his lay activity in the Church of Christ.

That he chose to interrupt his hectic schedule to include oral history interviews reflects a reverence for history he developed as a small boy at the knee of his maternal grandfather. Sisk felt a responsibility to posterity in providing the highlights and insights of his twenty-four years (1955-1979) as a member of the U.S. House of Representatives.

The first seven chapters of *A Congressional Record* deal with Sisk's memorable "down home" years in Texas, a boyhood flavored with morning pony rides to school, an intimate network of family ties, diligent religious training, and a feeling for the land.

"Diverse" is the word for the young Bernie Sisk: high school valedictorian, horseman, oil roustabout, business college student, cotton plant manager, trucker, gas station attendant, baseball buff.

Sisk recounts marrying his high school sweetheart, and how the new couple faced the twin calamities of the thirties, the depression and the severe drought that followed.

Episodes of that time linger: Ailing with what was then called yellow jaundice and too weak to drive his truck, Sisk yielded the wheel to his wife Reta who, with their baby on the front seat beside her, hauled a load of crated glass 125 miles, enabling her husband to collect his paycheck.

The themes reflected in Sisk's youth permeate the book: a sense of tolerance, the resourcefulness of one reared in the Southwest, faith and fundamentalism, a fondness for the agrarian spirit.

Sisk emerges as a figure of transition, a man who spans eras in twentieth century America, moving from a Dust Bowl boyhood, via his own bootstraps, to the highest councils in American government.

1

1.
Origins

AID:*   *What do you know about your ancestors?*

SISK: Most of my information has been put together by other members of the family; my granddaughter and my older daughter. It looks like the Sisks came to this country around 1670. They are basically of Scottish-Irish-English descent.

The Sisk name was not a very common one. George Sisk, a building contractor in Ireland, wrote to me many years ago, asking where my people had come from. Some friends in Fresno were flying to Ireland. I said in fun, "Why don't you look up my cousins?" They made a point to visit this George Sisk who learned what I looked like, my height and build and coloration. He said, "He is one of us. He is definitely one of the clan." He told them that we are descended from Spanish sailors who were shipwrecked around 1300 A.D. off Ireland and some of the sailors stayed in Ireland.

My paternal great-grandfather, David Sisk, came down from the Carolinas about 1850. The initial Sisk family apparently spread out around the line of where North and South Carolina are today, around Shelbyville. I understand I have a relative by the name of Sisk who was killed in the Battle of Kings Mountain. Before Great-grandfather David there was apparently a Robin Sisk, my great-great-grandfather. Robin was a name that seemed to be characteristic of that time. My grandfather's name was Benjamin Franklin Sisk. He was called Frank; I don't think they ever used the name Ben. He was a native of North Georgia. Grandfather Sisk was too young to be in the service during the war, but he took the family cattle and horses and drove them into the mountains, and stayed with them to keep Sherman and his troops from capturing them. He saved most of their animals. Their nearest town of any size was Chattanooga, which was, of course, a big battleground.

My paternal Sisks and maternal Dodds and Hawkinsons worked on the railroads. Grandfather Sisk and a great uncle of mine, Bud Sisk, both worked for the Southern Railway. My great uncle had been a conductor and retired on pension, after more than forty years with Southern Railway. Uncle Bud and Aunt Lou Sisk came to visit us when I was just a

---

*A. I. Dickman is indicated as "AID" throughout the transcript.

little kid. They had a pass on the railroad. I thought that was great because they could go anywhere they wanted to go.

Around 1912 Grandfather Sisk decided to retire. He went up to Burk Burnett on the Red River that, at one time, was the biggest oil boom town in the world. We always called it Burk. Oil was discovered around 1917. My grandfather had this little house on twenty acres out in the suburbs of Burk. Then all of a sudden, they discovered oil at 140 feet. When I went there they had six pumping wells on my grandfather's place. I guess at one point he was worth quite a lot of money. The in-laws all swarmed in. (Neither my father nor his brother went to Burk. They stayed away because they weren't inclined towards oil at all. They were basically farmers.) His daughters had husbands, several of whom rushed in to take care of my grandfather's business. Grandfather Sisk went down to Duncan, Oklahoma, where he passed away. He and my grandmother are buried in the Duncan cemetery. Grandfather Sisk died, I believe, in 1923. Grandmother Sisk died in 1935.

AID: *Was there any inheritance that came down to you or your brothers or sisters from the oil money?*

SISK: No; there was some money divided eight ways because there were eight children, six girls and two boys. Nothing got down to the second generation.

AID: *What was your mother's maiden name?*

SISK: Lavina Thomas. She was born in Montague, Texas, also my birthplace, on November 7, 1884. Her father was Richard Orden Thomas.

AID: *What was his occupation?*

SISK: I guess you would say, a farmer. His father, John Thomas, was in Texas before the Texas revolution. He apparently went there as a youngster, sixteen, seventeen years old, around 1820. Of course, the Texas revolution, when Mexico was defeated at the Battle of San Jacinto, was in 1836. He was there at that time. My Great-grandfather John Thomas was the first sheriff of Lamar County, Texas. Apparently, in those days, county sheriff was a pretty lucrative profession because Great-grandfather Thomas at one time had quite a large estate. In fact, it is reputed that near the time of the Civil War he owned some two hundred slaves. He freed them all at the time of the Emancipation Proclamation. They had no place to go so they stayed on the plantation. There, they ate them out of house and home because the plantation shared whatever food it had. Great-grandfather Thomas, who passed away shortly after the war, pretty well lost everything he had—which was not unusual during that period of time, the late 1860s.

My grandfather was one of four boys and several girls. Grandfather Thomas enlisted in the War Between the States and got into the cattle business after the war. The Thomas family may have been related to Cynthia Chisholm, who lived in the vicinity of present-day Dallas.

Sisk's Grandfather and Grandmother Thomas in 1891.

According to Texans in that area, her name was given to the Chisholm Trail. My grandfather herded cattle up into Kansas to the railheads in the 1860s and 1870s. Montague, Texas is where Grandfather Thomas settled after he was married. My grandmother was Martha Mitchell. My wife was a Mitchell. People kid us that maybe we are distant cousins although we don't have records that say it is true. Montague, her birthplace, is only about seventy-five miles outside of Fort Worth. It is on the Red River, just across the river from Oklahoma. It was Indian territory in those days, of course.

AID: *What were the dates of deaths of your grandparents Thomas?*

SISK: Grandfather Thomas died in 1923 around January twentieth. He died just a few days before his eightieth birthday. Grandmother Thomas died in December 1931, not long before my oldest daughter was born. She was buried in Clarendon, Texas.

5

Arthur Lee Sisk, B. F.'s father, in 1905.

William Jennings Bryan Thomas, Sisk's only living uncle.

AID: *Did they have family plots?*

SISK: Yes, a number of my mother's people settled around Clarendon. My Uncle Frank Thomas is buried there; so is my Uncle Dick Thomas and my Uncle John Thomas. In my mother's family, there were four boys and three girls. Her two older sisters, named Mary and Mattie, are both buried in Lubbock, Texas. All the boys are deceased, except one. My mother's baby brother Bryan is still living in Electra, Texas. He is in his eighties so I go to see him when I can.

Grandfather Thomas served during the major part of the Civil War and was wounded in the Battle of Shiloh in Mississippi. It was a peculiar wound because the bullet cut open his forehead but ricocheted off. Another bullet at the same time split his foot open. He carried these scars to his grave.

AID: *In what town was your father born?*

SISK: Plainville, Georgia.

AID: *Do you remember his date of birth?*

SISK: August 30, 1883. His name was Arthur Lee Sisk.

AID: *Did he have any brothers or sisters?*

SISK: He had a younger brother and six sisters. There were two boys and six girls in my father's family. The girls were rather prolific; they all had rather substantial families. His brother never had any children. My father lived in Georgia until he was around twenty years old. My father's family,

6

Arthur and Lavina Sisk mark their fiftieth anniversary in 1956.

after the War Between the States, was typical of southern people; they were very poor. (In those days people didn't know they were poor; I was a poor kid with patches on my pants and I didn't know it because I had plenty to eat. Nowadays everybody knows if he or she is poor; people are poverty-line.) My father had very little basic education. He told me that it was, at the most, a third grade education. Where they lived they would only have about three or four months of school each year. Perhaps because of family need (I don't know exactly), he went into the cotton mill when he was only twelve years old, sweeping and so on. His sisters worked in the cotton mills in Dalton and Calhoun and Plainville.

Before Oklahoma became a state, my father worked on the railroad in the Choctaw nation and the Chickasaw nation. Then his parents came down to Texas and my grandfather bought a farm in Montague County. That is where my father met my mother and they were married in 1906. She was a native of Texas. In spite of my father's lack of formal education, I think he was a very brilliant man. He educated himself and was an excellent businessman later on, when he got into the cotton gin business. He was excellent in math, and in his head could do more figuring than I could do on paper.

AID: *What about family health traits?*

SISK: My family was fairly healthy. Grandfather Sisk died of a heart attack in his seventies. Grandfather Thomas never had any heart problems but as a

7

youngster he had a kidney problem. However, he was over eighty when he died. My father had a serious heart attack in his sixties. My father's youngest sister, a very lovely woman named Hazel, who had long blond hair to her waist, died at a fairly early age of pellagra, something you never hear of today. It is caused by a faulty diet, yet she married a rather wealthy man who certainly could afford the best food. I don't understand what happened.

AID: *What are the family food preferences?*

SISK: When my wife wants to be real nice to me she fixes what we call a Texas dinner, consisting of roasting ears of corn, black-eyed peas, corn bread, fresh cucumbers, fried okra and bacon and buttermilk. I love it.

My mother's baby brother, who lived with us, came along about the time of William Jennings Bryan, a man his parents thought was one of the great men of his time. They named him William Jennings Bryan Thomas and he is known as Bryan Thomas. Years later, when I was in Congress, I was in Lincoln, Nebraska. I was chairman of the Veterans Affairs Hospitals Subcommittee and the Veterans Administration was trying to move the veterans hospital out of Lincoln. (This story has to do with Bryan so I am telling it here.) This was in the mid-fifties and I was there with their congressman. Governor Anderson, a friendly man, had a reception for us at the capitol and on the way we came to a huge statue of William Jennings Bryan—at least twenty, maybe thirty feet high. I mentioned something about my grandfather and my uncle named Bryan and that night they inducted me into the Great Navy of Nebraska. Nebraska sits on an ocean of underground water—hence, the navy. Andy Devine, the gravel-throated comedian, was inducted with me. It was quite a show and the governor made a speech expressing the appreciation of Lincoln and the state of Nebraska for my efforts in retaining the hospital there. He presented me with an official document that gave me title to the statue of Bryan. The only problem was that I had only forty-eight hours in which to move it!

AID: *Your grandfathers on both sides played an active role in your life?*

SISK: They did. Grandfather Thomas had the greatest impact on me because I was closer to him at the period of my life when I was more subject to influence. My grandparents Thomas and my Uncle Bryan lived with us. My well-educated Grandfather Thomas was well-versed in history and took an active part in local county affairs. He may have been tax collector or assessor.

I just loved to sit at Grandfather's knee while he talked about the Civil War and Texas history. In fact, I had a kind of hunger for it. I still read all kinds of history books, including historical novels.

Grandfather Thomas' activity in the courthouse gave him considerable knowledge in the law and he helped all kinds of people in a variety of ways. Naturally, he was a Democrat; he was also a rebel and could let out the rebel yell. To him, "damnyankee" was one word.

AID: *What natural disasters happened to members of your family?*

SISK: Montague County was like a tornado alley. My Grandfather Thomas' house was blown away one time and my Uncle Oscar Sisk's house was totally destroyed. They were in the storm cellar underneath the house and the house just took off, over their heads. He had two wagons, one very old one and the other brand new. The tornado picked up the new mule wagon and tore it apart; pieces were found over a mile away. The old wagon didn't even roll off its tracks.

2.
Growing Up Years

AID: *Now let's get you into the picture.*

SISK: I was born on December 14, 1910, in the county of Montague, one of the earliest settled counties in Texas, on the Red River south of what was once Indian territory, now Oklahoma. Nearby is the town of Montague, the county seat. I remember clearly the old courthouse on the square, a barber shop, a blacksmith's shop and a little market. It hasn't changed much even though the county has had a decrease in population. Because of the competition between the towns of Bowie and Saint Jo, neither could get enough votes to become the county seat. My wife and I visited the old courthouse several years ago and she still kids me that when we entered the building, a hen came wandering down the hall. My oldest sister is buried in the Montague cemetery. She died during her first year of life, before I was born.

AID: *Incidentally, does your will give instructions as to where you wish to be buried?*

SISK: Yes, we have acquired our plots in Belmont Gardens in Fresno.

AID: *What about your name?*

SISK: I have the same initials as my Grandfather Benjamin Franklin Sisk, but my mother, for some reason, had a strong feeling against the name of Ben. They compromised and I was given his initials, but my name is Bernice Frederick. Like the song, "A Boy Named Sue," that led to certain situations for me I won't go into here.

I have two younger sisters, the older one born when I was three years old. Her name is Lloyd. The family has remarked that my mother was mixed up on names. My other sister, Opal, is eight years younger than I am. She was born during the rough winter of 1918 when we were living on a cattle ranch sixty miles east of Amarillo in caprock country. Tens of thousands of cattle froze to death that winter.

9

AID: *Please describe the house in which you were born.*

SISK: It was about two miles east of Montague in fairly rural country. Italian people around the turn of the century had moved into the area and improved the land and planted vineyards. Some of my earliest recollections are about my playmates, the children of the Barney and Andrew Fenoglio families.

AID: *What crops did your father grow?*

SISK: Cotton, corn, milo, and peanuts. We had a large family garden and a pear orchard that covered several acres. My father would pick the pears and load them into the wagon. Mother would pack him food to take along and he would leave early in the morning and be gone from three days to a week, peddling pears across the river in Oklahoma, which was still called Indian territory. He would make several trips each pear harvest season.

AID: *What kind of stock did he have on the farm?*

SISK: My father loved good stock and wanted the best horses and mules he could get. He always had a riding horse so he could saddle up and ride.

AID: *When did you learn to ride?*

SISK: Probably, they put me on a horse when I was a couple of years old. Later, when I was about six, we moved to the panhandle, where I rode horseback to school. I was practically raised on a horse.

I was about six years old when we moved up to the Amarillo country. My father was a kind of pioneer, I guess. Things were getting a little close for him in Montague, people moving in so our neighbors were within a mile of us. My mother's brother lived in Alanreed and another brother lived in Clarendon, the county seat of the adjoining county. Dad went up and looked over the situation and liked it; it would give him room for more cattle and stock. So he bought some land and leased some about seven miles from Alanreed. This was practically all ranch country located in what was called "the breaks." Amarillo is in the north plains and is as

Reta Sisk pays a visit in March 1955 to the old Sisk homestead in Alanreed, Texas.

level as a billiard table until you come down to Jericho, about fifty miles away. Then it breaks off into the caprock country, with creeks bringing down a lot of water to grow good grass. The Rock Island Railroad went through Alanreed, which is where we got our mail. It was a trading post for the ranchers and cowboys and had a pretty tough reputation. In fact, it was called "Gouge-eye" because of some rough fights that occurred there. I remember that three or four men were killed in a shootout. Later, the bank was held up.

The move to this country from Montague was made by what was called an "immigrant car." All of our furniture was loaded into a boxcar and the horses and mules were loaded into the center of the car. Dad rode in the freight train so that he could water and feed his stock. The rest of us took the passenger train. Today the trip would be about a three-hour drive. Then, we got on the Fort Worth-Denver train across the edge of Oklahoma, where we changed to the Rock Island Railroad. The trains would switch around and it took three days to make the trip. But we always traveled by train if the trip was any distance. Indians used the train a great deal.

AID: *From what tribes?*

SISK: Shawnees, Chickasaws, Choctaws, Seminoles, among others. Oklahoma had a great mix of Indians. Anadarko was and is today a large Indian center. In those days, Indians wore native dress and long hair that hung clear down to their belts. I would stand very close to my mother as they passed by. They attended school in the Indian territory. None attended our school.

AID: *How many head of cattle did your father have?*

SISK: There were times when he had as many as two or three hundred head, mostly beef cattle, Herefords, although he milked from twelve to fifteen Jerseys. What milk we didn't drink went into the hand-turned separator, but it turned so hard it's no wonder my father suffered a heart attack later on.

Our only refrigeration, if you could call it that, was good cold West Texas water pumped from 200 feet underground by a windmill. The well water went into a milk trough made out of two-by-twelves and lined with bricks. Mother put the milk and other perishables in that fresh cold water. Dad would take the cream about seven miles into town to a small creamery where it was tested and paid for. The creamery put it on the train to Amarillo where it was made into butter.

AID: *You fed the skim and whey to the hogs?*

SISK: It was great hog feed. Late in the spring my folks would decide to butcher six or seven hogs and these were fed accordingly. Hog-killing time followed a good hard freeze, usually in November, and I would stay home from school. Dad would go over to the neighbors' and four or five families would get together. Of course, all of the kids loved to watch

11

what was going on. Once, Dad shot the pigs; I wasn't allowed to watch. Anyway, after the hogs were stuck and hung up, Mother would use practically everything, but she would never put sausage in hog gut. She made bags out of cotton or duck cloth, turned them inside out and stuffed the sausage in them. She cured her own meat. Man, we would eat that sausage and ham all winter long.

AID: *Tell me about your early schooling, please.*

SISK: I rode to school on a horse named Beauty. She was a little bay pony and when my sister started school she rode behind me on the pony. The Whitefish School was about four miles away and was anchored by large guy wires to keep it from blowing away in the seventy-mile-per-hour winds that blew there. My father became head of the school board and persuaded the ranchers to build a more substantial schoolhouse. In the old schoolhouse when the wind blew hard, the blackboard would bend and sway as you wrote on it. One teacher taught seven grades and once in a while would try to carry an eighth grade. Usually from fifteen to twenty-five students were in attendance. Kids would go to school about five months out of the year—they were picking cotton until nearly December and in March they were helping with all of the spring jobs in the fields. However, during my last few years, it had become a seven-month school.

I had one teacher named Jerry Phillips; he was about six feet eight inches tall and was a pretty good baseball player. I was a natural left-hander and Phillips was bound and determined to change me to writing right-handed. I had a terrible time and would slip the chalk back to my left hand. When he saw me doing that, he would throw erasers at me.

We had some young beautiful female teachers, probably only seventeen or eighteen years old. I understand about falling in love with your teacher. Hiring teachers was difficult because you had to find a family willing to board the teacher. When I was in the sixth grade, my Uncle William Jennings Bryan Thomas became the teacher and remained for many years. Because I was his nephew, he was pretty rough on me.

I was a happy youngster even though I was a bit of a lone wolf, having no brothers to play with, and my sisters were younger. I spent Saturdays on my horse; Mother would fix me some lunch and I would take off across the country. I would ride to the let-down where you could trip the fence wire loose and lead your horse across and go to the canyon containing a lot of petrified wood. I loved it.

Later, my father allowed me to ride Nell, an excellent riding mare who was high-spirited and, of course, much larger than my pony, Beauty. We also had a junior-type rodeo where the son of Bunk Stubbs (the man from whom my father bought the ranch), who was older than I, taught me how to ride yearlings. We used a loose surcingle, just a rope around the horse's belly, that you could hang on to. Although I had already ridden calves, this was different and I went scooting across the corral on my nose. The older boy said I was doing real well so I tried again and was thrown off. I was ready to call it quits but my friend insisted I try it again. This time, I was not only thrown off but stomped on. My mother came out and cleaned off my bruises and the dirt. Later, I learned how to rope yearlings and to race our horses.

The two creeks we had to cross to get to school would freeze over in the winter and all of the dirt roads would ice up, too. I knew better than to ride my horse over ice, but one day I was in a hurry and my horse slipped and fell, catching my leg underneath. She tried to get up but her hooves would slip; there we were until a cowboy came along and got the horse up and off me. I was late getting home and my family had worried, but that was the atmosphere in which I grew up.

One night, after I had forgotten to round up some cows during the day, my father sent me out in the dark. I saddled up my pony and about a half-mile from the house she stepped into a hole and stumbled. I flew over her head and hit my head on the ground. I was knocked out for a while. Fortunately, my father had trained all of the horses not to move once the reins touched the ground, so when I came to, I climbed on her back and rode home. By this time, the family was out looking for me.

AID: *Did you have regular chores?*

SISK: Yes. When I was about eight or nine I milked cows—two of the gentlest Jerseys we had. We had a hired hand as milker who was paid thirty dollars a month and "found," which meant money plus board and room.

AID: *Were these all Anglo-Saxon hands?*

SISK: Oh yes, I don't remember seeing a non-white. There were no blacks or Hispanics either. You would see Indians occasionally, but they stayed to themselves.

AID: *What was your religious background?*

SISK: Both sides of the family were straight-laced religious people, rather strict and conservative-thinking. The Sisk family, as far back as we have found, were Methodist. The Dodds, my maternal grandmother's family, were Baptist. She was dominant so Grandfather Sisk became Baptist. My father was originally a Baptist, but on my mother's side, the Thomases as far back as my great-grandfather were members of the Christian church. I, too, am a member, as was my father.

The Church of Christ was the conservative branch of the Christian church when it divided over organization and congregational autonomy and the question of music within the worship service. I went to Sunday school regularly as a child and have been very active in the Church of Christ all of my life.

AID: *What was the role of the Bible in your upbringing?*

SISK: We read the Bible regularly and I have always kept a Bible on my desk although I don't read it as often as I should. My mother and father taught in Bible school and I did, too, later, at Abilene Christian College. Traditionally, at the table, you always expressed your thanks for your food.

AID: *Do you believe the Bible is an adequate guide for many of life's problems today?*

SISK: Basically I think that is pretty much true. My parents taught us faith in God although they frowned on miraculous healings or religious cults. But they taught the Bible as a way of life meant to be adhered to. They believed deeply in the divinity of Christ and that all of the things we enjoy from nature are God-given. I have never felt they were extremists.

AID: *In addition to giving thanks at the table, what was the role of prayer in your life?*

SISK: On occasion because of a family crisis or illness, they would pray, not for a miraculous healing but simply as a reflection of their faith in God.

AID: *Did they permit drinking of alcoholic beverages?*

SISK: No. My father never drank. After he suffered his heart attack he would drink a little port wine. I do remember a bottle marked "bottled in bond" that was in my mother's kitchen cabinet; Grandmother would very carefully measure out about an ounce and made a hot toddy for my grandfather. He would gulp it down and then go to bed. No card playing or dancing were permitted, either.

AID: *How old were you when you took your first drink?*

SISK: Probably around age nineteen. About the time I went to college they were making home brew and that stuff must have been thirty percent alcohol. The liquor was bootleg and they would drink the white corn liquor or bourbon straight, no ice or anything. Maybe I was a softie but I just didn't like the taste—or the after-effects. Today, while I still don't like the taste, I will drink a cocktail once in a while and I keep wine and serve it. I drink an occasional beer in the hot days of summer.

AID: *How about smoking?*

SISK: My father didn't smoke when I was young, although later he did smoke a pipe occasionally. Grandfather Thomas smoked a pipe. Grandfather Sisk, as far as I know, never smoked at all. I started smoking when I was in high school and I smoked cigarettes for nearly fifty years. Under pressure, maybe two packs a day. My annual physicals at Bethesda Naval Hospital were all okay, no sign of disease in my lungs, although the physicians urged me to quit on general grounds. Well, about four years ago, I had an abdominal aneurism. The main artery expanded from a normal inch and a quarter to about three inches. On my way to the hospital for the necessary surgery, the thought hit me that now would be a good time to quit. I smoked my last cigarette going to the hospital and I have not smoked since.

AID: *The surgery did the trick?*

SISK: I was out of commission for a couple of months. But I am fine now.

AID: *Did you inherit any characteristics other than your left-handedness?*

SISK: Only that. But I am the only one in the family who is. Neither of my sisters is, nor is anyone in my father's or mother's family.

AID: *Your family was made up of traditional southern Democrats?*

SISK: Yes. I remember that when I was a youngster, a family reputed to be Republican moved in. I was curious to see them because I wondered if they had horns or something. My impression, as a boy, was that they were odd and unusual because they were Republicans.

Getting back to the religious thing, once a Catholic family moved into the neighborhood. I was a kid and had never seen a Catholic. This was the atmosphere in which I grew up—everyone was white and Protestant. When my wife and I came to California after both of our children were born, we realized neither one of us had ever seen a person of Japanese descent. There are still portions of this country that are parochial and far from a melting pot.

AID: *Were there any Jews?*

SISK: I had some Jewish friends in Clarendon in Donley County. There were Jewish synagogues in Lubbock and Amarillo but none in the small communities.

AID: *Do you consider yourself to be tolerant toward other races and religions?*

SISK: I think I am, yes. One of the things said of the members of the Church of Christ was that they were supposed to be anti-Catholic. Perhaps some of them were, but I never felt that way or had any problems. My former administrative assistant and now my successor, Tony Coelho, is Catholic. He was studying for the priesthood when it was discovered he is a controllable epileptic, and that ruled him out. He finished college as a political science major and I took him to Washington with me as an aide in my office.

AID: *Where did you get your tolerance?*

SISK: My father was a very tolerant man. I have never heard my father criticize anybody. Of course, he never cussed at all. He always said that a man has a right to his opinion so he never criticized anyone for his religion or politics. He felt he had an equal right to his opinion but that if he disagreed with someone, it would be an agreeable disagreement. This has also been my personal philosophy. I guess I can be very bull-headed when I take a position, but I respect the rights of others.

As I think now of my friends and supporters, many are Catholic and many are Jews. I have many friends among blacks, Mexican-Americans and other Hispanics. Yet maybe I am not as tolerant as I think I am; introspection is always difficult. Let me be honest. If someone asked whether I would want my child or grandchild to marry someone who is black, I would have to say no. I have seen too many tragic mixed marriages. If that is intolerance, I am sorry.

I have been hurt by the occasional intolerance of others. Emilio Canales

15

of Fresno was my friend. I have eaten many times in his restaurant. He had supported my candidacy and that helped me because he was rather prominent among other Mexican-Americans. Later, Phil Sanchez, who was running against me, sold Emilio on working for him. I got word that Canales was saying I pretended to like Mexican-Americans but that I am a native of Texas and all Texans hate Mexicans. This wounded me not only because I had considered him my friend but also because I wondered about the disappearance of tolerance. When I asked him about his statement, he tried to deny it.

AID: *Please talk some more about your childhood memories.*

SISK: I remember, about the time I was seven, going with my parents in the Model T to the Baptist church in Alanreed, to listen to a new invention called a radio. My sisters and my grandparents were along, too, and the church was crowded. When the radio was turned on, there was a crackling sound but you could hear frogs croaking and some people talking. On the way home my grandfather said to my mother: "Why Vinie, you know that was the biggest fake in the world; there was somebody in the back room making those noises. Vinie, you know that." I'm not sure that my grandfather was ever convinced about the radio before he died in 1923.

Talking about that Model T, I remember my father learning how to drive it. My father had gone over to my uncle's to help him put up some hay and called my mother on the phone to tell her he would be home for lunch. We had telephones, a party line of about fifteen families. My uncle loaned him his Model T to drive home and had explained how to use the three pedals and how to fix the gas and spark and crank it, etc. We lived on a hill, at the foot of which was a wire gate that closed off our large yard. I watched for my father and saw him driving along the road, but instead of stopping at the gate to open it, he drove right through it, ripping it apart, and continued right up the hill through the yard. The dog and chickens knew he was having problems—the dog was howling and the chickens were squawking. Mother yelled at me to run into the house before Dad ran over me. Anyway, my father drove around the house and back down the hill and through the ruined gate before he could stop that car. That memory is still so comical that I can't think of it without laughing.

As I have mentioned, my father was a deeply religious man who had never learned to swear. Well, that is a disadvantage when it comes to handling mules. Old Tobe had been in the family for ages—he was probably thirty-five years old when he died—and he was generally a steady old mule with streaks of stubbornness. On this particular occasion Old Tobe was pulling a butcher knife wagon—a high narrow wagon with narrow steel treads used to pull bales of cotton. Old Tobe decided he wasn't going to pull it any more and just quit. My father got exasperated and shouted everything within his vocabulary to get Old Tobe started again, but he lacked the right cuss words. Finally Dad, who rarely lost his temper, decided he was going to move that mule and he built a small fire under him. When the flame and heat touched his flanks, Old Tobe lunged ahead a few feet and sat down. Well, that placed the wagon directly over the fire and Dad had to crawl under it to put out the fire. He hustled sand and dirt and it is one of the funniest things I remember. I didn't dare to let him see how funny it was to me, but later Dad could laugh about it.

I told you about Jerry Phillips, the schoolteacher who threw things at me to get me to stop using my left hand. Well, I became afraid of him and that gave me trouble with my multiplication tables. I had no problem with reading or history but I had one heck of a problem learning those tables. My uncle and mother decided I ought to repeat the grade but all of a sudden, one morning when I woke up, I knew my multiplication tables. Something had clicked and from that moment on I had no more trouble with math, getting top grades in plane and solid geometry and algebra, later on.

In the winter of 1918, the snow got so deep we couldn't get off the place and we didn't have much of a Christmas because we couldn't get into town. It was twenty below zero and the cattle were starving—thousands of head were lost, although we were more fortunate than some and didn't lose many of our own. I remember seeing stacks of dead cattle piled up.

AID: *How did you get along with your two sisters?*

SISK: Fine. Lloyd would ride behind me on Beauty. She was not a quarrelsome girl and usually did what I asked her to. My youngest sister was eight years younger than I and I thought of her as just a kid. She now lives in eastern New Mexico and the other sister lives close by in Dinuba. We still get along just fine.

My old English teacher, Mrs. Burleson, is living in a rest home in Meadow, Texas. She still is quite active and has retained her sense of humor. We all just loved her. In fact, we are planning to attend our fiftieth class reunion in Meadow this October and we are looking forward to seeing her. She exerted a great influence on both my wife and me. Her brother-in-law, Omar Burleson, and I both attended Abilene Christian College although he graduated in 1928 and I didn't start there until 1929. (It is Abilene Christian University now.) Incidentally, he served in Congress for thirty-two years and retired when I did in 1978.

AID: *What else do you recall about your childhood years?*

SISK: I used to go hunting at night for oppossum, raccoons, skunks and bobcats. And I trapped a little, too. I learned how to skin animals and dry the skins on a rack and sell them. With the small amount of money I made I'd buy stamps or books. Dad would always see that I had a few nickels to spend when I wanted something. He and I were very close, perhaps more so than most fathers and sons. But once he used a razor strap on me. My father, who was a very kind, loving person, had given me ample warning

17

about my bad habit of playing on my way home from school. The two creeks we had to cross had high bluffs and we would dare each other to jump off into the water. Or we would catch fish. It was easy to forget what time it was. One time I arrived home after dark. My parents were really worried. Dad asked me what had happened. I told him the truth and he said, "Son, you are just going to have to remember. We have talked about this and you know it." Then he took the strap to me. It was the only time my father ever touched me. I know it hurt him more than it hurt me.

One of my closest friends was a cousin who lived only four or five miles away. Jack Thomas was about my age and we were in the same grade. He died a foolish death that just about broke my heart. One day he had a stomach ache and they called old Dr. Coffage, because he was the closest physician even though he had whiskers and was a thousand years old, or so it seemed to me. My mother would call Dr. Montgomery, who lived in McLean, fifteen miles away, for anything she thought was serious. Anyway, old Dr. Coffage came out to treat Jack for his stomach ache and he put a mustard plaster on him. Well, Jack had appendicitis as it turned out and got worse until my mother threw a fit and insisted they call Dr. Montgomery. When he arrived he tore

Sisk and first cousin J. K. Jackson display knickers, 1925.

off that mustard plaster and put an ice pack on Jack, but it was too late. His appendix ruptured before they could get him to surgery, where he died.

AID: *This was your first experience with death?*

SISK: Yes, although I had another sad experience at about the same time. Another cousin, Velma Thomas, about my age, pretty with long curly hair, who lived maybe ten or so miles away, died when she was just eleven years old. I don't know the cause of her death. I couldn't understand why this had happened to my two cousins. I was too young to understand.

AID: *Were your clothes homemade or store-bought?*

SISK: Homemade. I wore overall bibs with straps and often had patches on the knees and on the seat. Sometimes Mother would patch patches. She was a stickler for cleanliness. Patches didn't matter as long as they were clean. She supervised my Saturday night bath in the washtub. She would spank me occasionally for getting into the dirt and getting my clothes dirty.

~

3.
High School

AID: *At school, did history remain your favorite subject?*

SISK: Oh yes, I loved history and I still do. As I have said, I learned history from my Grandfather Thomas—Texas history, United States history from the southern point of view. We re-fought all the battles in the Civil War. I knew Texas history from start to finish—the Alamo and San Jacinto and Sam Houston. In high school and college, I took all the history courses they would let me take.

AID: *Where did you go to high school?*

SISK: I was going to tell you. All of a sudden, the same way he had decided to leave Montague, Dad decided to leave our place near Alanreed. I know now that it was my parents' concern for my and my two sisters' education. I was completing seventh grade when my father put the ranch up for sale and we moved to Abernathy, Texas, a pretty good-sized community about sixteen miles from Lubbock. It had a good high school with four or five hundred students, and to me, coming out of a one-teacher country school, that high school was a big one. My father went into the cotton gin business with my uncle, the husband of my mother's sister. It was called the Jackson and Sisk Gin Company. They built a new gin in Abernathy. Then after two years, my father and my uncle sold that gin and we moved to Meadow, Texas, where my father bought another cotton gin. Meadow is twenty-eight miles southwest of Lubbock.

Meadow High School is where I finished my last two years. I made a straight-A average and wound up the class valedictorian. Yet I wasn't a brain; I don't recall studying a lot. Meadow is where I met my future wife and we had a lot of fun.

AID: *Was she the first girl you ever dated?*

SISK: No. I hadn't dated in Abernathy because I didn't drive and mostly we played group games at school and had little parties. But at Meadow I fell head over heels for a little girl there and we double-dated with a girl named Reta and her fellow, who worked for my father in the cotton gin. Well, Reta and I soon found out we liked each other better and became engaged to be married before we graduated from high school. Actually, I had gone two years to college before we married.

AID: *How did boys growing up then learn the facts of life?*

SISK: My parents never discussed those matters with me. You found out by gosh and by guess and by accident. Kids would talk. To tell the truth, I was in high school before I thought about it from a sex standpoint. I don't remember even kissing a girl at Abernathy. I must have been a kind of 'fraidy cat, because I was in college before I did any experimenting— guess I was a little scared.

19

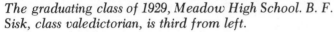

The graduating class of 1929, Meadow High School. B. F. Sisk, class valedictorian, is third from left.

Bernie Sisk, star high school southpaw.

The frankness of today just was not present in those days. For example, in my home, the word pregnant would never have been mentioned. Even after my sister was married and having her first baby, my mother would not discuss it. I can't remember, until we had children, ever hearing my mother use the word pregnant in a conversation. Those were the mores by which we lived then. Today it's vastly different—there have been many changes. We had a grandson's birthday recently and the kids sat around and talked about this kind of thing.

AID: *How did young couples court in those days?*

SISK: In old jalopy automobiles. My father's first car was a baby Overland, back in 1916, and then a Model T. I told you about the first time he drove a Model T. Later he bought a beautiful blue Chevrolet, the prettiest car I have ever seen. He would let me borrow the car and I used it to date the girl I mentioned, with Reta and her friend double-dating with us. Young couples usually went to a movie, or if daring enough, to a dance. Since neither my wife nor I were permitted to attend dances, we didn't go to them very often. Strictly chaperoned parties were held in friends' homes, yet kids being kids, you had the good and the bad as you have today. The same kinds of things happened then as now. I don't think the young of today are worse than we were, maybe even better. I just don't know.

AID: *That was during prohibition days, wasn't it?*

SISK: Prohibition was a tragic mistake. I can remember when you would pay twenty-five to thirty dollars a gallon for old homemade corn liquor. You had to drink it quickly so you wouldn't be caught with it, and that fast drinking caused immediate drunkenness. And, of course, bootleg liquor brought on the syndicated type of organized crime.

20

AID: *Had you thought about politics as a vocation when you were young?*

SISK: I never had any interest in politics whatsoever. My grandfather had inspired my love for flag and country and my interest in government. I wanted to go to the naval academy and felt slighted because I had no opportunity to apply. Probably the congressman, whoever he was at the time, simply picked the applicants from the large high schools in Amarillo. It's funny how things turn out because I felt that if I ever had anything to do with selection, I would give everybody a chance. So, as a member of Congress, I made certain that every high school in my district, regardless of size, knew the dates and procedures to follow for its candidates.

4.
Post-High School

AID: *What were your plans after high school?*

SISK: During my senior year I had been doing some bookkeeping for my father and recognized the value of learning methods and techniques. To get that knowledge, I enrolled at Draughn Business College in Lubbock and spent the entire summer of 1929 attending school there. Lubbock was just twenty-eight miles away and I came home on weekends. In that short period of time I studied typing, double-entry bookkeeping, advertising, and sales. It was an intense, practical training.

My basic expenses were paid by my father, but I wanted to reduce the financial load on him. I was boarding in a private home and since I grew up understanding the value of a dollar, I thought it would be mighty nice to make a few on my own. We only went to school half a day so there was time for work. The school employment office told me to apply for a job at a restaurant in town. I was told to come to work at two in the afternoon and I washed dishes until ten in the evening. I was paid a dollar fifty for those eight hours. That was enough to pay for most of my board. Things went along well until the chef told me that starting the next day, my job would be to clean and dress a dozen chickens. While I had seen my mother wring a chicken's head off, I had never killed or cleaned one. The live chickens were in chicken coops and I tried wringing their necks but they would get up and run off. I finally put a chicken on the floor, put my foot on its body and jerked its head off. Brutal, but I couldn't figure out any other way to kill it. Then I skinned it and cut it up. That's the way I killed and butchered chickens.

It wasn't a bad job. I not only earned my dollar fifty but I got all the food I could eat. The chef got drunk about every other day and he had a temper. They had delivered thirty dozen crates of eggs to the restaurant

Upper left: Sisk, far right, stands with employees of the A. L. Sisk Cotton Gin Co., Meadow, Texas—the family business—in this 1929 photo.

Upper right: Amid the orchards around 1928.

Right: Sisk with first car, in Texas in 1928.

and the chef had a quick way of breaking them, half a dozen at a time. This particular day the first eggs he broke were bad and he got mad and picked up those crates of thirty dozen eggs and threw them into the alley. Eggs were all over; you have never seen such a mess. I stayed on that job about three weeks.

By early fall, my high school principal, Leland Martin, encouraged me to go to college because I had received a scholarship as the class valedictorian. My parents were also interested that I enroll in college. As a result, I enrolled in Abilene Christian College at mid-term for the 1929-1930 session. My plan was to spend two years there and then transfer to Baylor University at Waco, Texas. Baylor had a good law school and I wanted to attend that school eventually.

Abilene was the first time I had really been away from home. It was 170

Men's dormitory at Abilene Christian College, Abilene, Texas, around 1930. Sisk attended the school for two years.

miles from Meadow, too far to get home weekends as I had while at the business school. I was a very homesick young man living in the dormitory there.

AID: *Probably lovesick, too?*

SISK: Naturally, of course. I went to summer school in 1930 to make up for the mid-term enrollment, and by then, the depression was making itself felt. West Texas was also under severe drought conditions. Banks were closing. One incident occurred when I was working for my father at the cotton gin a year later. He told me to run down to the First National Bank, the only bank in Meadow, and get the money for the payroll. We always paid in cash by the week. The bank had a sign on it that read: "Closed until further notice." I was startled. Everything we had was in that bank. I returned home and told my father. He was a calm man who never got excited. He took a big deep breath and said, "We have to get payroll money because our people have to buy groceries." He went to the safe and took out a bundle of cotton yard slips. Like the pink slip on an automobile, these were considered title to a bale of cotton. He peeled off a hundred slips and handed them to me with the instruction to take them to the First National Bank in Lubbock. I arrived around nine in the morning and took the yard slips to an officer of the bank. He looked at me a little questioningly because we had no account there. I told him that our bank hadn't opened that morning. He turned white and started to tremble all over. Another man had to relieve him at the window. I received ten dollars a bale for a total of one thousand dollars, which was actually a loan

23

on which the yard slips were the security. All of the money went for payroll. We had fifteen or twenty persons on our payroll at a salary around fifty or so dollars a week. This happened before Roosevelt closed the banks in 1933.

The banks in Abilene also went belly-up, causing tremendous hardship for the colleges there. There were four church-supported schools: Abilene Christian, Simmons University (which later became Hardin-Simmons), MacMurray College, and St. Joseph's College. The first was run by the Church of Christ, the second by the Baptists, the third by the Methodists, and the last by the Catholics. Most of the some twenty-five thousand persons in the community were dependent on the colleges in one way or another. What saved them was a man named Hardin. He was an oil millionaire and he gave liberally to at least several of the colleges, including Abilene Christian. That's why Simmons changed its name to Hardin-Simmons. The Hardin family did a lot of good in that part of the world.

Abilene is also the headquarters for Herald of Truth, a nationally-broadcast program of the Church of Christ. Batsel Barrett Baxter heads up the program; his father was president of Abilene Christian when I was a student there, and the son was a senior in the academy the final year I was in Abilene. I have kept in touch with these people.

AID: *I haven't asked you about your participation in sports.*

SISK: I tried out for practically everything. My lack of wind and slow speed made me mediocre in track; I was too light to play much football. My tennis was much better and in high school I won the county championship. But baseball was my real love. The coach needed a southpaw so I became a pitcher. But too many pitching arms are destroyed because the coach doesn't know enough to protect the youngster with a good arm. I pitched and won a nine-inning game early in the high school season and damaged my arm so that it was never as good afterwards. West Texas in April is chilly and the coach should never have permitted me to pitch the whole game. However, I continued to play baseball in college and, although I was never a great player, I love the game.

In high school my future wife watched me pitch and was embarrassed because opposing players weren't able to hit what I was throwing. She wasn't that knowledgeable about baseball, but she learned a lot about the game when we 'were in Washington.

AID: *How did the depression change your college plans?*

SISK: I've mentioned the banks closing and the drought. As the depression worsened it was clear that my father was in financial difficulty. So the second year of college, which I completed in June 1931, turned out to be my final one.

~

5.
Courtship and Marriage

AID: *When were you married?*

SISK: On April 20, 1931, when I was in my second year at Abilene. We were married without telling our parents and, as kids will sometimes, we ran off to New Mexico to get married because Texas had a three-day waiting period. I returned to Abilene to finish my second year and my wife returned home to her parents.

AID: *Please tell me about your wife and her family.*

SISK: Her name is Ireta Mitchell. I never liked her first name so I dropped the first letter and that made it Reta. She was the seventh of nine children. Her father, George T. Mitchell, was a rather well-to-do farmer in Altus, Oklahoma, where she was born. Then they moved to Meadow, Texas, where he owned a farm and later built a little hotel in Meadow. He owned a Ford dealership and a service station, most of which he lost in the depression. Her mother, Lulu Mitchell, passed away here in California some years ago at the age of ninety-six. Her maiden name was Wilson and she was distantly related to Woodrow Wilson. Reta's father, George, was born in Illinois but I never could figure out how he came to be born there because his father was a Confederate veteran. On one of our early dates in high school, Reta was at my house for Sunday dinner, and a favorite entertainment was to get out the family album. She looked at a picture of Grandmother and Grandfather Thomas sitting with two other persons and she said, "See that couple next to them. That's *my* grandmother and grandfather." It was a group picture of Confederate veterans and their wives at a reunion in North Texas.

Right: Ireta Mitchell (Reta Sisk) as a high school senior.

Far right: Bernie holds his first daughter, Bob-bye, at their home in Texas.

25

AID: *When did you tell your folks about your marriage?*

SISK: As soon as I returned home from Abilene. It was evident that going to Baylor University would put too much of a burden on my folks even though they encouraged me to go and were willing to make all kinds of sacrifices, although they were already making sacrifices. The depression provided some interesting experiences. For example, there were times when Reta had to wait until I collected my pay before she could afford a two-cent stamp to mail a letter. But most everybody was in the same pew. Bartering returned to style. You traded eggs for bacon or a chicken for something you needed. We moved out to a little farm my dad had and we carried eggs to town and at the rate of six cents a dozen we traded them for groceries.

6.
Depression and Drought

I started to look for work. While things were pretty tough, we had a lot of friends in Meadow, including one friend who was a diabetic and ran a Magnolia gas station. (Magnolia was a forerunner of Mobil.) My friend's diabetic condition got worse and one night he shot and killed himself. His widow leased me the retail part of the station; I couldn't finance the wholesale end of it. We got through the summer quite well. Regular gas was nine cents a gallon; premium gas (or what was called "red gas") was twelve cents a gallon. We rented a small apartment in Meadow, an extra bedroom in Mother Brown's house. She was in her eighties. We shared her kitchen.

In addition to running the service station, I would take my pickup to Lubbock and load up with 300-pound cakes of ice and sell them to families in the country. My route was about twenty miles long. That was our main income; the service station produced very little. People just had so little money. I remember selling tires on special for three dollars each.

What I am talking about now happened the following summer. In between the two summers at the service station we moved back to Dad's house on the land outside of Meadow. Our first child, Bobbye Corene, was born there on February 29, 1932. Corene was the name of my sister who died in infancy and my parents wanted my daughter to have that name also.

We hardly missed having gas or electricity in that farm house. A good Coleman lamp furnished our light. We heated water on the stove for bath water. It was a coal-burning stove. Our baby was born at home and I was there during her birth. As I remember, she was rather ugly when she was first born, but she became beautiful quickly.

We had a hog that we butchered later; we had a milk cow and fifty white leghorn chickens that literally turned to eggs. As I remember it, every hen laid an egg a day. We exchanged them for meat, ten dozen eggs for five or six pounds of bacon. We baked our own bread and grew our own vegetables. The only things we had to buy were salt, pepper, sugar, and fruit. Bananas were ten cents a dozen. We made our own butter. We took our grain and corn to the mill where it was ground. I used my dad's tractor to farm two hundred acres of cotton, also grew a little milo, and we harvested 115 bales of cotton. Cotton was nearly worthless—five cents a pound—and I gave the last twenty bales to an uncle whose rather large family was far worse off than we were, paying for the harvesting.

I also worked again for my father in the cotton gin. But 1934 was the last year he ran it; the country suffered from a severe drought and only one-third of a normal crop was ginned. He sold out to the Lubbock Cotton Oil Company and worked for an uncle of mine running his cotton gin. Those were very bad years for all of us. It got so that there were just no jobs to be had.

I had an uncle who was related to the people who owned Miller and Miller Freight Lines in Wichita Falls, Texas. I saddled up and went down there and got on what was called the "extra board." It was standby, and if they put out an extra load you could work for a day. This was called "bucking the extra board," which I did until late August, when I got on regular driving at the grand sum of fifteen dollars per week.

We rented a small furnished apartment in Wichita Falls so I would be closer to my work. I worked hard and was placed on the main line express run from Wichita Falls to Amarillo. I would leave Wichita Falls at 7:00 P.M. and work nine warehouses to arrive in Amarillo about 7:00 A.M. the next morning. I had no helper but juggled the freight alone. One day I was feeling really sick—it turned out that I had yellow jaundice—but I had to make this haul of a load of glass, crated on end, for a town 125 miles up the highway from Wichita Falls. After I got loaded up, I stopped at my house and my wife saw the shape I was in. She just took the baby, got in that truck, drove it, and then helped me unload that heavy glass. When we returned home my wife called a doctor, who gave me some medicine. Suddenly, on about the third day, I got up hungry and that was the end of it. I went back to trucking and was raised to eighteen dollars a week, later twenty dollars. Our daughter Marilyn was born on February 21, 1935. The doctor's bill for delivering her was thirty-five dollars.

My wife bought a new Singer sewing machine and I thought she had sunk us with the hundred-dollar debt to be paid off at the rate of four dollars a month. But it proved to be one of the best buys we ever made.

Reta made all the children's clothes, as well as many of our own clothes. She was thrifty and managed our finances. Without her management we might have starved, because I was never good at saving money.

By this time I was one of the two top drivers, and when the company bought two new White trucks, I got one of them. I drove for almost two years, accident-free. That was a sort of miracle, because at times I would fall asleep while I was driving. I will never forget one such night; I had been out for forty-eight hours after getting stuck in the black mud on the north plains. I didn't get into Amarillo until 5:00 P.M. instead of 7:00 A.M. They just loaded me up and turned me right back on the road again. I must have dozed off, because when I came to, right in front of me was a big concrete culvert. I managed to pull out and missed it by a hair.

Wichita Falls is a miserable place to live because of its climate. I requested a move to Amarillo, and after the company okayed it, we put all our household goods in the cab of the truck and moved into a little house, where for the first time we had electricity and natural gas. One Saturday afternoon, after working all day, I was taking a bath. The water heater was old and liable to blow up. All of a sudden there was an explosion and I jumped out of the bathroom, stark naked. Well, it wasn't the water heater. It was a nitro truck, jarred crossing the Santa Fe tracks, and it literally disintegrated. The largest piece of that truck was a hunk of rubber from one of the tires. It took the Santa Fe twenty-four hours to repair the damage to the tracks. These nitro trucks were one way you could make money in those days if you were willing to make a nitro run. They paid twenty-five dollars a day and that had looked awfully good to me. But after that explosion it didn't look good any more. The drivers were a little crazy. They had red flags on their trucks, and if you didn't get out of their way, they would run right over you.

By August my wife was getting fed up and I couldn't blame her. I was gone all of the time. She never saw me except on Sunday, and half the time when I was home, I'd fall asleep. It was a miserable life and so I just called it quits and we moved back to Meadow. Lubbock Cotton Oil, the company that had bought out my father, offered me a job keeping books and I wound up managing the plant. Gins closed down around the first of February in that part of the country. The drought was still bad and 1937 had been another poor crop year. Things were really dismal around there. Some people were in the Works Progress Administration. I never was— too much pride, I guess, although I might have been better off. My people had always struggled to make it on their own. I guess we were born that way, yet I don't belittle those on WPA because some would have starved to death without it.

There were absolutely no jobs anywhere. I said, "Well, something has got to give."

My wife's now-oldest living brother, another fellow who had a little house trailer, and I teamed up and went into the oil fields at Hobbs, New Mexico. It was called the "Monument area," south of Hobbs just across the line from Texas. I started out stringing pipe but the only money I really made—and the reason why I didn't stay long—was bucking mud for Halliburton. One day there was a big blow south of Monument. It woke us up that morning—the ground was shaking. We could hear the roaring even though it was six miles away.

Halliburton was hiring anybody. Mud was actually a special kind of clay dumped into a wild well to seal off the gas. My job was bagging this mud and placing the bags on trucks that hauled it as close as possible to the well site. I worked forty-eight hours straight; three hours of work, then a thirty-minute break. We ate sandwiches the company brought us. Once that gas well was closed there wasn't anything else to do.

Part 2:

CALIFORNIA, HERE I COME

Confronting a shortage of jobs every bit as acute as the prairie's lack of water, Bernie and his father joined the Dust Bowl migration to California, with the younger Sisk vowing to accept the first job offered him. When a fruit-picking assignment was tendered, Bernie grabbed it.

Starting from scratch in a new environment, Sisk rapidly became acclimated, securing permanent employment as a winery worker. A pioneer union organizer at the Tulare County plant, he became the charter shop steward.

When war intervened, Sisk rendered service as a flight dispatcher based in Visalia.

Shortly after the war, the General Tire and Rubber Company distributor in Fresno hired him as a salesman, a position from which Bernie swiftly advanced to general sales manager.

Contacts with customers during his rounds had brought to Sisk's attention the unmet water needs of farmers on the San Joaquin Valley's west side. That awareness coincided with efforts by a few Fresno Democrats to enlist Bernie, an admitted political neophyte, in the service of the party.

His maiden campaign, challenging incumbent Republican Congressman Oakley Hunter, was under-financed by today's standards, but rich in raw energy and door-to-door persistence. It paid off.

As a newly-elected California congressman, Sisk had to part with a remnant of boyhood days: his old nickname, "Tex."

7.
Apple Knocking

SISK: I returned to Meadow. My father said, "You have talked about going to California. There just has to be a place where things are better, where a man can find work." I had a wife and two babies and I wasn't about to sit there and starve to death. While we had saved a little money, it would soon be gone. Mr. Brock, father-in-law of one of my wife's brothers, wanted to go, too, so the three of us—Brock, my father, and myself—took off in a pickup truck. Before we left, John Cadenhead, brother of our former banker, asked me why in the world I was going to California. He said, "What are you going to do when you get there?" Right off the top of my head, I told him I was going to take the very first job offered me. When you are out of work, you will work at anything. He was skeptical and said I would be back within a month. I was determined to prove him wrong.

When we left home, I wasn't feeling good but didn't say anything about it. I didn't want to hold us up.

AID: *When was this?*

SISK: The last day of March 1937. I continued to get worse so I rode in a bed we had in the back of the pickup. I had the most horrible sore throat you can imagine and I was really sick. We spent the night in a motel in a small town whose name I won't mention, and the next morning Dad looked at my bed and it was absolutely brown from my sweating during the night. He rushed me to a doctor, who took one look at me and said, "Let's get him out of here. You follow me." He jumped in his car and we followed him in our pickup. We had met him in the drug store and he had his office in his home, where he asked my father, "Do you know what's wrong with this young man?" My father said, "No sir, that's why we are here." The doctor said, "He has scarlet fever. He may have passed the toughest part but he is still contagious and legally I should quarantine him for ten days. But in view of the fact that you are going to California and plan to be there tonight . . . " Dad said he wanted me taken care of as a first consideration. The doctor gave me some medicine and something to put in my eyes and Dad bought a pair of sunglasses for me because my eyes hurt. I got back in that pickup bed and we drove right through to Visalia, California, stopping only for gas. We got through the port of entry near Blythe without having them more than glance at me. We took a motel and I got into bed and stayed there for the next ten days. I made no contact with anyone and I am certain that I didn't infect anyone. I was so weak that I could hardly sit up to take a little nourishment, but soon I was recovering my strength.

One day I was sitting on a park bench and a fellow came over and asked me if I were looking for work. I told him, "Yes, sir." I didn't ask what it was or anything—I was carrying out my promise to take the first job offered me in California. He told me to be at that spot at six the next morning. He drove me to an orchard about two miles east of Cutler and put me on a ladder thinning nectarines. I had never seen a nectarine before. Anyway, this was my first job.

I was paid thirty cents an hour, five cents above the going rate. There were about thirty of us thinning nectarines and other fruits. Each morning he let some go until one morning I was the only one there. He was almost manufacturing work for me to do. The only reason I can think of is that I was a hard worker, probably the hardest worker in the crowd. I was hungry and glad to work hard. I stayed until there was absolutely no more for me to do.

After that I picked oranges, chopped cotton, picked peaches and apricots. You name it, in connection with farm work, and I did it. Most of us working in the fields and orchards were from Texas, Arkansas or Oklahoma, and occasionally someone would be from Kansas or Missouri. All white Anglo-Saxons, no black or brown persons in the group. Each one had a nickname—mine was "Tex." For the next twenty years I was Tex to everybody; I even used that nickname on business cards.

AID: *When did you goose figs?*

SISK: Oh, dear, who told you about figs? [*It was Mrs. Sisk.*] I didn't do that very long. They were a variety of black mission figs. In early spring, although mature in size, they are still green as can be. But this farmer wanted to beat the market in the East, so I put a little olive oil on the blossom end of the fig and it turned dark overnight. They looked ripe. Later, laws were passed prohibiting that practice.

A better opportunity for more permanent work was provided by the California Growers' Wineries, a plant two miles from Cutler. It was a co-op but its managers were Dutch Leonard, Sox Setrakian, and Charlie Clap. Dutch Leonard was a famous baseball player who had played with the Senators and the Yankees. His nephew, Leonard LaBlanc, was doing the hiring, and I applied for a job. While I was waiting to hear about it, I kept working steadily, sometimes holding down two jobs. I was trying to save enough money to bring my wife and children to California.

My father was getting anxious to return to Texas but stayed here to help me get started. We went to Cutler and rented a house for fifteen dollars a month, partly furnished with a bed and stove and table. I bought the rest of the essential furniture with a dollar down and dollar-a-week payments. I sent my wife enough money to buy the train tickets to California, and as soon as that was settled, my father went on back to Texas. When Reta arrived, she thought I had gone crazy to come to this country. She had never been to California and had taken the train at Lubbock through Clovis, New Mexico, and Barstow, California. Whenever she looked out the train window she saw nothing but desert or mountains. Then darkness fell and she never saw the great Central Valley until she arrived in Fresno at night. Of course, the next day I showed her around and she immediately saw the tremendous difference.

Shortly thereafter, the winery told me to come to work. It was late summer before the crushing, for which I was paid forty cents an hour. It was steady and I worked ten hours a day. Four dollars *a day*, after *weeks* when I hadn't made four dollars. My wife got a job in the packing shed, piece work, and some days when she was handling rotten fruit, she didn't make fifty cents. That wasn't enough to pay the babysitter. And the hours she worked—some days until ten or eleven at night. Even though it was rough, we were saving money because we wanted to buy a house. We have always despised paying rent, having been taught it was a waste of money.

A local merchant in Cutler named Lem Glover, a partner in the Goodman and Glover general merchandise store, where they sold everything from shoe tacks to wagon wheels, had a proposition for us. (Reta had worked in his store and had become acquainted with him.) He wanted to sell us a lot he owned in Cutler. We had just started our savings, so he decided to build a house on his lot. After it was built, we went to Visalia and talked to the manager of the Bank of America. With our meager savings and by hocking everything we had, we came up with nine hundred dollars. We bought that little house and moved in and even had enough left to buy furniture. We were very proud of that house because it was the first one we ever owned. It was across from the Cutler park and was a white, two-bedroom house with green shutters. It soon had a lawn and a hedge around the yard. The total price was $3,000 and we had a mortgage to keep up.

We didn't worry about our monthly payments because I had a steady job at the winery. I had no car and needed transportation, so we went down to Visalia to Mr. Mahoney, the Ford dealer there. He sold us a late model V-8 Ford with a little down and payments of around twenty dollars a month. Incidentally, this had occurred before we bought the house.

All of a sudden, the winery board of directors decided it must reduce expenses and let go four or five of the most recently hired. That included me. Although the directors said they would put us back on as soon as business improved, I was out of a job. My wife and I got in the car and drove to Visalia to see Mr. Mahoney. I told him we would have to return

Looking a shade like Bogart, Sisk poses in a Tulare County field in 1938.

Bernie, Reta, Marilyn and Bobbye in front of the family's Cutler home in 1942, their first California residence.

Three generations gather outside Sisk's Cutler home in 1942. Flanking him are daughters Bobbye, left, and Marilyn. At right are parents Lavina and Arthur Sisk.

the car. I told him what had happened at the winery and that there was just no way we could meet the car payments. He asked, "How are you going to look for work?" I said I would do what I had done before, hitch-hike or walk. He studied us a little bit and said, "You take that car and go back home. When you get a job and some money, bring the money in to me." You know, we were almost in tears to be treated like that by a man who didn't really know us—he had only seen us one time. So when I got a few dollars ahead, I would give him five or ten or fifteen dollars. Finally, the next summer, the winery called me back and from then on my job was very steady. But we will never forget Mr. Mahoney.

There had been no union at the winery when I started but we organized one. I was a charter member of the Winery and Distillery Workers Union. They broke us one year, but we came back and made the union stick the second year. I was the union's first shop steward. Today that union is international. Our first union contract called for sixty-two and one-half cents an hour and the next contract for one dollar, two and one-half cents an hour. The women had been working for twenty cents an hour and we got their wages increased considerably.

The winery had its three managers but Sox Setrakian ran the show. Later he and I became friends and he was a supporter during my years in Congress. Although we have had our ups and downs, I respect him. He did a lot for the raisin industry. I also came to know Charlie Clap well. He owned a ranch and wanted to hire me as ranch foreman. If he had offered a decent wage, maybe I would have taken it. He wanted to pay only seventy-five dollars per month and I wouldn't work that cheaply.

8.
World War II

As 1941 came along, I held a fairly responsible position in the winery. Of course, in December the Japanese attacked Pearl Harbor! I had a wife and two children so I went in the draft as a 3A. The winery cellar manager, my supervisor, was Gail Huffman. We were good friends and decided we would go up and volunteer for OCS, officer candidate school. Over the objections of our wives, we went to the Fresno army base where the old air terminal used to be.

AID: *You were thirty-one years old at this time?*

SISK: Yes. We put in our applications and they scheduled us for all the pro-cedures: a written test and then a physical and an officer interview. You walk in and sit down and they start asking you questions. Gail flunked out, I don't know why. He then joined the Marine Corps and served with distinction. Anyway, they okayed me. They said, "All right, your papers

A Ryan PT (primary trainer) soars above Sequoia Field in Visalia, California in 1943. Sisk dispatched such aircraft from his Sequoia Field post.

are being sent to Western Defense Command in the Salt Lake City headquarters and you will be notified when to report." In the meantime, they said, "You report to Sequoia Field where they are training flying cadets. We want you to go there until you are called by Western Defense Command."

I went back to the winery and resigned and reported to Sequoia Field. They immediately put me to work as a flight dispatcher. The flight dispatchers technically had charge of the cadets on the ground and in the airplanes.

AID: *But you were civilians?*

SISK: We were civilians, but we wore pinks and more or less dressed as officers. We got the sum of seventy-five dollars a month.

AID: *Which was a second lieutenant's pay?*

SISK: That was about a second lieutenant's pay. We were, for all practical purposes, equivalent to second lieutenants. Cadets were required to salute us and all this sort of monkey business. We were under direct orders of the army. They pushed us hard. We put the first sixty-five hours on the green cadets. Technically, my job was on the ground. What I would do was report to the flight line and immediately get on the phone and call the tower and order my planes.

AID: *Were they little PTs (primary trainers)?*

SISK: These were primary trainers. We thought we were a hot outfit because we had monoplane Ryans. They were pretty hot compared to Stearmans. We had as many as 600 planes. Man, we were turning out cadets like you wouldn't believe. We only had forty-five days to get those cadets in and out.

The wing commander was Saul Sweet, now in his eighties, who still flies out of Visalia Airport. Murrell Gallagher of Visalia was my flight commander. We had flyers and instructors from all over the country.

AID: *Did your OCS orders ever come through?*

SISK: I kept waiting in 1942 and when 1943 came along I was still wondering what in the heck was happening in Salt Lake. Finally, in the fall of 1943, I got a form with a few blanks filled in. In other words, I was disqualified.

AID: *Overage?*

SISK: It didn't give a reason. It just said I had been disqualified. I took it to our base commander. He checked around and told me, "They are overloaded with OCS applications. They have nothing against you. You better just stay where you are and keep your mouth shut and your nose clean." I stayed right there until the end of the war. Then they closed the base and I was out of a job. However, that was one time you didn't worry about jobs; jobs were looking for you in those days.

At that time, Bobbye was finishing elementary school. They had no high school in Cutler. We were determined to give the kids a better educational break, so we started looking for a place to move. We talked about selling our Cutler house. It was hard because the house meant so much to us. We had kept it in pretty nice shape. We didn't know what price to ask. We thought we might get $4,000, $1,000 more than what we paid. I called our insurance agent, Earl Friend, who had become a good friend. I said, "Earl, what should we ask for this house?" He said, "If I were you, I guess $4,500 anyway or maybe $5,000. You know, things are going up." That night we talked about the price we would ask and decided on $6,000. This was double, mind you, what we had paid. Mr. Reed, a local barber, looked at the house, walked in that afternoon and said, "I will take it." It was cash on the barrelhead.

AID: *Oh, you are rich!*

SISK: Wow, brother, I will tell you that we were shook! Reta shed tears. Somehow she had a feeling that if she ever let go of that little house she would never own another home. In the meantime, I had a relative in Fresno who wanted us to come up and look at the property there. I still didn't have a job. We finally made a deal and bought out here by Roosevelt High School. We moved about the first of June 1945.

9.
The Tire Business

I had people wanting me to go to work for them before we moved in. Glenn Smith of the LeMoss-Smith Tire Company, General Tire distributor down on Broadway, had been told by a mutual friend that I was moving up here, and Reta always complained that I went back to work

General Tire and Rubber Co. sales managers meet in San Francisco in 1948. Sisk is third from left.

before we ever got through moving. The kids started school in Fresno and I started working for the tire company.

We covered a five-county area for the General Tire and Rubber Company. We had a lot of big accounts, many located on the west side area. I did some selling but basically I was the service manager.

AID: *What was your pay?*

SISK: Somewhere around $350 to $400 a month at that time. As we built up, I became retail sales manager and finally general sales manager in charge of all sales, retail and wholesale. In fact, I was general manager there when I filed for political office.

AID: *What was your salary then?*

SISK: I would guess about $800 a month.

AID: *Were you living in the house you had recently bought?*

SISK: Yes, in fact we still own the same house. It is for sale right now. We have owned the house almost thirty-five years.

AID: *When did you join the Kiwanis service club?*

SISK: About thirty years ago I was sponsored by Ray Pryor, then the Lincoln-Mercury dealer here in Fresno.

AID: *Was there only one Fresno Kiwanis Club at that time?*

SISK: There was only one club, the Downtown Kiwanis. The club was getting too big, so it sponsored a new club called the North Fresno Kiwanis Club. I was a charter member of the new Kiwanis Club.

The North Fresno Kiwanis Club, the organization which helped launch Sisk's political career, honored the congressman in 1976 as one of only two charter members still in the club. At a dinner to celebrate the club's twenty-fifth anniversary—and his twenty-fifth year of membership—Sisk is joined by Max Hessmann, left, (the other active charter member) and his wife, Dick Hunt, president, and an unidentified woman. Sisk and Hessmann were enrolled in the Legion of Honor.

AID: *How many members do you have?*

SISK: We started in north Fresno with about forty members, as I remember. I was the third president. The first president was Carl Duffy, an optometrist here. He actually switched from the Downtown Club and became president of the new club in order to help us get off the ground. He was a wonderful guy and the father of Gordon Duffy, the present assemblyman. His vice-president was Bob Barnard, who was the son of Judge Barnard, a superior court judge. When he moved up at the end of the first year to become president, I became Bob's vice-president. I followed then as the third president of the club, in 1952 or 1953.

10.
The First Campaign

AID: *Like out of the blue, they suggested you get into politics?*

SISK: Really what happened was this: I had always been interested in government and Reta and I always voted. We took an interest to that extent, but I

41

had no interest in appointments or elections or anything like that. I didn't know a single member of the Democratic Central Committee. I didn't even know they had a central committee. I didn't have any idea how politics was organized.

After I became general sales manager, I made many trips to the west side. Our service salesmen were knowledgable in both service and sales. These men would go out in fast van-type trucks, well-equipped, and would pull into one of the ranches on the west side. Maybe the rancher would say, "You can have those Ford tires recapped if you pull them off." I made trips with them to find out what was going on and became well-versed in the water problems of the west side. It was evident to me that if it didn't get more water, there would fast approach a time when the land was going to dry out. That would be the end of the line as far as the great west side was concerned.

AID: *How was it getting water then?*

SISK: They were pumping it out of wells, but the water table was going down and down. Where wells had once found water at one hundred-fifty, two hundred feet, the wells were down as deep as seven hundred feet, which was approaching the economic limit.

My recognition of what was going to happen caused me to explore why we couldn't get more water projects. We had Shasta-Keswick up north and we had the Friant-Kern Canal taking water down there. We had the Friant-Madera Canal taking water up to Madera. I began to make some inquiries to educate myself on what was going on out there.

In the meantime, Wally Henderson, with whom I had become acquainted through union activities at the winery back in the 1930s, came into the picture. He had served as the business agent for the Winery and Distillery Workers Union. Later on, he became secretary-treasurer of the Central Labor Council. Finally, he wound up in the Assembly. Wally was also a charter member of the North Fresno Kiwanis Club. Along about January 1954, I walked into the club one day a little bit early, and it happened that Wally Henderson and Elmo Willeford were there. All three of us were Democrats. Most members of the club were Republicans. I said, "I just made a trip out to the west side and, Wally, I am thoroughly disgusted with you and your party." He said, "What do you mean? It's my party, but it's your party, too." I said, "What's the matter? You can't elect a Democratic congressman for this area; you can't even get one nominated!" I reminded him about the Republican incumbent, Congressman Hunter, who wouldn't even support a water project out here. I said, "The last time Hunter ran, he won a double nomination. You couldn't even get your candidate nominated."

Wally said, "I agree that we have a lot of problems but if you don't like it, why don't you do something about it?" I wasn't paying much attention to him. I said, "If we don't get some water out on that west side, this county is in trouble economically. It is at the point where the cost of lifting well water has reached its economic limit." That was the end of the conversation. I never thought anything more about it, but later, around late January, the girl in my office said, "A gentleman on the line is calling about having lunch with you." So I got on the phone. He told me his name, Charlie Clough, but I had never heard it before. I said, "I can meet you for lunch Friday." He said, "That's fine. I will meet you at the Sequoia Cafe."

I got out my tire book and my papers regarding our latest discounts. I thought the man was a trucker who was flat broke and had to buy tires and needed credit. I had already figured the best deal we could offer that day on truck tires. I walked in and here are two men. They introduced themselves as Charlie Clough and Ken Andreen. (Charlie Clough was the first husband of the woman who later ran my Fresno office for twenty-five years. Later she became Betty Cornelius.) Charlie was congressional district director of the California Democratic Council and was editor of the *Fresno Labor Citizen*. I didn't know any of this at that time. Ken Andreen was a young attorney in the office of Peckinpah and Peckinpah, which was at the time one of the city's big law firms. He is now [July 1979] a superior court judge.

We sat down and ordered lunch and I laid my tire book over on the side. I was assuming they wanted to buy some tires on credit. Charlie Clough finally said, "Mr. Sisk, the reason we're here is that we understand you might possibly be willing to be a candidate for Congress." Man, I almost fell out of my chair. I said, "You people are mixed up—I work for General Tire and Rubber Company."

"We understand that's the work you do, but we have been told that you're a Democrat and frankly, we're needing a candidate."

They put it that bluntly. I said, "You're right on one basis, I'm a Democrat—I came from a country where if you weren't, you were disenfranchised. I don't know anything about your problems needing a candidate. Charlie said, "Let me explain. Wally Henderson called and indicated . . ." I said, "Oh yes, with friends like him, I don't need enemies." They explained the situation to me. I won't go into all the details. I was curious, even though I didn't know anything about politics and I felt it was totally outside of my consideration.

They insisted: "Would I be willing to think about it?" I finally said, "Okay, I will give it a little thought." As far as I was concerned, that was the end of that. But they called a fellow in Kerman who was a member of the Democratic Central Committee. A few days later, a big, tall, lanky man came in the office and introduced himself as Walt Lambrecht. Again, I thought he wanted to buy tires, but he also wanted to talk to me about running for Congress. I said, "Come on, now. I'm not candidate material; I don't know anything about it." Several other people called me up. As the old ego started working, at some point I went home and told my family about it. That's when Reta called a family meeting to vote on the issue. We had four members of the family, and the two girls voted for Papa to try for Congress.

I was asked to appear before the Democratic Central Committee, where I was introduced to the chairman, Lionel Steinberg, a farmer and fruit packer. The California Democratic Council, CDC, had been formed the previous year by Alan Cranston, now a U.S. senator. The council was an attempt to produce a procedure making it possible for Democrats in the state to be nominated. Under the cross-filing system, which was then in existence, we had a frequent situation where a Democrat couldn't get nominated. In fact, two years before, the Democratic candidate running in the primary had not even won his own party's nomination. The CDC was organized on a statewide basis with local Democratic clubs. This meeting was organized as a nominating convention so the Democratic Party could get behind one candidate, get him nominated and on the ballot in the general election.

My wife was still quite concerned, but she and my daughters went with me. Joe Manning, a friend of mine who now lives in the Bay Area, drove us up. Marvin Baker, a farmer from Madera, was also interested in the Democratic nomination. Both Baker and I spoke to the thirty or so delegates assembled there. After a good deal of discussion, delegates recessed and held a caucus. They got Baker in one corner of the room and me in another. My supporters said, "We can get you the majority of the votes on this if you will agree to run." My wife was still pretty unhappy with the idea of my candidacy. I didn't realize how unhappy she was. I finally said, "If the votes go in my favor, I will be willing to file." As I recall, there were three votes for Baker and twenty-seven votes for me.

AID: *Do you recall Baker saying if he ran and was elected, he would return his salary?*

SISK: I think that is right. He got his three votes from Madera people who later became supporters of mine. In fact, his nephew, Aubrey Baker, and his wife, Georgia, became my Madera representatives and close friends.

AID: *Were there any other candidates?*

SISK: There were no other candidates known at the time. That is why they were out searching for a candidate and found me. I would needle them later by saying they needed a sacrificial lamb. The two of us were the only names placed in nomination by the CDC endorsing convention. The CDC later became a left-wing outfit, in my opinion, but I was one of the first CDC-endorsed candidates to win an election in California.

Jimmy Roosevelt simultaneously received the same type of CDC support that I did. Jimmy and I were the two new Democrats elected in California in 1954; we were the babes of the new process of endorsement. He took the seat held by Sam Yorty, who was giving up his post to run for the U. S. Senate.

44

I was running against an incumbent so I was deemed to have very little chance. I had set up some pretty substantial requirements: if I was going to run, CDC would have to raise enough money for a good public relations man to run the campaign. I was simply not going to run unless the party was willing to support me financially to that extent.

We held a meeting at the Belmont Inn, the first political meeting since I had filed for the election. A Fresno attorney, F. Nielsen, wrote a check for fifty dollars for me, which was a lot of money in those days.

Al Thomas was made campaign treasurer at that first meeting—and is to this day. The few persons present were Charles Clough, Elmo Willeford, Al Thomas, Bud Eickholt, Nielsen, and myself. Someone said, "All right, who are we going to get to run this campaign?" Somebody thought of Ed Piston, a popular public relations man out at Fresno State College, who some felt might be too busy to be interested in running a campaign. Despite this, they called him at 10:00 P.M. and Ed came down and visited with us for a little while. "I have taken on an associate," he said, "who is going to be interested in getting involved with political campaigns if there is sufficient money involved."

"Who is this?"

Piston said, "A fellow by the name of Jackson Carle, who is an attorney and a former newspaperman and has worked for the government (most recently the Bureau of Reclamation), but has been fired by the new Eisenhower Administration." It was decided we would call this man the next morning. That was my first contact with Jackson Carle, who was a godsend as far as I am concerned. We wondered at times whether he was going to be paid, but we managed to pay him all right.

It became clear right away that Jackson knew more about politics than the rest of us, who were strictly amateurs. But he had a program. I owe my political life to Jackson Carle; he had the knowledge, understanding, and patience. Other people recognized this, too.

AID: *Had you talked to your employer, the General Tire distributor?*

SISK: Yes. Although they had reservations because they recognized some of the problems I would run into, they said, in a sense, "Use your own judgment; go ahead if you want." Glenn Smith, manager of the business, gave me a lot of support although he might have doubted I would win. The idea was that I would continue to work at least through the primary, which would have been in early June. Some friends of my opponent threatened to cancel their tire business. That was when I got my first understanding about this political game. I was appalled, to tell you the truth. I went to Glenn and said, "I know what is going on and I think it is terribly unfair to the company so I am going to leave. I am going to give this campaign all I have, although I may not win."

I realized I was an amateur and had gotten into something I really didn't know very much about. If I had known better, when they asked me to

45

run, they couldn't have run fast enough to catch me. But my father always said, "If you are going to do something, give it all you've got; if you lose, you won't have any regrets that you didn't do a little more." So I was going out there and campaign hard. We agreed that I would leave the company on the first day of April. If I didn't make it, I would be rehired.

AID: *You were involved in the campaign in earnest, but how did you support your family?*

SISK: I did have a little help from friends here and there. We also had a little savings. We had a lot on which we were planning to build. I sold it and used all of that money. We had a cabin up at Yosemite National Park that we sold. I also talked the committee out of some money to at least pay my gasoline bills. In fact, I wore our automobile out in that campaign.

Incidentally, I lost my nickname, "Tex," during the campaign. My advisers didn't think that was a good political name for Californians. That's when I became "Bernie," although I had been "Bernie" to my wife since we first met.

The total amount of money spent in the campaign, for both the primary and general election, was $12,000.

AID: *And who were some of your contributors to the campaign?*

SISK: I remember the first big check, for $500, was from Jack O'Neill, a farmer on the west side. As I have said, my criticism of my opponent, Oakley Hunter, was about his refusal to support the San Luis Project. I didn't know Jack O'Neill that well, although one of his sons was a customer of ours. I knew he was a registered Democrat but like many conservative farmers, he voted Republican at times. My support of the San Luis Project helped me. In addition to Jack, Russell Giffen and Jack Harris were among the others who had been working for years to get supplemental water to the west side. I came along at a good time because they were unhappy with Hunter's unwillingness to lead the fight to get the project authorized. He had introduced a bill but just let it sit. The general feeling was he did this because of the influence of "Mr. Republican," Lloyd Harnish, who was bitterly opposed to the reclamation law and the acreage limitation.

We also had labor help; I was labor-endorsed. I always had been considered a good friend of labor although, as a political novice, there was no record on me. I had walked picket lines and been active in the winery labor union.

I've mentioned that Wally Henderson was the Democratic assemblyman for the Fresno district and I had walked picket lines with him back in the 1930s. We had hired him as the business agent for our union.

The Teamsters supported me, as did the building trades, the milk drivers, and the retail clerks. It was pretty much across the board for me because Hunter was considered anti-union.

AID: *What other contributions came from corporations?*

SISK: None from oil companies. I'll tell you about that. I came into the office in September and found everyone dancing for joy. They said they had gotten a call from Frank Desmond in Madera that we were going to receive a $2,000 contribution. That was a lot of money in those days. I didn't know the source of the funds and it wouldn't have made any difference if I had. A day or two later, I made a speech in Kerman or Riverdale reiterating my position supporting a reduction in the oil depletion allowance. When the oil people heard about it, that was the end of the $2,000 contribution.

A year or two later, Superior Oil found itself in trouble. A bill deregulating natural gas had passed in 1955 or 1956 (over my opposition), and this was to the oil companies' liking. After it passed both the House and Senate and had gone to President Eisenhower, Senator Carl Curtis (R-Nebraska) announced he had been offered money by Superior Oil for his vote. That blew the bill right out of the water and Eisenhower vetoed it.

I just remembered a contribution of $400, made directly to my campaign committee, from a Superior Oil Company lobbyist. Evidently, this came in before the incident I have just related about the $2,000 we never received. Later, this lobbyist came into my Washington office. Natural gas deregulation was again a national issue and when I told him I was going to vote against the bill because of my long-standing commitment to this regulation, he became nasty and insulting. I was pretty thin-skinned in those days and I blew up and escorted him out of my office. He never came back. He seemed to think that he had bought me for $400.

AID: *Any other major supporters?*

SISK: Yes. Sox Setrakian, from my days at the winery. He was a raisin grower and head of the raisin administrative committee which controlled marketing under the federal marketing order. Sox was "Mr. Raisin" for thirty years in this valley. He was a successful Democratic businessman. I don't remember the amount of his contribution.

Earl Cobb, the winery manager where I worked, made a small contribution. And this was in spite of my walking a picket line against him years before. Most of the contributions were small, from individuals. The campaign finance committee raised the money and I wrote to each contributor, thanking him. This was my general practice after each election, I didn't care if he gave one dollar or a thousand.

AID: *I'm told that your minister wrote letters in your behalf.*

SISK: I had forgotten about that but I believe our minister, Albert Lovelady, did write to other ministers.

AID: *What other issues, besides water, came up in the campaign?*

SISK: The right of collective bargaining was a hot issue. The original Wagner

47

Act passed in the 1930s was considered the Emancipation Proclamation for labor. However, the National Labor Relations Board made major modifications in it. While I was in support of labor, I was also very strong in my support of agriculture.

Another major issue concerned the kind of farm bill we were to have. Do you remember the battle over farm price supports for such commodities as cotton, wheat, feed grains, dairy products, and others? Having lived through the depression and knowing what happened to agriculture then, I was basically for some type of national farm program where the valleys could be leveled out and a reserve established to provide for crop failures. This problem is still not resolved. I have some ideas and believe action can be taken to help the situation.

Another big issue was McCarthyism. The poor secretary of the army was taking a terrible beating. Hunter made the mistake of supporting McCarthy. I beat him over the head with it. I kept hammering away at McCarthyism. Reaction against McCarthy had set in and although he was still on the rampage when I went to Washington, his wings were soon clipped. During the Eisenhower campaign of 1952, communism and fellow travelers had been a big issue. His opponent, Adlai Stevenson, was our good friend.

AID: *How did you campaign? Any house-to-house?*

SISK: Yes sir! I rang doorbells. Walt Lambrecht had an idea about a farm bill that I thought was somewhat extreme and would have been hard to adopt, but Walt wanted to sell it. So we walked the streets of Selma, Kingsburg, Reedley, Sanger, Orange Cove, Riverdale, Caruthers, Coalinga, Kerman, Burrel, and almost every other small community, particularly in Fresno County.

Between the time that I filed and the June primary, we concentrated purely on population. We were too thin and broke to go out in a big campaign. We did need billboards but were told the company was sold out. In desperation, I went to Hugh Burns, a power in the state Senate, although I wasn't particularly close to him and some of my associates didn't like him. Hugh apparently said the right word to the billboard company and we got them. However, as I recall, that event occurred in the general election, not in the primary.

During the primary, we concentrated on the Fresno area. I went to Madera, where Frank Desmond was chairman of the city's Democratic Central Committee—a wonderful man. He and his lovely wife, Lucille, broke their backs for me. Alan and Sadie Roberts worked mighty hard, too. We went to every farm, every household, and every business in Madera County. I would give out a package of matches asking for a vote. To the extent we were able, we did the same kind of campaigning in Fresno County but couldn't get to every house because it was just too big.

We had a lot of other people who walked precincts for us. Labor

Fresno headquarters for Sisk's maiden campaign in 1954.

furnished people, the retail clerks especially. They placed bumper stickers on their automobiles and hung placards on doors throughout the city. However, we hardly did any campaigning in Merced County during the primary.

AID: *It was the Twelfth District then?*

SISK: Yes. After election day I had not only been nominated but had defeated Hunter in total Republican and Democratic votes by a very narrow margin in Fresno and Madera counties, but he beat the heck out of me in Merced County. Merced County and the northern end of Fresno County had gone Republican for years and years. Bud Gearhart, a Republican, had been in Congress fourteen years before Hunter. In the last thirty years, only one Democrat had served and that was for only one term.

AID: *Did the primary result surprise Hunter?*

SISK: Hunter had apparently been told by his people to go ahead about his business since no one had ever heard of Bernie Sisk. So I guess the results came as a shock. They got out here then and began to put a campaign together. During the primary, Hunter once referred to me as a "country bumpkin." That was probably more truth than fiction. My response was: "Maybe he is right, but I would rather be a country bumpkin than a city slicker." That caught on. People do not normally appreciate someone who makes fun of someone else, so Hunter's comment backfired.

Believe me, we didn't quit working in the general election. I continued to campaign hard throughout the summer months and October, ringing doorbells, walking the streets, talking to people and asking them to vote for me. The mistake of my opponents was that they had made me mad. They had threatened my tire company. I simply was determined to give it all I had, win, lose, or draw. I couldn't have done it alone; I had a lot of friends. Winning the election was simply hard work.

Even the day before the election, I was still campaigning, still ringing

The Associated Press captures four grins of victory following Sisk's successful 1954 campaign; from left, Reta, Bernie, Marilyn and Bobbye.

doorbells on election eve. Ted Nix, a farmer near Selma, was chairman of my farm committee. The only TV ad we could afford had Ted driving up on his tractor and commenting favorably about this fellow Sisk. His wife organized with her neighbors eight coffee hours over a four-hour period in eight different locations. The smallest attendance was fifteen and the largest was thirty-two women. I'm sure we got more than a few votes out of those coffees.

When I walked into the campaign office on election eve, everybody was there and we were all worn out. They wrote their predictions about the outcome on a piece of paper. Mine was that we would win or lose by no more than 2,000 votes, out of 160,000 votes cast. While I thought it would be close, I wasn't at all confident that we were going to win. But we had done our best; there would be no regrets. We won by 9,008 votes. That is the only election, of the twelve I was in, in which I remember the exact count.

Part 3:

MR. SISK GOES TO WASHINGTON

In an affable, folksy style, Bernie traces his coming-of-age as a U.S. congress-man. He hit the ground running in 1955, immediately advocating the San Luis Project, the centerpiece of an election campaign that had also zeroed in on farm price supports and collective bargaining.

Convinced that the valley's west side faced economic ruin without the supplemental water the San Luis would provide, Sisk soon became enmeshed in the complex maze of water issues peculiar to California and in an equally intricate process of congressional give-and-take.

Through the ensuing discussion, Sisk illuminates the dark corners of water development in California, a labyrinthine topic of historical and current import to the state. Indeed, much of the history of California can be told through the history of its water development. The Central Valley Project remains among the most formidable rearrangements of the natural landscape yet attempted.

In his memoir, Sisk speaks colorfully of "getting your ducks in a row," the coalition-building necessary to steer the San Luis Project through hearings and past recalcitrant lawmakers. From his post on the House Interior and Insular Affairs Committee, he forged alliances with Republican and Democratic legislators alike—Sen. Thomas Kuchel, Rep. Howard Smith, Sen. Clinton Anderson, Rep. Wayne Aspinall.

Bernie sketches with precision the other key actors in the drama: the Metro-politan Water District of Los Angeles, Kern and Contra Costa counties, area growers, then-Governor Edmund G. "Pat" Brown, and activists who would later organize National Land For People.

Five years of reconciliation efforts bore fruit in 1960 when Congress author-ized the San Luis dam/reservoir as part of the Central Valley Project, furnishing water to farm land in Merced, Fresno and Kings counties. The legislation sealed an agreement between California and the federal government insuring the San Luis of 2.1 million acre-feet of gross storage capacity, one million of which was earmarked for federal use.

(An acre-foot—the amount of water required to cover one acre with one foot of water—can be understood in this way: 1,000 gallons of water are required to produce one pound of food, and the average person consumes roughly 1,500 pounds of food annually. Accordingly, one acre-foot of water is required to produce the amount of food a family of five is likely to eat in a year's time.)

The reservoirs of the San Luis Project were designed to augment the underground water table on the west side, where subsidence, salinity and a falling water table imperiled a half a million acres of farm land.

The pact providing for joint federal/state construction and ownership of the project—and use of the water—marked the first such cooperative undertaking in U.S. history. The 600,000-acre Westlands Water District is the principal contractor for federal water in the San Luis service area. The U.S. Water and Power Resources Service (formerly the Bureau of Reclamation) delivers some 6.5 million acre-feet for irrigation on two million acres of valley land served by 130 irrigation districts. The dam was completed in 1967.

Sisk expands on his thinking regarding enforcement of the bitterly-disputed Reclamation Act of 1902, the definition of an "economical farming unit," his work with Kings River water districts to develop equitable contracts for water storage in Pine Flat Reservoir, and what he describes as "the ongoing war" between state and federal officials for control of California water.

While still one of the newer members of the House, Bernie played a pivotal role in forming the Democratic Study Group, an attempt to give the party's liberal wing cohesion and bargaining power. As chairman of the organizing committee that spawned DSG, he was persuasive in convincing then-Speaker Sam Rayburn the group would work harmoniously with the leadership.

Wrapping up the account of his early service in the House, Sisk recalls how the launching of Sputnik in 1957 induced the Congress to move with alacrity in assembling a select space committee, on which he served. Through his assignment on the standing Committee on Science and Astronautics, he worked to apply the principles governing "the law of the sea" to mankind's newest frontier.

11.
The New Congressman

SISK: The Democratic Party was kind of startled. Telegrams began to flood in from Washington and from all over the country. It is hard to describe the feeling of elation, but I was also relieved; it had been a tough situation to go through. Jackson Carle, my campaign manager, did a masterful job.

I immediately contacted Ed Piston, who had recommended Jackson Carle to us, and asked if he objected to my offering Jackson a job. He said, "No, I think he might appreciate it." The administrative assistant was the top man and the salary was $9,700 in those days. I offered it to Jackson and he took it. With his help, I put together a staff. We developed some theories and policies. Jackson and his wife went back to Washington a week ahead of me. We had no staff except Betty Clough, who had worked as a volunteer throughout the campaign. She had headed up our office during the campaign, had directed the volunteers and did all the things that had to be done. Betty had a job as far as I was concerned. She went to work on January 3, 1955, the first day you technically take the office.

Charles Clough, Betty's husband at that time, was very active in the labor movement. He worked for me throughout the campaign. Charlie is now in publishing.

Jackson Carle's wife, Eunice, had been office manager of the Harris Construction Company. When I called Jackson in Washington, asking him whom I should hire as a secretary, I thought of asking what his wife did. Jackson said she was filling out job applications in Washington. I said, "If she is interested in working, I would be happy to hire her." Jackson said, "I don't want to impose on you because sometimes a person doesn't like to hire a husband-and-wife team." I said, "I am confident that whatever is going to be done is going to be done right. She is available so I will put her to work." Eunice Carle continued to work with me for seventeen years. She worked longer than Jackson did; she came back and worked in the office here. She was still working for me when she died of cancer. Eunice was a wonderful person. Jackson has been lost ever since she passed away; she was a tower of strength for him.

I had never been to Washington, D. C., when I left here around the

53

twenty-sixth of December, 1954 to take my office as a member of Congress. I had a friend who rented an apartment for me. It was a whole new ball game; I had trouble finding my way to the office.

I was sworn in on the third of January, 1955. Afterward I received a lot of invitations because everyone wanted to get acquainted with the new members. As a new member, you had to accept them all.

My wife said we had to get a few things for the house, so we went shopping for some pillows in a supposedly good department store. The sales clerks were lackadaisical; they couldn't have cared less. I asked about a pillow and the sales clerk just threw the pillow across the room to me. My wife was tickled. That was my first impression of Washington.

We lived south on Indian Head Highway in Maryland. It was quite a ways out, beyond Bolling Air Force Base. I was still having trouble finding my way because there were diversions in traffic and crossing bridges was quite a problem in Washington in those days. I got on the wrong bridge one day, getting in the wrong lane. I found myself way out in the suburbs, in an entirely strange community, but managed to get turned around and back on the correct route. In the meantime, my bladder needed to be relieved. By the time I returned to the right road, I had to get home badly. I finally got to the complex where we lived, a huge brick building where every apartment looked exactly the same. I got out of the car and went to what I thought was my apartment. I struggled with the key, but it wouldn't open the door. Finally, a woman opened the door and I rushed into the living room where a man was sitting with three kids. I apologized and got out of there and finally got to my own apartment.

To get properly established in Washington as a new member, you need good committee assignments. Tony Coelho, my successor, and I did a lot of work early on committee appointments for him. In contrast, when I ran, no one had expected me to win, so none of the preliminaries had been done. When Dwight Eisenhower was elected in 1952, he brought in a Republican controlled Eighty-third Congress, both in the House and Senate. We turned it around and gained Democratic control in the Eighty-fourth. The Republicans have not controlled it since.

Clair Engle, a famous cowboy from Northern California and a wonderful person, was ranking minority member of the House Interior and Insular Affairs Committee during the Eighty-third Congress. With the change-over in power, he became chairman of that committee. He helped me in whatever way he could. He preceded Harold "Bizz" Johnson, representing all that area from the Oregon border all the way down to the San Bernardino County line (all the eastern and mountain area). He asked me if I wanted to be on his committee. I said I definitely wanted to be on it, if I couldn't get on Agriculture.

Harlan Hagen, a Democrat from Bakersfield, who then had a term's seniority on me, was seeking Agriculture. He got that assignment over me.

As a member of the State-hood Subcommittee of the Interior and Insular Affairs Committee, Sisk helped lay the ground-work for Hawaiian state-hood. Here, the subcom-mittee—Leo O'Brien, right, Sisk and E.Y. Perry —joined by Senator Hugh Scott, second from left, confers with Admiral Harry D. Felt in Hono-lulu.

So Clair helped me get the top spot possible on the Interior and Insular Affairs Committee. When a party changes control, the percentage of party committee members shifts. Each committee is balanced according to the percentage of Democrats and Republicans in the House. The member who ranked just below me was Stewart Udall of Arizona, older brother of "Mo" Udall (the present member of the House). Stewart Udall later served as secretary of interior under Jack Kennedy. Edith Green of Oregon, elected the same time I was, was also on the committee below me.

The assignment gave me a lot of help because it was right in line with water programs and had jurisdiction over the San Luis Project, which I was advocating. An ideal appointment for me; I enjoyed it very much. This committee has a broad jurisdiction in domestic matters, with five subcommittees in those days. Power and Reclamation was the most important subcommittee. The next key subcommittee was Statehood (or what we called territories), which had jurisdiction over all of our offshore territory, including the islands (Hawaii was then one of them). It also had an Indian Affairs Subcommittee, National Parks Subcommittee, and the Mines and Mining Subcommittee. I got on the Power and Reclamation, Statehood, and Indian Affairs subcommittees right away.

Here is a list of Democrats who were on the Committee on Interior and Insular Affairs of the Eighty-fourth Congress: Clair Engle of California was chairman. Wayne Aspinall of Colorado was chairman of the Sub-committee on Power and Reclamation. Leo W. O'Brien of New York was chairman of the Subcommittee on Statehood or territories. Walter Rogers of Texas was chairman of Mines and Mining Subcommittee. Gracie Pfost of Idaho was chairman of Parks and Bureau of Land Management Subcommittee. James A. Haley of Florida was chairman of the Indian Affairs Subcommittee. George Shuford of North Carolina was another member of the committee, but was not particularly well-known. Adam Clayton Powell of New York was the next ranking member. He outranked me by two or three places.

Others included, in order of seniority: Ed Edmondson of Oklahoma and Lee Metcalf of Montana (Metcalf later served many years in the Senate and recently died in office); George Christopher of Missouri; myself; Stewart Udall of Arizona; Charles C. Diggs, Jr. of Michigan; J. T. Rutherford of Texas; Edith Green of Oregon; and Bob Bartlett of Alaska (he was a delegate from Alaska because it was a territory at that time). A. Fernos-Isern was commissioner from Puerto Rico. Mrs. Joseph R. Farrington was a delegate from Hawaii and a Republican.

The election of 1954, which changed control of the House to the Democrats, did not change the total balance in California; we had eleven Democrats and nineteen Republicans. The only two freshmen Democrats from California at that time were Jimmy Roosevelt and myself.

AID: *Did it give you a kind of nostalgic feeling, going to Congress with the son of Franklin Roosevelt (knowing how you admired F.D.R.)?*

SISK: Naturally, there was a bit of nostalgia there. I have a personally autographed picture of Mrs. Roosevelt. Although a lot of people were critical of the Roosevelt family—and probably rightly so—I developed a lot of respect for Jim and we are good friends. I have been to his home and met his wife, a very lovely person. He was a hard worker, studied hard and knew his legislation. He was always on the floor, attended meetings, never neglected his duties. These traits appealed to me. On the other hand, his brother Frank, a nice guy, was nowhere near the pusher that Jim was. He later became secretary of commerce.

During my second term, we were concerned about the Republicans outgunning us. We feared they could gather enough conservative Democrats from the South to outnumber us on committees and even on the House floor, so we set up the Democratic Study Group, which is still in existence today. Jimmy Roosevelt and I were charter members of DSG. I chaired the nominating committee which formally organized the DSG, which at first was just an informal group. Eugene McCarthy (a good solid man in those days, of whom I thought a lot), John Blatnik of Minnesota, Chet Holifield of California, Lee Metcalf of Montana, Frank Thompson of New Jersey, and the delegate from Puerto Rico were some of the original members.

We all worked together informally, but Speaker (Sam) Rayburn wasn't happy with it because he never liked caucuses or organizations within organizations. However, Mr. Rayburn was losing too many battles on the floor. In fact, several of us told him, "We have to get organized or otherwise we will continue to be shot down." Although hesitant about the idea of the group, he gave some type of signal, meaning that he would not

Sisk meets 4—H Clubber Jo Ann Jensen of Laton in 1957, a session typical of many held during his visits to the state.

Prior to the advent of jet-age commuting, stays in Washington tended to be lengthy and required every last suitcase—as this 1956 scene suggests.

Left: Valley sheep rancher Phil Erro confers the title "Honorary Sheepherder" on a grateful B. F. Sisk in 1959. Sisk received the recognition for his work on behalf of area sheep ranching.

Sisk meets with Fresno representatives of the AFL-CIO in his Washington office in 1958.

Left: For a two-year-period, from 1957 through the end of 1958, Democratic members held all five Central Valley congressional seats. The Democratic lineup, from left: John McFall, Sisk, Clair Engle, John Moss, and Harlan Hagen.

Below: San Joaquin Valley congressmen Sisk and Harlan Hagen, right, demonstrate the fine art of shish-kebabing to Rep. Harold Cooley, then chairman of the Committee on Agriculture and one of the most powerful men in the House.

The California congressional delegation, 1958. Sisk is in first row, far left.

oppose the group if it were put together in the right way. In 1956 or 1957, we decided to formalize the group, with officers, etc. I was selected as the chairman of the organizing committee. The committee was composed of ten members, including Edith Green, Frank Thompson, Jim Roosevelt, Henry Reuss (of Wisconsin and now chairman of the banking committee), Al Ullman (now chairman of the Ways and Means Committee), and others.

The second or third year after we were formally organized, it became my duty to tell Jim Roosevelt he couldn't be president of the organization. This was tough to do, but I was selected because we were colleagues. Jimmy did a good job but many felt he was a little too far off in left field, too liberal. Rayburn wouldn't have liked him as president, either. I called Jim and he came up to my office. I told him, "Jim, I think you know how I respect you, but the group feels that it is not appropriate for you to be president for reasons you can understand." This was very tough for me to do.

Some of the freshmen congressmen elected with me included: Charlie Teague, a Republican from Ojai, California, who is now dead; Republican Johnny Baldwin from the Bay Area, also now dead; Ludlow Ashley of Ohio, still in Congress and active on the banking committee; Charlie Diggs from Michigan, who recently resigned, one of the first blacks in Congress (Diggs served with me on the Interior and Insular Affairs Committee and later became chairman of the District of Columbia Committee). Also in the Class of '54 were Dante Fascell of Florida, still in Congress (he is active on the Foreign Affairs Committee and has done an excellent job); Edith Green from Oregon, now retired; Martha Griffiths of Michigan, a former judge, now retired from Congress and practicing law in Michigan. Robbie MacDonald from Massachusetts died of cancer a number of years ago. Paul Rogers of Florida retired the same time I did. J. T. Rutherford is gone. Frank Thompson of New Jersey is still there and is chairman of the House Administration Committee. Stewart Udall, whom I have already mentioned, has retired. Charlie Vanik of Ohio is still there and is on the Ways and Means Committee. Jim Wright of Texas is majority leader of the House.

Rayburn, who knew I was one of the marginally elected freshmen (I won by 53 percent), recognized that I needed all the help I could get and gave me a second spot on the Veterans Affairs Committee, which is considered a minor committee. However, this committee deals with a large cross-section of Americans and Mr. Rayburn knew that spot would help me out politically in my district. I served six years on the Veterans Affairs Committee and was chairman of the Hospitals Subcommittee during the last couple of years I was on the committee, an interesting experience since it involved all of the veterans hospitals across the nation.

During this period of time—from January 1955 to January 1961 (the year I became a member of the Rules Committee)—I was also on the District of Columbia Committee, where I had a hassle with Lyndon Johnson over home rule. Rayburn again helped me by getting me on the Export Control Select Committee. We were having a problem with the exporting of ideas, especially to Russia, regarding research information. There are certain laws which govern what can be exported in terms of research, knowledge, factual information, etc.—anything in the sensitive area of national defense had to be licensed. Many people thought Russia was getting too much information from the U.S. The select committee which was set up was called the "Kitchin Committee," named after its chairman, A. Paul Kitchin from North Carolina, who had been in Congress for a number of years. Del Latta, currently a Republican member of the Rules Committee, served with me on that "Kitchin Committee." Eddy Boland of Massachusetts, who is still in Congress and one of the ranking members of Appropriations, was also on that select committee, as was Republican G. P. Lipscomb of California. We held a whole series of hearings and published a report.

12.
Blue Ribbon Committee
on Space: A-OK

In October 1957, Russia launched Sputnik. I don't know what the rest of the country thought about it, but it jarred Washington quite a bit. Eisenhower, Rayburn, and Johnson, as well as others, were concerned. Rayburn moved faster than anybody else. In a matter of hours after Sputnik was in orbit, questions were being raised about what had happened to us. The navy, under normal procedures, was given the responsibility for getting a satellite into orbit. Unfortunately, the navy wasn't having much luck. In a matter of hours, Rayburn named a "Blue Ribbon Committee," and I was appointed to it. This Select Committee on Astronautics and Space Exploration included Democrats John W. Mc-Cormack, Massachusetts, as chairman; Overton Brooks of Louisiana, a famous member of Congress at that time; Brook Hayes, who became well-known; Leo W. O'Brien of New York; Lee Metcalf of Montana; William H. Natcher of Kentucky; and myself. On the Republican side, there was Joe Martin of Massachusetts, a former Speaker of the House during the previous two Republican-controlled Congresses; Leslie Arends of Illinois, the minority leader of the House; Gordon McDonough of California; Jim Fulton of Pennsylvania, who is now dead; Kenneth Keating of New York; and Gerald R. Ford, Jr. of Michigan. Jerry and I were the two junior members on the committee.

Official U.S. Navy photograph

Above: The full standing Committee on Science and Astronautics assembles in its chambers in 1959, shortly after the panel was officially formed. Sisk is seated, fifth from left.

Left: In line with his duties on the Space Committee, Sisk was on hand when North American Aviation rolled out the first of its experimental X-15 aircraft in 1958.

Below: Members of the select committee on space gather around a miniature mock-up of an early U. S. space probe. Sisk is standing fourth from left; Gerald Ford is standing at extreme right. Seated at right is John McCormack, later Speaker of the House. (1958 photo)

During the period from late 1957 to 1959, the space committee took up a lot of my time. I was also serving on the Interior and Insular Affairs Committee and the Veterans Affairs Committee. On each of these committees, I was also serving on several subcommittees. Admiral Hyman Rickover spent hours before our committee. Werner von Braun, the father of the V-2 rocket, also spent hours before the committee. He headed the space research team.

We immediately took the space program from the navy and gave it to the army. This wasn't playing one branch of the armed services against another; the navy had simply been unable to get any of its vehicles into the air. It was decided that the space program was to be placed under the Redstone Arsenal, an army base in Huntsville, Alabama. I spent a good deal of time commuting to that base in Huntsville. Von Braun and his team, whom we grabbed before the Russians following World War II, were called the Penamunde Group. These German scientists and technicians were the founders of our space program to a large extent; they miniaturized and made possible the launching of our early vehicles into space. The Americans just didn't have the know-how the Germans had. All of the early hearings were held in executive session. Everything was very QT. We were trying to catch up with the Russians. There were many things that had military significance, even early on. I still can't talk about some of this information.

Johnson, as majority leader in the Senate, appointed a like Senate committee, which he headed himself. The committee formulated legislation after extensive hearings and put together a package, then carried it to the floor. We passed it through the House and the Senate. We had House-Senate conferences, as I well remember.

This was the first time that I recognized what an operator Johnson was in connection with his legislative ability. I had felt very strongly about certain aspects of the Space Act. Leo O'Brien of New York, a friend of mine on the committee, had joined me in support of an amendment the House had adopted. Johnson opposed this amendment in the Senate. It got hung up in conference. McCormack called me on the telephone and said, "Bernard (he always called me that), you are going to have to go over and sell Johnson on that amendment because we have to come to some sort of an agreement." I called O'Brien and then I called Johnson and asked for an appointment. We had lunch with Lyndon Johnson and later met in his majority leader's office on the floor of the Senate. We had quite a little friendly set-to over this amendment. Johnson charged up and down the floor. The truth of the matter is, we actually worked out a compromise. He gave a bit and we gave a bit. We maintained the basic part of the amendment although we did modify it. That is what finally settled the differences between the House and the Senate and sent the bill

Members of the House Science and Astronautics Committee pose with military personnel at the Redstone Arsenal in Huntsville, Alabama in 1960. Sisk is seated, second from left.

An early Redstone rocket lifts off the pad in Florida.

on to the president. I cite this because I did get a good picture of how obstinate Johnson could be and, frankly, he was an operator.

AID: *Can you be a little more specific about what he said?*

SISK: Johnson spoke what you could call *real* Texan. He could swear—he had quite a command of that type of language. Later on, when I was on the Rules Committee, I had another head-on with him. I'll talk about that when we come to it.

Upon the signing by the president of a bill creating the space agency [National Aeronautics and Space Administration], the select committee

63

went out of existence. The permanent standing committee was approved and the rules were amended to set up this committee, of which I also became a member. That committee was chaired by Overton Brooks. The name was changed at that time to the Science and Astronautics Committee.

Overton Brooks' selection as chairman had certain interesting aspects. Carl Vinson of Georgia was chairman of the Armed Services Committee and had been for years and years. In fact, Carl had served in the Congress for fifty years. He had become "Mr. Armed Services" for all practical purposes. Overton Brooks was a ranking member of Armed Services. One of the things that has been said—and probably correctly—is that Carl Vinson refused to retire from the House (he is still alive and living down in Georgia and is approaching one hundred years old) because he didn't want Overton Brooks to be chairman of Armed Services. There were some rather obvious reasons for that. It is always said that a deal was made at the time Overton Brooks became chairman of the Science and Astronautics Committee in order to get him off of the Armed Services Committee. When Overton became chairman, he had to give up his position on the Armed Services Committee.

AID: *So Carl Vinson could retire?*

SISK: Carl Vinson then retired.

AID: *According to a newspaper story, the permanent committee was adapting sea law to space. Do you recall that?*

SISK: Yes. The committee was dealing with something that nobody had been too concerned about—outer space. We had dealt with worldwide regulatory air travel but that was within air space of a nation; for example, the rights of one nation's aircraft to fly over another nation. When you are talking about satellites hundreds or thousands of miles out in space, at what point does this control of air space end? We established in a sense the law of the sea; there are international waters and international space over which no one has control. Bitter debates did go on. My memory fails in regard to the details, but in essence, we operate in outer space as we do in international waters.

AID: *The newspaper story said that there were two projects in contention: the Mercury project versus the project called Dinosaur. You favored Dinosaur. Do you recall that?*

SISK: The early history of the Mercury project did not look good to me. I was chairman of the subcommittee dealing with space travel on the permanent standing committee, but right now, I can't recall the reasons for my position regarding the Mercury program.

One of the special committee studies pertained to unidentified flying objects. There was a lot of speculation and concern about UFOs at that time. The chairman, Overton Brooks, appointed a committee of three to investigate UFOs. This investigation was done secretly, although I don't understand the reasons for the secrecy. The UFO investigation was very interesting because it was difficult to unravel fact from fiction. There were many astounding occurrences which put some doubt in your mind. However, most of the objects were illusions caused by reflected light creating unusual figures. These light reflections didn't account for everything, though. We came back with a statement that we had not been visited by beings from other planets. There are no little Martians out there, but the fact remains there are some unusual happenings.

AID: *You left the committee when you went on the Rules Committee?*

SISK: My direct participation in the problems regarding space ended in January 1961 when I became a member of the Rules Committee.

13.
The San Luis Project

AID: *Let's talk about the San Luis Project.*

SISK: As we have already discussed to an extent, the San Luis Project is the reason I got into politics. As the west side wells became deeper, factors emerged making it simply impossible economically to justify the production of crops; you could not produce enough to pay the power bills. I recognized what was going to happen in that area; it was simply going to dry up and blow away, reverting back to what it was when the land first began to be developed. It was at that point that I expressed grave concern about the position of the incumbent congressman, Oakley Hunter, who did not feel a reclamation project was the answer. I did. That was the key issue throughout the campaign.

I was elected to the Congress in the fall of 1954. Shortly after the Eighty-fourth Congress convened on January 3, 1955, I introduced the first San Luis bill, of which I was author. That bill called for construction of an off-stream storage project. This project was different from the normal reclamation projects with which people are generally familiar. Normally, you build a dam across a flowing stream for two purposes: 1) to stop periodic flooding because of excessive rainfall or snow melt, etc. and 2) to conserve water for a later period or in a more orderly way. This project did not call for the damming up of an existing stream because there is no stream of any consequence in the west side area. What the bill did propose was to pick up water through pumping plants at Tracy that were in existence as part of the Delta-Mendota Project. Those pumps would be utilized in winter when enormous volumes of storm water from rainfall and snow melt were coming down the northern mountains of California into the American, Sacramento and Trinity rivers and into the other rivers flowing into the delta. After picking up that water through these pumps,

Two scenes of the San Luis Project area prior to construction: general view of San Luis Reservoir area in 1961, looking northeast, shows debris scattered along Cottonwood Creek bed (top). San Luis Creek area, south of Highway 152, shows medium to light clearing of trees and shrubbery. Both areas were inundated as reservoir was filled in late sixties.

the water would be transported into a storage area. This San Luis site was a logical storage area. Engineers had examined many sites for a storage area to hold a substantial amount of water and that would permit construction of a dam, at reasonable cost, for a reservoir. They selected this site.

There was a lot of misunderstanding about the San Luis Project. Even in the initial phases, we had a selling job to do, both to the Congress and to the people.

AID: *Could you describe the San Luis Project physically and geographically?*

SISK: Let me distinguish between the dam itself and the whole area affected by it. The dam is in an area about twelve miles almost due west of the city of Los Banos, California. It is just on the edge of the coastal foothills on the west side of the San Joaquin Valley. Because of the geography of the hills, there was a rather narrow point on which we could build a dam connecting these hills. There would be a few saddle dams in addition to the main dam and the whole area forms a beautiful amphitheater or reservoir for water. The dam filled with water provides something more than two million acre-feet of storage. An acre-foot is the amount of water that it would take to cover one acre of land one foot deep. In volume, that equals approximately 326,000 gallons, so when the dam holds two million acre-feet of water, you can get an idea of how many billion gallons of water that is.

The area affected directly by the San Luis Project runs generally south or southeast of the dam site. That area is served today by the Westlands Water District, the San Luis Water District and the Panoche Water District, which cover something like 700,000 acres of land. Westlands Water District alone includes about 600,000 acres. These districts run a number of miles south of the dam site across western Merced County, western Fresno County, and into western Kings County. The division of the water in the San Luis Dam is 50 percent federal water and 50 percent state water. [The Westlands Water District contracted for federal water from the project.] The San Luis Project provides supplemental water—by supplemental I mean that it is not now and never was expected to supply the total amount of water needed year in and year out. The wells there, before we put in the San Luis Project, were running so deep and cost so much for the power to lift the water that far, that you could not grow enough produce or commodities to pay the cost of the power. The land would have reverted to desert were it not for the supplemental supply which, with the wells, provides the overall amount of water needed. So if you come up with a dry year where you do not have an ample supply of water coming out of the delta, as happened two years ago [1976-1977], you have to pump that much more. The more you pump, the more water you are pulling out of the ground. Before the San Luis Project, as the water was pulled from underground, wells had to be drilled deeper. More water was pulled out than was being put into the ground; therefore there was an overdraft. After we brought the San Luis in with its supplemental supply, the water table began to rise. Because of the reduction of the amount of supplemental water owing to the drought, we had to increase our pumping as the water table began to drop again.

AID: *If I were to dig a well today on the west side, how far would I have to go?*

SISK: Today, you would still have to pump lift from about 450 feet, which is very costly. The average price of wells on the west side today is $150,000 to $200,000.

Now may be the appropriate place to emphasize that it is important for

67

Above left: Before completion of the San Luis Reservoir and the Pleasant Valley Canal, "fill 'er up" in Coalinga, California, referred as much to water as to gasoline. Because its underground water supply was brackish and undrinkable, the city operated two desalinization plants producing 38,000 gallons of water daily. Residents of distant farms were required to obtain adequate drinking water supplies from city dispensing stations such as this one (1968).

Above right: Mrs. Lou Niboli, a Coalinga housewife, fills her saucepan with water from a "third tap," a product of the city's dual distribution water system (1968).

As the San Luis Dam nears completion in 1967, Sisk chats with Coalinga officials about the city's water needs and the reservoir's capacity to alleviate the community's water shortage.

people to understand some of the political and economic problems of western water and in particular this project. We talk about putting a family on 160 acres. (There are even some groups who advocate only twenty or forty acres—years ago you heard about what ten acres and a mule would do for everybody.) First of all, a person in that position would find uneconomic the enormous cost of a well. I have supported the 160-acre limitation through the years, provided you use reason and judgment. People testified at the hearings and supported this project on the assumption we would continue to apply the law as it had been applied for the last fifty years. You could lease land and sell off your land under the "ten years provision" of the recordable contract. In turn, you could have 160 acres for each family member and you could farm a management block within the family. This would permit farming an economical unit. If you limited land ownerships to 160 acres—much less twenty to forty acres—and you had to drill a well on the land, you would have to consider the cost of that investment, plus the fact the federal government may require residency (which the National Land For People crowd is demanding) and that means you have the cost of a house to consider as well. To build a house today costs $50,000 or more. Then you have to consider the cost of equipment. The average farmer needs a planter, harvester, cultivator, and the ordinary kinds of tools. I don't mean the elaborate ones. He could easily wind up with $150,000 to $250,000 in equipment alone. Plus a house and a $150,000 well. You see the ridiculousness of some of the suggestions in connection with farming only 160 acres in this area. I am strongly in support of the family farmer. Surprisingly enough, where previously the bulk of the land was farmed by less than fifty people, today there are probably two thousand different landowners there.

At the present time, most of the land in the Westlands Water District is under recordable contracts. This means you sign a contract upon receipt of water that you will divest yourself of all acreage in excess of 160 acres, within a ten-year period.

There has been a great deal of misunderstanding about the 160-acre limitation. Let's say that a man and his wife have a large family of eight or more children. Each one is entitled to 160 acres, so combined they could wind up owning 1,600 acres or more. That is legal—there is no change in the law.

Now I don't have a particular reason to carry a candle for the Southern Pacific or Standard Oil or anybody else. An enormous amount of land *was* owned in very large blocks. For example, Standard Oil owned over 100,000 acres, as did Southern Pacific—far more. Russell Giffen was probably the largest individual landowner with 100,000-plus acres. Russell Giffen, in my opinion, is one of the finest men I have ever known, and the community, state and country owe him a great deal. Russell, in truth, is a big man in more ways than one. Giffen testified in Washington in support of the San Luis Project and stated he would sign a recordable contract—thus requiring him to divest himself of his holdings—because otherwise, he said, without a supply of supplemental water, the west side would simply go back to dust. He signed such a recordable contract after the San Luis Project became operative and today doesn't own an acre of land in the Westlands Water District.

Another large landholder, Jack Harris, has signed a recordable contract. In addition to Standard Oil, other oil companies owned fairly good-sized blocks. Southern Pacific has put its lands up for sale after signing recordable contracts. In fact, right now [July 1979], there is a whole string of them to be approved which the present secretary of interior, Cecil Andrus, is holding up by quibbling over minor matters.

AID: *Who are they selling their land to?*

SISK: To individuals who can afford to purchase it and who then usually lease it. We argue about what is an economical farming unit. Is it 1,000 or 2,000 or 5,000 acres? I think it depends on what you grow and where your land is located. I have difficulty following the reasoning of the people in opposition.

As I've said, San Luis was different—it was off-stream storage, which is now a commonly-used term. What Governor Jerry Brown and Ron Robie [Ronald B. Robie, director, Department of Water Resources for California] are talking about in connection with the California water proposal currently pending before the state Legislature is basically a broad use of off-stream storage. Hungry Hollow is another suggested site. There are a number of others as well.

The San Luis Project was very difficult to sell because of its unique nature and because of the area's large land ownerships. Naturally, when you propose a project in which federal monies are to be used, even though every dollar of this project—construction, irrigation costs, the systems themselves—was reimbursable, the monies for construction were still interest-free. To that extent, even in those days of low interest, it still was a subsidy. That's where the 160-acre law came in under the 1902 Reclamation Act, limiting the amount of subsidies an individual or corporation could receive. Because of the large ownerships, this was one of the things Congress explored very carefully.

AID: *I have here the Public Affairs Report, Institute of Governmental Studies at Berkeley, Volume 19, October 1978, Number 5. The author, who is a Department of Agriculture and Resource Economics professor, says in effect: In addition to the interest subsidy (which you have already mentioned), the water users are not required to repay the full construction cost plus interest. For example, on those projects completed between 1903 and 1976, the total irrigation construction cost—excluding costs of flood control and recreational wildlife refuge—amounted to $3.62 billion. Yet water users were only originally liable for 60 percent of that, or two billion dollars. The rest was to be paid out of revenues from hydroelectricity sales. The Public Affairs Report claims that water users haven't been repaying that because of the impact of inflation on project operation and maintenance costs. If the total operating and maintenance costs accrued between the years of 1903 and 1976 are subtracted from total payments made by water users during the same period, it is found that only $700 million dollars of the $2.9 billion have been repaid (three and three-tenths percent). At current collection rates and costs, and assuming no further inflation, it would take 432 years for water users to repay their share of construction costs. The report goes on to state that for the Westlands, the newest of the projects, water users repay all irrigation construction costs and receive no explicit subsidy from electricity revenues.*

70

SISK: Dick, let me first say that at the time that this material came out, it coincided more or less with the time the Department of Interior under the new administration [Secretary Cecil Andrus] was projecting some figures. To be a little brutal about it, both Congressman [Harold T. "Bizz"] Johnson, chairman of the reclamation subcommittee early on, and myself felt the figures were as phony as a three-dollar bill. In the first place, they were predicated on improper basic figures. Also, they did not take into account, in our opinion, many other aspects of the overall program. At any rate, some of the figures that this particular professor is quoting were requoted by the Department of Interior. We, along with some other interested parties here in California (irrigation districts, etc.) had an independent analysis made of those figures and found them at variance by almost two billion dollars. Their calculations were absolutely not correct.

To break this down into dollars and cents and to disprove these figures off the top of my head would be difficult. However, there is no question that there are reports and factual material which rebut this argument substantially.

On the other hand, let me say this: the Committee on Interior and Insular Affairs had an understanding at the time it approved the San Luis Project in 1960 and when signed into law by President Eisenhower, that it would be required to stand on its own feet and not burden the Central Valley Project fund. The Central Valley Project, which included Shasta, Keswick, Trinity, Millerton and other projects—such as San Luis when it came along—was becoming an integrated program.

These projects were conceived with the idea of producing a great amount of hydroelectric power. As the power was sold, it would help repay the cost of the projects. This was a dedicated type of program; it was part of reclamation law. This type of repayment would assist the growers and the taxpayer, and in the final analysis, it provided the easiest and simplest way to pay across-the-board. As each project was added, if the benefits-to-cost ratio was less favorable on a given project than in others, that project would become a burden on the total CVP fund. The CVP fund was accumulated from power revenues along with payments by farmers and other assets of the CVP. The Congress wanted to make sure that the San Luis Project did not become an undue burden on that fund. This is where the report is correct: provisions were written in connection with the Westlands contract, providing that water users of the San Luis would have to guarantee the total repayment of all the reimbursable costs without becoming a burden (or leaning) on the CVP fund.

AID: *Is it also the philosophy of CVP funding that the repayment by agricultural water users be based upon their ability to pay?*

SISK: That is correct. Going back to the 1902 Act, the law very specifically states that repayment is based on farmers' ability to pay. This is true in the earliest reclamation projects ever authorized. This has been traditional; the aim of these projects was to develop and to bring people to the West by creating an economy here; helping create customers for railroads and merchants and other business establishments.

The hearings on the San Luis Project went on for years. The first hearings I was involved in occurred in 1955. We had hearings through 1960. It became evident, certainly by 1956, that we still had a lot of basic work to do if in fact we were going to make this project go. It was to be the largest single reclamation project in total cost authorized by the Congress up to that time. It would create the largest agricultural irrigation district, in acreage, in the world—the Westlands Water District. Recognizing the problems, I came back to California on many trips. I sat down with people from Kern County and the Metropolitan Water District in Los Angeles—which is, by the way, from the standpoint of industry and people involved and monies overall, the largest and most powerful water district in the world. Basically, MWD's big use is for industrial and municipal water, not agricultural water. If you have ever been in Metropolitan Water's headquarters in Los Angeles—the board room is more elaborate than those in many state legislatures. So I met with those people because it became evident that we had a whole variety of problems to settle. Clair Engle had won election to the U.S. Senate in 1958. Wayne Aspinall of Colorado then became chairman of the Interior and Insular Affairs Committee. He came to me right after the assumption of his chairmanship and said, "Bernie, I am for your project. I believe in it and think it is necessary, and I will help you in any way I can, but there is no way that we are going to move on it until you get your ducks in a row out in California. You have to get unanimity and you have to come back here in lock-step with all Californians—the state administration, the Legislature, and all the various water agencies—agreed. When you do that, we will move this project."

We had been struggling with this since my election in 1954. We eventually agreed, for the first time in reclamation history, to put together a joint federal-state operation—a first in the history of federal water development that permitted intermingling of federal and state waters in a single reservoir. We had proposed a million acre-foot reservoir at the San Luis site; once we recognized that we had to work out some kind of a federal-state joint operation, we doubled the size of the project. We went to two million acre-feet, in fact, 2.3 million acre-feet total storage, 50 percent to be state and 50 percent to be federal. By this time Pat [Edmund G.] Brown had become governor of California. He was elected in 1958. I had a friend to deal with there because I had always worked very closely with Pat. What brought the Metropolitan Water District around was that it was going to receive a substantial portion of the state's water. It also brought Kern County around because once we agreed to an additional million acre-feet of water in a holding basin for water southbound to Kern County as well as to Southern California and Los Angeles, that took away Kern's concerns and the county joined ranks. We then went before the committee with California in lock-step as Aspinall had asked.

We had succeeded in pulling California together but we still had obstacles. We were talking about a multi-million dollar project that we were going to have to sell to the Congress of the United States. I dealt with people like Senator [Henry] "Scoop" Jackson, who was very active on the Senate's Interior and Insular Affairs Committee. I dealt with New Mexico's [Clinton P.] "Clint" Anderson, the chairman of that committee. I worked with Tom Kuchel, who was then senator from California. I already mentioned Clair Engle, who had been elected to replace Bill Knowland when Bill left the Senate to run for governor of California. They were going to replace Knowland with Goodwin "Goody" Knight. Unfortunately for them, the swap didn't work. I think it was the worst mistake the Republican Party ever made. It lost control of the state of California through one unfortunate maneuver; at least, unfortunate on its part.

In connection with legislation, often you run into some peculiar situations. To get this project out of the Committee on Interior and Insular Affairs, we needed the help of John P. Saylor of Pennsylvania, who had been traditionally considered one of the great enemies of reclamation. Saylor was the ranking Republican on the House Interior and Insular Affairs Committee and had been elected to Congress in 1949. He was finally sold on going along with us. That is the first and only reclamation project he ever supported, that I know of.

We made it very clear in the bill that no one was going to be individually enriched. John Saylor's support gave me a great deal of help on the floor. Even with that help, we stalled before the Committee on Rules. This, in spite of my talks with chairman Judge Howard W. Smith of Virginia, one of the great legislators of all time in my opinion, although he and I didn't vote together very often. I talked to other members of the Committee on Rules. Still, we didn't get a rule. As it happened, the Democratic Party was having a big congressional affair in Washington. We from California felt it might be of help if we bought a substantial block of tickets to that dinner. As a result, shortly thereafter, we did secure a rule for the San Luis Project. I want to make it clear it was simply a matter that in the past, California had not done as much, party-wise, as a number of other states. I think this had been resented a little. The bill went to the House floor; we got a good vote and passed it by a substantial margin. It then went to the Senate.

There it got out of committee rather quickly. Clinton Anderson handled the bill expeditiously in the Interior Committee. He worked closely with Clair Engle and Tom Kuchel as well as with "Scoop" Jackson and others from the West. On the Senate floor, it stalled again, and continued to be stalled for quite a long while. Senators Engle and Kuchel continued to try to work out problems to get it to the floor. Finally, in the closing days of the session in 1960, in the Eighty-sixth Congress, we were bucking the deadline. Engle and Kuchel called me and asked me to come over and I met them in the cloakroom of the Senate. They said, "Bernie, we have done everything we can. How well do you know Clint Anderson?" I had been acquainted with Senator Anderson in a general way. He and his wife had been guests in our home on one occasion. I knew of no reason why Clint would be unfriendly to me, and I didn't have any particular axe to grind with him. I said, "I will talk to Senator Anderson." I went into the cloakroom where he was seated. He was a diabetic and had serious health problems. He was sitting at the end of a big long sofa. In order to get his attention so he could hear what I was saying, I knelt down. I actually got down on one knee. It was symbolic, I guess. Senator Anderson was not a person who talked much, but was rather reticent. He sat there and looked at me. Anybody who knew Senator Anderson knew that he had a way of looking directly at you without blinking. I explained the matter as briefly as I could because I knew I had only a few minutes. His time was valuable. He was very much involved in the nuclear program, for example, and a whole variety of other things. I explained to him as quickly as I could the essential nature of San Luis. After listening to me, he said not a word, but sat completely quiet. It seemed like forever. Finally, he said, "Okay." He got up and walked on to the Senate floor and almost within a matter of minutes, they passed that bill through the U.S. Senate. It went to President Eisenhower, who signed the bill into law in practically the closing days of that Congress.

The problem that the bill had had previously in the Senate involved a man with whom I had travelled. I had joined him on the platform and had shared duties with him. He was Wayne Morse of Oregon, and he had some problem with this project because of the nature of the landholdings. Morse visualized the enrichment of these big landholders and the oil companies. It happened that Wayne Morse was out of town on that particular day, although I was not aware of it at the time. Senator William Proxmire, a compatriot of Morse's, was on the floor when Senator Anderson brought this up. (The matter was handled expeditiously and there was no roll call vote.) Proxmire raised some questions but I guess he was caught off-balance without any backup materials, and Morse wasn't there. The general feeling of the Senate, which was nearing the end of the session, was that it was time to act, so it went ahead and voted it through. Had that bill not passed that year, I believe it would have had to start over in the next Congress and it might never have been authorized. It was almost a miracle.

Let me give you some clarification. Clint Anderson, although he was chairman of the committee, was not at fault for not bringing it to the

Senate. There were dissenting members of his committee, with whom Clint was trying to get along. Clint Anderson himself was a great friend of reclamation and had supported California, New Mexico, Arizona, and other upper basin projects. Senators Morse, Proxmire, and Paul Douglas of Illinois were raising questions brought forth by those who later formed the National Land For People group. We still have trouble with them today. This group wanted to carve up land ownership into ten- or twenty-acre plots. There was a difference of philosophy. Anderson kept getting requests from Morse and Proxmire to hold it up. There is a tendency for a chairman of a committee to protect his own membership; the chairman will adhere somewhat to the wishes of his colleagues. My contention with Anderson was that this project was simply too important for one or two senators to hold up. I argued that the opponents were not in line with the basic concepts of reclamation. Senator Anderson was willing to listen to me because the argument conformed to his own philosophy and he finally made up his mind that he couldn't delay it any longer.

AID: *In talking about the position of the Eisenhower Administration on the San Luis Project, can you give details?*

SISK: The Eisenhower Administration supported the project. Under Secretary Fred Seaton, the Department of Interior supported this project generally throughout, although they had recommendations and asked for amendments at the time of the hearings. In most cases, the committee went along with most of Interior's amendments. The Bureau of Reclamation [now the Water and Power Resources Service] also supported the project. So actually, at no point did we have any problem with the administration. Once we had the bill passed, there was no question of Eisenhower's signature.

AID: *You mentioned getting your ducks in line in California, and Pat Brown's cooperation. However, you didn't mention Governor Knight. Was he opposed to the project?*

SISK: No. Governor Knight basically supported the project. As far as the state's administration was concerned, we didn't have any serious problems. Our problems were with irrigation groups up and down the state, putting together a program we could all agree on, moving in lock-step.

AID: *How about the Farm Bureau?*

SISK: The Farm Bureau generally supported the project.

We had objections from the CCID, Central California Irrigation District, which was headquartered in Los Banos. The CCID is a carry-over of the old Miller and Lux holdings. It received its water through the Delta-Mendota Canal by virtue of giving up waters out of the San Joaquin when Friant Dam was built. The dam diverted water from the San Joaquin to Madera in the north and Kern in the south. As a replacement for these waters, the CVP intent was to bring down water from the Tracy pumping plant through the Delta-Mendota Canal to CCID. CCID's concern was over drainage; it had too much saline water and its lands were reverting back into salt. CCID was concerned about the lands to be irrigated in the Westlands; the Westlands, being above CCID lands, would tend to destroy them.

A famous water attorney in Merced, C. Ray Robinson, was the attorney for CCID. Robinson was a tough customer; he was a hurdle that we had to overcome. There were people from that group who believed they had been walked over. The drain became the crux for settling the problem. The CCID and its attorney had us stymied until we could get an agreement on drainage. As a result, we had to be very careful about the language used in writing the bill. CCID's key people attended a meeting in Washington with the Bureau of Reclamation, representatives from the Department of Interior, members of the committee, and myself. We hammered out an agreement requiring the simultaneous construction of a drain along with the irrigation district. The decision satisfied the CCID people—and justifiably so—because it is foolish to create a project for the good of some people but to the detriment of others. After the completion of the dam, we started distributing water. At the same time, we started digging the drainage system. We had to have appropriations for the distribution of water and the digging of the drain simultaneously, as we moved along with the project.

AID: *Why was the drain delayed so long?*

SISK: Early on, I don't think the drain was delayed. As the pressure built up in later years, it was delayed; the Appropriations Committee wanted to cut back because of pressures on the budget. Some of the members didn't realize the importance of the drain and were inclined to cut back on the funds for the drain, but to continue with the distribution system. People in the East are not aware of the saline problems we have in the Central Valley. As a result, during some years you had a larger appropriation directed to the construction of the distribution system and a lesser amount to the drainage system. [In 1967 California withdrew from the joint development of a master drain with the bureau, and the bureau began building its own San Luis drain.] The CCID lands were protected generally; they had to be under law. At the present time, the drainage system is still only partially completed. We are dumping the drainage into the Kesterson regulating reservoir, located midway between the valley area and the delta. There is controversy on what to do with the agricultural effluents. There are alternatives to the use of the San Joaquin River as a drain: 1) create one or more salt sinks in the valley; 2) build a gravity canal to the ocean. There is a lot of opposition to dumping it back into the delta. I don't blame them on that score because we have enough problems trying to keep the delta cleaned up, which I strongly favor. There is a fight going on right now about how much more water can be taken out of the delta, and how much additional water should be put in for flushing

Courtesy Fresno Bee

President Kennedy addresses a crowd gathered at the Fresno Air Terminal prior to officiating at the San Luis Project groundbreaking in 1962. Sharing the speaker's platform with him are, from left, Gov. Edmund G. Brown, Sr., state Senator Hugh Burns, U.S. Senator Clair Engle, Fresno Mayor Arthur Selland, Sisk, and Ralph Brody.

purposes. The congressman from Contra Costa County at the time the project was approved was John Baldwin. Later on, Jerry Waldie became congressman after John passed away. He opposed any further removal of water from the delta on the basis that it was affecting the water quality there. After Jerry ran for governor, George Miller became the congressman and is today. We have had our problems with George; we are at opposite poles politically in connection with some of the water problems. The drain is not completed partly because we haven't agreed about where it should go; the battle in the delta is about where the outlet should be.

I want to mention one satisfying experience. President Eisenhower had signed this legislation in 1960. In 1962, I had the good fortune to fly with President Kennedy on Air Force One out to California where we landed at Castle Air Force Base in Merced. President Kennedy was taken by helicopter to Yosemite National Park, where he spent the night. I flew with Governor Pat Brown to Fresno, where Secretary of Interior Stewart Udall, accompanied by a lot of prominent federal and state people, attended a big dinner that night, celebrating the groundbreaking of San Luis, which occurred the next day. The next morning after this big affair in Fresno, Governor Brown, Congressman "Bizz" Johnson, who had worked with me all the way on this project, and I flew by helicopter to Yosemite and met the president again. We flew with him to Los Banos and the San Luis Dam site where we had the groundbreaking ceremonies.

A sudden elevation to higher office? No—but a high point in Sisk's career nonetheless, as he addresses the crowd assembled for the San Luis groundbreaking in 1962. The presidential seal is displayed for President John F. Kennedy, who later pushed the plunger at Sisk's elbow, detonating the charges that marked the beginning of construction on the massive project.

That project continued to occupy a great deal of my time, effort and energy. Every year I had to go before the Appropriations Committee and fight for sufficient money to keep the construction going, to get the dam built, to get the pumps installed, to get the forebays and afterbays built. Once you had those built, you went back fighting for money to construct and complete the distribution system.

AID: *The original amount authorized for the distribution system was $192.6 million dollars. This amount wasn't indexed [a measure of the inflationary rise of costs] although a lot of reclamation projects were.*

SISK: I will have to take part of the blame; some of the blame should go to the staff and the members of the committee. However, I don't want to pass judgment at this point. There was no earthly reason why it shouldn't have been indexed. The treatment of the San Luis Project was different from that of other projects. We had to adhere to a much tighter line. This had to do with repayment; this project could not become a burden on the CVP fund. Members of the committee deliberately kept the pressure on the project so we would have to come back to get reauthorization, which made us more accountable to the Congress on a year-by-year basis.

AID: *Will you talk about the roles of John McFall, "Bizz" Johnson and, more recently, John Krebs and Alan Cranston?*

SISK: John McFall was the first of that group to be elected [in 1956] in an adjacent district along the northern boundaries. He was not on the Interior and Insular Affairs Committee and was not on Appropriations at that time. John was not directly involved in any way. In the 1960s, as a member of Appropriations, he did support and help the project because we had common irrigation and district problems. That is, there was a kind of an imaginary line up there. In later years, I represented 85 percent of the people in Stanislaus County. He represented 85 percent of the land area in Stanislaus County. We were all around each other and had common problems.

View of the San Luis Dam looking south, with a portion of the San Luis Reservoir on the right. The dam is three and one-half miles long and 320 feet high. At the time of this photograph (March 1968), the reservoir held 180,000 acre-feet of water, against a projected 2.1 million acre-feet.

View showing construction progress of the intake and trashrack structures of the San Luis Dam, the major feature of the huge San Luis Unit.

The Bizz Johnson situation was a little different. He was elected in 1958 and served on the Public Works Committee but later joined the Interior and Insular Affairs Committee. Being on Public Works and representing an area which was involved in water development (this was the area from which we were seeking to get water in the valley), he understood the problems of water development and was a strong friend of the CVP. He inherited Clair Engle's old stand on the CVP. When Clair went to the Senate, Bizz came in representing his district in the House. Bizz was not

Above: While the entire San Luis Project wasn't operational until 1968, Sisk was present in 1965 to dedicate the Los Banos Creek Detention Dam, first unit of the project to be completed. Joining him in the formal ceremonies are John Buchholz, left, the project's chief engineer, and Floyd E. Dominy, U.S. commissioner of reclamation. The dedication marked the twenty-fifth anniversary of the first delivery of water from the Central Valley Project.

Left: On hand to dedicate the San Luis Project in 1968 are Sisk, Rep. John J. McFall, Lt. Gov. Robert Finch, Secretary of Interior Stewart Udall and U.S. Sen. Thomas Kuchel.

Photograph shows completed San Luis Dam with components identified.

U.S. Water and Power Resources Service

Reach I of the San Luis Canal, a few miles from Los Banos, California. The Dos Amigos Pumping Plant may be seen in the background. The 103 mile-long canal measures more than 200 feet wide and thirty-six feet deep.

U.S. Water and Power Resources Service

Aerial photograph looking southerly provides overview of San Luis Project as it appeared in 1979. Rebuilt Highway 152 sweeps by base of dam and reservoir. O'Neill Forebay is at upper left; Romero Overlook, a visitor center open to the public, is in foreground.

involved in the early days of authorization because he wasn't yet on the Interior and Insular Affairs Committee. Bizz got on the committee by a maneuver on my part, an arrangement in early 1961 with the Speaker, along with certain other members, to take my place on the committee when I went to Rules. I wanted Bizz there because he understood the problems of water development and we had like philosophies. This was accomplished despite other people's wanting that spot on the committee. Bizz had been trying to correct some of the matters unfortunately left undone at the time. (We referred to the indexing.) He has consistently tried to get more appropriations by testifying in support of San Luis.

Krebs and Cranston came along much later. At the time we were trying to get authorization and early monies, Kuchel and Engle were for the project. Although I am a Democrat, I was a very strong Kuchel man. Cranston was never particularly involved with San Luis; he supported appropriations requests, with which we were primarily concerned. Cranston is still essentially supportive although he is not as strong on the position as Kuchel and Engle had been.

Although Krebs was basically in support, he had commitments to those who later organized National Land For People, which I felt created a bad situation. He and I had very different opinions about some of the ongoing rules and regulations for reclamation. We are at odds today as to our philosophies. I say that we have to maintain commercial agriculture. I am not in conflict with the 160-acre limitation, but at the same time I don't think Congress ever meant to limit the size of a farm, because that would mean limiting success. You don't limit the size of a service station or any other type of business, although we do limit subsidy (i.e., water). I agree with the right of limiting subsidy.

At the time the Interior and Insular Affairs Committee, and more particularly the subcommittee on reclamation, was considering the San Luis Project, the cost to users of San Luis water was discussed. This was a big item. Traditionally, we had a postage stamp rate for CVP water that was $3.50 an acre-foot. This was established years before. Any landowner, from Northern California clear down to the Tehachapis, who was receiving CVP water (from the Madera, Orange Cove, and the Central California water districts and others) was receiving federal water from a federal project. This $3.50 per acre-foot postage stamp rate was based on the farmers' ability to pay, predicated on costs at that time. It was thought this amount could be repaid by hydroelectric power revenues in line with the requirements of the law under this forty-year contract. When the San Luis came along, it was a new ball game even though it would be a continuing part of CVP. An early issue was that recipients were going to have to pay more for water; costs and interest rates had gone up so there had to be a change. The postage stamp rate was no longer fair and equitable.

After months and years of discussion, it was written into law that the rate would be $7.50 per acre-foot. This was agreed to by the Bureau of Reclamation, the Department of Interior, and the water users. In addition to that, there would be a fifty-cent per acre-foot charge to take care of drainage costs. At the time, it was understood the costs would be based on the cost of the drainage systems for the three water districts which dealt exclusively with the San Luis Project. Most of the water from the federal San Luis Project went to the Westlands Water District, but the other two water districts were involved also. These districts were paying for the cost of a drainage system for the whole San Joaquin Valley.

The Pat Brown Administration, at the same time, was proposing a state-wide project to drain the entire valley, starting down in the Wheeler Ridge area in the south and going up to the delta in the north. At the time the bill was authorized and signed into law by President Eisenhower, it was contemplated that there would be a master drain for the valley, built by California, which would reduce the burden on the CVP fund. However, the federal government by law had to back this up by providing a drain if the state did not. The state never has, even to this day.

Getting back to the rates for water, a permanent contract was consummated with the Westlands Water District in 1963 by Secretary Udall, setting the rates at $7.50 per acre-foot of water, fifty cents for a drainage system, and additional costs for the distribution system; $192.6 million was allocated for the distributing system. This would be about five dollars per acre-foot extra, making the total cost thirteen dollars per acre-foot. After the water is brought to a grower's farm, he would have to absorb the additional cost for distributing the water throughout his farm.

The five-dollar figure for the distribution system is not firm; as inflation sets in, the cost will rise. So today, if you are paying $7.50 for the canal side and fifty cents for the drainage system, you are probably up to eighteen to twenty dollars per acre-foot as the total cost.

I want to make this perfectly clear: fifteen to twenty dollars per acre-foot for a farm isn't what you call cheap water.

Anyway, $7.50 per acre-foot of water was set as a firm price. This is why there is a big fight going on right now [July 1979]. People testified before the committee that they had predicated their operations (i.e., equipment, lands) on this price. However, the government did not live up to this contract; the present administration is trying to change the rules in the middle of the game. In my opinion, you don't do it that way. I think in the future we may have to adjust prices, but the $7.50 per acre-foot of water was the basic fact of life at that time. This amount was double the price of the original postage stamp rate which had been in effect during the previous decades.

AID: *It also must be considered that this water is only supplemental and they still require their own wells.*

SISK: They still require these $100,000 to $200,000 wells because the San Luis Project was completely supplemental.

AID: *In terms of total water, is there enough water during most years to grow most crops, even alfalfa?*

SISK: There is no way that there will be enough water to put the whole area into alfalfa. One and three-tenths million acre-feet during a normal year were expected to be delivered to the San Luis Project service area (Panoche, San Luis, and Westlands water districts). If this amount of water is delivered, experience indicates the water tables will not be overly depleted by wells. In this way, the grower can farm most of his land; you would not have to summer fallow very much. This theory is predicated on cotton, grain, or an overall diversified operation. If you grew only the heaviest crop water users, you couldn't farm most of your land.

AID: *At the present time, are there any federal or state controls on overdrafts of underground water?*

SISK: In California at the present time, no. We are one of the few states which has not attempted to control ground water. Growers in California have bitterly opposed ground water control. An upcoming battle concerns this. Ultimately, we are going to have controls. In many states you cannot drill a well until it is approved.

AID: *What was the effect on farm subsidies when the west side got water? I understand that you can transfer land you own as long as you stay in the same county. Was there a tendency to transfer cotton-growing acreage from one part of the valley to another, from the east side to the west side?*

SISK: Yes, if circumstances were such that it made it economically feasible and there were willing sellers and buyers for purposes of transfer. Today, you have very few cotton gins, which are the initial processing plants for cotton, left on the east side. There was a time when practically every little town on the east side had a cotton gin or two, but it has now all gone back to grapes, oranges, other kinds of fruit, and vegetables.

14.
California Water Issues

AID: *Regarding the Peripheral Canal, in 1972 a bill was introduced for $1.6 billion in additions to the CVP: $1 billion of that was for the east side canal, $240 million for the Peripheral Canal, $200 million for the Cosumnes Unit, and $50 million for the Alan Camp Reservoir. Initially, the bill would move 1.5 million acre-feet from the Sacramento, American, and Stanislaus rivers to the San Joaquin by the Auburn-Folsom South Canal and the project in Five Lakes. First, your comments on that whole project.*

Above: Friant Dam and Millerton Lake, initiation point of the Friant-Madera Canal.

Right: Releases from the lower sluice gates of Pine Flat Dam thunder into foam in the Kings River. Pine Flat Reservoir sprawls behind the dam.

SISK: We are dealing with a very expensive project here. At the time several co-sponsors and I introduced that legislation, there were various bills put in. We were feeling our way; we were trying to get the issue before the Congress so there would be a simultaneous analysis by the state of California and the federal government. We wanted to coordinate the project in order to have joint use of facilities and to have the project state- and federally-funded. When we hammered out the original agreement concerning the San Luis Project, I mentioned it was the first time in the history of reclamation going back to 1902 there was a joint federal and state operation. This was done by necessity—to get California into lock-step. The project to which you refer was the second venture in California of a joint state and federal operation. The Pat Brown Administration supported the Peripheral Canal of Bill Warne—Pat Brown's water man. The Reagan Administration wanted the Peripheral Canal too. This, too, is Jerry Brown's position. Yet the price of it has constantly gone up.

85

Here is the situation as it developed: Because of the battle over the Peripheral Canal, the majority of us felt we had to share in the benefits if we were to help pay for it. We need an additional 1.5 million acre-feet of water since we are running at a deficit today. Bizz Johnson wanted the Alan Camp and Cosumnes projects because they were important to his constituency up there. However, there was some question about the benefit-to-cost ratio of those projects, according to the studies of the Corps of Engineers and the Bureau of Reclamation. But people in the area needed them and Bizz wanted them, so the projects were included.

The east side project, which had been visualized for many years, was thought to be the ultimate solution. It would hook together all of the projects, starting from the American and Sacramento rivers to the Cosumnes, Tuolumne, Stanislaus, Merced, Fresno, and San Joaquin rivers, all the way down to Kern County. Hungry Hollow and other reservoirs would be holding reservoirs for this water. Many say this east side project must come so that the valley's agricultural economy can be maintained.

At the time I introduced the legislation, it was assumed there would be a sufficient water supply; additional state and federal waters would supply this project. But now there is not enough water to justify the project on the east side. People in the valley, and I myself, think we must obtain more water from the north, tapping the Eel, Russian and Klamath rivers. (There have been all kinds of proposals.) We have been foreclosed by recent actions of the state Legislature protecting wild rivers. This prohibits us from obtaining new water. Jerry Brown's administration contends we should get enough water from off-stream storage; that is, you hold storm water from unusually wet winters until it is needed. Many irrigation people in this area say that is not the answer. The Metropolitan Water District of Los Angeles, which serves the most people and is among the world's largest consumers of water, maintains that new water sources must be developed. To give an idea of the enormity of the undertaking, the Alan Camp, Cosumnes, Hungry Hollow, and Peripheral Canal projects would cost $2.5 billion today.

AID: *What is the effect of the New Melones service area on the CVP?*

SISK: I think it fits in very well. This is one time when John McFall and I crossed paths. McFall wanted to take care of some deficient areas in San Joaquin and northern Stanislaus counties. The area I represented in northern Merced and southern Stanislaus counties is at an elevation which could not be served unless it were out of the New Melones Reservoir. I wanted some water for that area.

The conservation group, "The White Water Boys," and the Jerry Brown Administration tried to block New Melones. They have tended to slow it down.

86

AID: *What was your strategy to overcome President Nixon's freeze on con-gressionally-approved funds for water projects?*

SISK: Our strategy was muscle. We felt it was penny-wise and pound-foolish to stop ongoing projects which were invaluable to help balance our import-export business due to the importance of exported agricultural com-modities. We immediately went to bat for the projects, insisting monies for them must be made available. The Congress overrode some of those freezes. Nixon's action was very unpopular with the people.

AID: *I have some questions about drought: The fact that the recent drought was the driest two-year period on record emphasizes California's long-term water shortages and need for conservation. I would like to know your thoughts on reclaimed water.*

SISK: I think we should not dump any water back into the ocean. At the Kesterson site, for example, rather than spending millions of dollars to dig a pipeline to bring that water to the ocean, we should spend our money on research on a way to purify that water so we can reuse it. Water is too precious to pump out of this valley. We need every drop we get. Re-garding our sewage systems, we are going to go more and more toward the reclamation of all waters for reuse. We have methods of doing it; scientific research proves that you can clean up any of this water, al-though it costs more.

AID: *What do you think of using surface water for cooling nuclear power plants? Should you use drainage water instead?*

SISK: If we have sufficient drainage water and we can impound it in such a way that it can be used for cooling purposes, it would be fine. But to take enormous amounts of class one water for cooling purposes is difficult to justify.

AID: *Would you say state and federal governments responded to the drought emergency rapidly or slowly?*

SISK: I think they responded very slowly. Both were negligent in not using enough foresight and waiting until we were in an emergency situation. Then they overreacted. Instead of having a positive plan, they sat back and reacted to an emergency situation. As a member of Congress, there may have been things I should have done. I think it is a legitimate criticism, whether or not I am part of the criticized group. When we talk about shortages in petroleum for gasoline and electricity and so forth, we see that people respond when they are told the truth and are convinced there is a need. Look at the cut in water usage. People cut back so dras-tically that some of the cities were complaining about a loss in water revenues.

AID: *The newspapers say President Carter was pretty slow to act.*

SISK: I think he was really slow. Carter finally admitted it. I sat at a meeting one morning for two hours with Carter, [Cecil] Andrus, and his other water people and about fifty or sixty of us westerners, both Democrats and Republicans. Carter was under heavy pressure to answer questions. He said, "I didn't realize how important water was to the West." For gosh sake, I think that there is something wrong with the president of the U.S. if he doesn't understand the significance of water in the western United States.

AID: *In light of water shortages and what you just said, should there be any new land brought under irrigation, particularly by federal water development projects?*

SISK: There are a lot of very rich and valuable lands available in the West. These arable lands will produce vast amounts of agricultural commodities when they are brought under irrigation. I think it should be kept in mind that there is a limited supply of water. The issue I am getting at is that there is some land under irrigation which shouldn't be; it is of low quality and therefore represents a waste of water. I think we should measure comparable value of lands, giving priority to richer lands. These are alternatives we must analyze more carefully in the future. When you have land on which you can produce six bales of cotton to the acre, you have to give it priority over land that only produces one bale of cotton to the acre. But again, you have to take into account the social aspects: What are you doing to that community if you are taking away what it produces even though it is inefficient and uneconomical? When are we going to look cold-bloodedly at the economics of the situation? When will the world's population demand that, in order to feed and clothe it?

AID: *Ronald Robie says there is no coherent body of statutory law on ground water. To what extent should federal water programs conform to state goals and policies?*

SISK: There should be more coordination with the states. This is a never-ending battle. I still remember, although vaguely, a hearing in 1955 or so, when Clair [Engle] was chairman of the Interior and Insular Affairs Committee. There was a battle going on about state versus federal control of water, particularly concerning California. A Mr. Morton, an attorney from the Department of Justice in the Eisenhower Administration, came before our committee and testified at great length. The testimony involved ownership of waters in the mountain rivers. He took the hard-line position that every drop of water in every navigable stream in the state of California belonged to the federal government under the Treaty of Guadalupe Hidalgo. You talk about a hot session. This goes back to the history of the Civil War, when states' rights were disputed. No controversy has been more keen—or as bitter—as the issue of who controls and owns water. This is especially true between California and the federal government.

The federal government's stipulation that it had sole jurisdicton over every navigable stream was bitterly attacked by people such as Clair

Engle, Wayne Aspinall of Colorado, myself, and many others. Since then, there has been a policy of give-and-take, meeting the problems of each issue without completely deciding the issue in every case. Many cases have gone to the Supreme Court, like California versus Arizona, which the Court settled. There have been many other cases, particularly concerning trans-mountain diversions or interstate operation of rivers—rivers which cross state boundaries. There has been controversy about who owns the water and how it should be allocated.

I think the states should have more say about planning projects. There are hearings going on today dealing with legislation on this very subject. A new senator from New Mexico and the junior senator from New York (of all people) have introduced a bill which would determine whether the state or the federal government would control certain waters. I believe we are going to have to establish better ground water arrangements. Robie is right about this. This will have to be done at the state level. I would prefer that the state government rather than the federal government make the determination.

The federal government has pre-empted a lot of positions. People may say I am a little inconsistent because of the way the situation developed in California. California was asked to develop its water resources thirty to fifty years ago. An actual act and an executive decree urged the federal government to do it. (This was prior to CVP.) Under the 1902 Reclamation Act, the federal government came in, authorizing the Shasta and Keswick dams and the dams on the American River. So it is easily understood why the state turned this program over to the federal government. Once this was done, I think the federal government had to protect its contractual obligations and its contracts from intrusion by the state, which was trying to overturn some of the agreements.

When the CVP, through the Bureau of Reclamation, made a contract to supply X irrigation district in Fresno County with X amount of water, it became a federal government obligation and the state could not come in and change the rules of the game. However, things should have been done differently from the beginning. I don't want to seem inconsistent here, but we have to protect the integrity of federal waters and developments by virtue of an agreement between the state and federal governments made at that time. This is the only protection an individual has in connection with his contractual obligation to the government.

AID: *Should it be up to the state, when you are talking about the use of water for fisheries, recreation and other industries?*

SISK: I think it should be. Again, you have both federal and state agencies involved. Conflicts at times seem inevitable. It is creating some problems right now. In the Department of Interior, you have the Fish and Game Department. The conflict between it and the states in some cases is unfortunate. You get a lot of duplication. These things about government are easily criticized, yet when you get down to the nitty-gritty you are dealing with whose turf is being violated.

AID: *Jackson Carle told me about a conflict: The Bureau of Reclamation was building some dams up in the foothills where catch water basins had been built for livestock by another agency.*

SISK: That would be the Soil Conservation Service in the U.S. Department of Agriculture.

AID: *The Bureau of Reclamation destroyed those dams.*

SISK: Yes, they maintained that they had prior rights to the water and the other projects were an usurpation of their rights.

AID: *Here are two federal agencies fighting.*

SISK: Yes, it is not unusual; federal agencies fight among themselves, too.

15.
The Kings and Other Rivers:
Acreage Limitation Issue

AID: *Please talk about the Kings River.*

SISK: We have had many problems on the Kings including problems of flooding even though Pine Flat Dam was dedicated the year I was elected. There have been never-ending fights over the contracts on the Kings and how they are to be paid for. It is very current; as late as this past week [July 1979], there was another meeting in Washington. I was supposed to have been there but I couldn't because of other business, but I am on the committee that is trying to work out the final contract on the Kings. When Pine Flat Dam was built, people were very much opposed to any kind of acreage limitation on the Kings. The Kings was one of the oldest established areas in the valley. The waters on the Kings were established by riparian rights as far back as a hundred years ago. Those holding water rights built their own canals, pumping systems and so on, with their own money. There was no question that they owned every drop of water that came out of the mountains into the Kings River.

Because of the very serious periodic flooding, Tulare Lake can overflow thousands of acres. In fact, I flew over Tulare Lake in the 1969 flood and thought I was over the ocean. You couldn't see the shore on either side. This valley in very early times was on the Inland Sea, connected with the San Francisco Bay. As the waters receded, Tulare Lake remained the lowest spot in the valley. In dry years, there is no water in it at all.

Pine Flat Dam was constructed to stop this periodic flooding and to give some control over the waters through conservation. Although this was authorized and construction started under the 1944 Flood Control Act, in 1948 Harry Truman decreed, by executive order, that the conservation benefits should come under the Bureau of Reclamation [which meant under the 1902 Act's 160-acre limitation]. The Kings people immediately contested this in court and have litigated it through the years. When I went to Congress in 1954, I inherited that problem. Pine Flat was in my district and so is much of the Kings River area, although in places it's the border between Fresno and Tulare, and Fresno and Kings counties. Tulare and Kings counties were not in my district. I had the north side of the river all the way down and therefore the people depended heavily on me.

I spent long and miserable hours, weeks and months throughout the years, negotiating with Douglas McKay of Oregon. Douglas McKay was Eisenhower's first secretary of interior. Then in 1956, Doug decided to resign as secretary of interior and return to Oregon to run for the U.S. Senate. He submitted his resignation to President Eisenhower and went back to Oregon and ran. Unfortunately, he was not elected. I had been working with McKay and he was about ready to sign a final contract on the Kings. When Doug decided to run for the Senate, he called me and said, "We've got a new man coming in and I think he should take a look at these papers." So he walked off and left the contract lying on his desk. Fred Seaton, a Nebraska Republican, became secretary of interior. Although Fred was a Republican and I was a Democrat, I had a lot of respect for him and worked very closely with him. I got Fred right up to the point of signing the contract, when lo and behold, in the election of 1960, Kennedy beat Nixon for the presidency. So Fred called up and said, "Bernie, we have a new party and a new secretary coming in. I feel that the new secretary ought to have a chance of looking at this before signing it." He, too, left it lying on the desk. Each time you have to go back and refight the old fights and revise and amend and change.

Secretary of Interior Fred Seaton (seated) looks over a contract between the federal government and the Kings River Water Association regarding water storage in Pine Flat Reservoir, as Sisk, Rep. Harlan Hagen, second from left, and William Docker of KRWA look on. Seaton did not sign the contract.

Sisk looks on as Undersecretary of Interior James Carr signs the first contract between the federal government and the KRWA providing for storage rights in Pine Flat Reservoir. Carr signed on behalf of Interior Secretary Stewart Udall.

Stewart Udall, who had been elected to Congress in 1954, had been with me on the Committee on Interior and Insular Affairs. Stu drew the next spot below me on the committee and sat at my elbow throughout our service in the Congress. He had been with me on the San Luis all the way. Kennedy appointed Udall secretary of interior. After many discussions, finally, in 1963, Stu and I agreed to terms by which the Kings water owners would pay the cost of conservation benefits. What was the government's cost for conservation benefits? After all, flood control benefits are non-reimbursable. The project costs were approximately thirty million dollars; how much of that should be conservation benefits? The department and I negotiated and we came up with a final figure around $14.2 million. The Kings River people accepted that and numbered the districts. There are twenty-eight districts on the Kings, some bigger and some smaller, up and down the river starting on the east side and clear down to the west side. They paid the $14.2 million off. Some of them paid in cash and some small farmers on the east side took a long-term, forty-year pay-out—which they had the opportunity to do. That was a fair settlement. I had no argument with that.

Udall had agreed to sign the contract subject to a court review, a so-called friendly suit. I had finally agreed to that, contrary to what some wanted me to do. In 1963, almost ten years after I got to Congress, we got a signed contract on the Kings and Pine Flat. That suit has pursued its way slowly through the courts. The U.S. district court in Fresno, under Judge Donald Crocker, handed down a decision three years ago in favor of the Kings, that it was never intended for the reclamation law or the acreage limitation to apply. It was a distinguished decision. It went to the appellate court and the appellate court reversed the decision, and the Supreme Court refused to hear it. So that leaves it to the Congress to settle. Senator Frank Church's bill pending before the House [July 1979] may be the final answer. It, once and for all, may exempt from reclamation law the Kings and the All-American Canal in the Imperial Valley and the Kern River Project. It further exempts from reclamation law all Army Corps of Engineers projects.

AID: *On what grounds did the appellate court reverse the decision of the U.S. district court in Fresno?*

SISK: The only justification in the overturning of the local federal court decision by the appellate court was that President Truman had issued an executive order in 1948 and that it should take precedence unless Congress legislated otherwise. That is why we are fighting to try to get the exemption through the Congress to meet that appellate court criteria.

AID: *What are your thoughts about the Church bill?*

SISK: I support a good portion of Church's legislation, but I have reservations about parts of it. Church is trying to recognize the new era in which we live, including the changes in economic conditions and style and types of farming that have occurred in the last fifty to seventy-five years. To restate, the law which governs the operation of the San Luis Project, the Westlands Water District, and most of the major reclamation projects throughout the West, is based on an act passed in 1902 by the Congress of the U.S. That policy is embodied in the "excess land," or 160-acre provision, of federal reclamation law which was modified by a 1926 amendment and again in the late forties, but the basic law has not been changed since 1902. It limits distribution of water to each individual to an amount sufficient to irrigate 160 acres. It needs an update.

Church is proposing a maximum farm size of 1,280 acres. Let me comment on this because it is important. It is a subject about which many people have been misinformed in connection with the whole western reclamation program and in particular the kind of propaganda that the National Land For People crowd and others disseminate. I have no objection to limiting the subsidies any one individual gets. I think we have tradition, we have precedent, we have law after law recognizing that where taxpayer monies are being used or where subsidies are involved, either state or federal, there should be some limitation on how much of that can be enjoyed by any one individual. The 160-acre limitation in the 1902 Act was that kind of a limitation. But the limitation was on the amount of subsidy that could be enjoyed per individual, not the limitation on the size of the farm. I think some people miss this substantial difference. For example, should we limit the size of a grocery store and say that a grocery store can only sell so much? Should we limit the size of an airline because a substantial proportion of air transportation is subsidized? We know that airports with their safety devices are financed by federal agencies through taxes that have been assessed. We all contribute to it and that's fine. I am only bringing out the fallacy of the thinking of some people in connection with farming, that if you are going to have a federal reclamation project you have to limit the size of the farm, that there is something wrong with success. This really gets on my nerves. In my opinion, America was built by virtue of the aggressiveness, the hard work of the American people to go out and develop something and be successful. The fact that we provide certain benefits through government, as we have in a variety of ways throughout our history, doesn't preclude a person from going ahead on his own and being successful. We should limit the amount of taxpayer subsidy that any individual receives, but it is right, then, to go ahead and grow and own more land or lease land, as long as there are no subsidies involved. I think that is most important and where the issue is confused.

To some extent, the initial Church bill violated this concept by attempting to limit forever the size of the farm to 1,280 acres. If you are in a reclamation area, that is all that you can ever have. The language of the bill provides that you can never get out from under the limitation even if you have a forty-year pay-out. When it is paid up, you will still be under the same restriction, limited in perpetuity.

The committee, in an attempt to get around some of this, has provided that you can lease land on an annual basis. Let's say you have 160 acres and a fellow over here has 1,280 acres; on an annual basis, under certain provisions, you could lease that land. What I am supporting and what Senator Cranston is proposing—and what I hope will be accepted—is a provision enabling you to go ahead and lease another hundred acres or another thousand or more acres, but you have to pay the full cost of the water on an acreage above the 1,280. In other words, you are limiting the amount of subsidy that any one individual can receive from the federal government, which is right. But let's not get into the business of what, to me, becomes socialistic beyond anything I can accept, that it doesn't make any difference what else you do, you can never grow beyond a certain size. What we're hoping for is that an amendment will be adopted allowing three-year leasing.

AID: *What is the estimated value of the subsidy per acre?*

SISK: There is a great deal of variation. The normal rule of thumb, traditionally, in connection with a reclamation project has been, say, that in a hundred million-dollar project projected over a fifty-year pay-out, the interest will about equal the payment. This interest cost is on government borrowing and is based on the days when the government borrowed for 2 to 4 percent. Of course, today the interest is high, and the subsidy would be substantially greater. But the subsidy is the interest involved. Reclamation law applies only to lands west of the one-hundredth meridian. East of the one-hundredth meridian, you have flood control projects. Flood control projects are not ruled out in the West, although we don't have nearly as many as in the East. A flood control project may be in a harbor or on a river (there are literally billions of dollars in flood control projects on the

Above: Constituents come in all ages and sizes.

Right: Sisk receives a spirited welcome at the Fresno Air Terminal in 1964 as his grandchildren turn out to greet him.

Mississippi, the Ohio, the Tennessee and other rivers). Literally, there is no payback at all. The government pays all of it. This is why we claim we are being put upon, here in the West. Subsidy is subsidy whether it is for flood control or for reclamation. Reclamation in the West requires full repayment of the cost of all conservation benefits.

AID: *Wouldn't the East be concerned that some day the West might say, "Look at the subsidy you're getting and you're not paying any interest at all?"*

SISK: There is no question. They have become increasingly aware of this within the last two or three years since the Carter Administration questioned the application of law in the flood control project on the Kings River. Further, the court has ruled that in the forty years since the Imperial Valley Project was built, to go back now and try to assess the cost would be ridiculous. All of a sudden, our friends in Mississippi, where they have vast flood control projects, the Tennessee Valley Authority, and Florida, which has an enormous project at the present time, are really taking a look at their own hole cards. If you assess flood control costs against them, it could cost them billions of dollars. That's why you have so much interest in Congress today in this matter. That's why the Church bill contains an outright exemption, across the board, for all Corps of Engineers projects in the U.S.

For some reason, as I have said, you still have people who demand their pound of flesh and say that because you own the water you should be forced to divest yourself of your lands. There are only a small number of so-called excess landholders on the Kings. Practically all of the east side landholders in the Consolidated Irrigation District are small farmers. There are only a few large landholders at the Tulare Lake basin: the Boswell interest, the Westlake farms, the Southlake farms, and one or two others. These five or six own very large blocks. Here is the problem with those big farms at the lake basin: the lake basin farms flood at least once in ten years, and there are larger floods at longer intervals, as in 1969. I flew over that area, as I have said, and I could only see the tip of a house or a barn sticking up out of the water, or the top half of a cotton gin. The gins were useless for two or three years afterwards. No small farmer can operate under those conditions. It is the kind of farming that is a big gamble. It's very rich land. If you could make a big crop, let's say two out of every five to seven years, you might make money. If you get lucky and get four or five crops in a row before you have a flood, you will really clean up. The point is, there are no small farm operators with family-type farms and farm houses in that area. It's just open country. I say to people back in Washington, "Come out here and look at this area and then tell me if you can break that up into 160-acre farms and get anybody to farm it."

AID: *What about the Peripheral Canal?*

SISK: There isn't any question but that California has to have a facility like the Peripheral Canal if it is going to meet its contractual commitments and obligations to the Metropolitan Water District in Los Angeles.

AID: *Does the delta have all it needs in the way of water projects?*

SISK: There are some water projects the delta still wants. Even though residents will run for cover on it, there is no question they still need the Kellogg Project. They have been receiving a free ride from the federal government for twenty years and even longer from the state government. This is why this lawsuit is pending. I am not sure if the state expects to collect six million dollars or any other sum, but I think we are going to see some contracts. Those contracts should have been signed a long time ago for all the benefits the delta has been receiving. I happen to be a staunch defender of the delta. We are dependent on good water quality in the delta. Where do we get our water? We get it through the Delta-Mendota Canal. Where do we get it for San Luis? We get it out of the delta. This idea that we here in the San Joaquin Valley are shooting at those people up there and want to strip the delta of all its water is so foolish that a person would have to be crazy to believe it.

AID: *Do you believe that the delta groups have been trying to get a free ride while they are against the Peripheral Canal?*

SISK: The delta has never paid anything back. Prior to the building of the Central Valley Project, including the Shasta, Keswick and American river dams, the delta area was nothing but a salt swamp in summertime. People say that salt water intrusion, at times, has gone all the way up to Sacramento. Those dams were built so there would be a steady stream of water coming down, holding this salt intrusion from San Francisco Bay and creating fresh water lakes up there. This is good for the fishing industry and other industries. But the people who have lived there haven't paid one dime for those benefits. They will even try to get you to believe the federal project has harmed them.

AID: *Should water delivered to the delta for water quality enhancement be counted as a benefit?*

SISK: Very definitely. The state has filed a lawsuit, as I have said, trying to get the people to pay for the benefits. I believe the federal government is also filing a suit.

AID: *In what ways did you compromise with George Miller of Contra Costa County?*

SISK: We never compromised too much on anything. In order to get water under a temporary contract in 1978, I agreed to set up a study commission to take a look at the whole San Luis Project. I agreed to this so he would back away; I needed the approval of the committee and he was holding up the interim contract. That was the only compromise I made with him. The commission was unfavorable; it was a loaded deal. The Department of Interior under Andrus was responsible. They chose people who had preconceived ideas and had fought the farmers from start to finish. The minority report was written by state Senator Rose Ann Vuich (whom I managed to get on the commission) and an agricultural commissioner in Kings County. They were my only friends on the commission besides an attorney in Sacramento.

AID: *What other water matters were you involved in?*

SISK: I was involved in a great diversity of projects. We had the question of Lake Millerton on the San Joaquin River, which holds something over five hundred thousand acre-feet of water. Friant Dam was authorized and built prior to my becoming a member of the Congress, but there were still contract problems outstanding on Millerton with which I had to deal. I fought to get final contracts for some of the local small irrigation districts in the vicinity of Fresno. I don't claim that I did it alone; we managed to get well over ten thousand acre-feet of water set aside in perpetuity for the city of Fresno if and when it is needed. It took me two or three years to get final agreement from the Bureau of Reclamation and the secretary of interior for a water contract for the Broadview Irrigation District, which is a small district at the edge of the foothills. We got some 3,600 acre-feet of water for a small district near Clovis which is very heavily involved in citrus. These were all matters that took a lot of effort and time, with the bureau against them because it was trying to keep flexible to hold water back for some of the larger districts which might need it.

AID: *Are these east side projects?*

SISK: This is all east side that I am talking about here. From Lake Millerton, formed by the Friant Dam, the Friant-Madera Canal takes water from the San Joaquin up to Madera County where it is distributed throughout the county. The Friant-Kern Canal, out of the same area, distributes water down to eastern Fresno County, east in Tulare County and all the way to the Kern River in Bakersfield. A number of these small water districts, lacking the legal representation the richer districts had, were left high and dry. I went to bat for them. We have a number of very thrifty and thriving areas in these small districts.

I proposed a flood control project on the Fresno River, which was important to Madera County, and had the first study authorized in 1956. Then we ran into some problems. I had to go back and get it reauthorized in 1960. We battled that back and forth. I finally went before the Public Works Committee, got the study completed, and got an approved project by the Corps of Engineers. I went before the Appropriations Committee and got the money to start construction. We built Hidden Dam on the Fresno River. We have conservation benefits of about 150,000 acre-feet of water in Lake Hensley.

At the same time, I was carrying on a fight for the people in the Chowchilla area, which includes northern Madera and southern Merced counties on the Chowchilla River, to secure a study and design like that on

Courtesy Fresno Bee

Heavy equipment places rock on Buchanan Dam across the Chowchilla River during construction of the facility.

the Fresno River. Some competitive hostility between the people of Madera and the people of Chowchilla required very careful balancing. If I got a dollar for Hidden Dam on the Fresno River, I had to get a dollar for the Buchanan Project on the Chowchilla River. I talked to the chairman of the Appropriations Committee: "You understand I have a problem. These people are my constituents and I can't use one at the expense of the other. Therefore, I have to have a little bit for both of them." We started construction on both projects at the same time with the same contractor. Both projects were dedicated on the same day. Bizz Johnson and I, with other officials, dedicated Hidden Dam on the Fresno River and then drove over by caravan and dedicated the Buchanan Dam on the Chowchilla River. Lakes Hensley and Eastman are beautiful lakes providing valuable conservation benefits. People go up there for boating, fishing, and water recreation.

Merced County has always had problems with water. There was a small project on the Merced River up above Snelling. I suppose I had one hundred meetings or more with the Merced Irrigation District over the last twenty-five years. We were able to get approval for the Corps of Engineers to construct an additional larger dam on the Merced River. That has long since been built and is full. It provides an adequate water supply for eastern Merced County. There are numerous recreational benefits from that project.

16.
Out-of-State Water Projects

There were many water and flood control projects outside the state. I worked closely with the upper basin states in the authorization of the upper basin development. A bill, with Wayne Aspinall as the principal author, authorized projects in Utah, Wyoming, Colorado, Arizona and Nevada. I did this in the face of vigorous and prolonged opposition from the Metropolitan Water District of Los Angeles. MWD believed California ultimately would lose the long legal fight with Arizona over Colorado River water. In other words, substantial amounts of water in the Colorado would be given to Arizona, and the Metropolitan Water District would not continue to have almost unilateral access to Colorado River water. It fought any further utilization of water on the Colorado at any level. This was simply a parochial and selfish position. On the other hand, if you owned property in Los Angeles or Southern California, it was in your interest to enjoy the benefits of Colorado River water in spite of the fact that you were taking water away from Wyoming, Montana, Idaho, Colorado, Utah, etc.

Because of the assistance and help I had through the years from westerners in connection with our problems, I couldn't turn those states down. Clair Engle and I just had to tell Southern California that, in this case, we couldn't go with it. The carry-over of some of those fights has continued to this day. This whole water subject is so complex, there are so many odds and ends to it. Some of the old-timers who were involved are gone, and we will see new people who don't know as much about it as some of us who fought these battles. Maybe we will be better off. In the West, a man would rather trust another man with his wife than with an acre-foot of water. That's just how precious water is.

AID: *What other out-of-state projects were you involved in?*

SISK: Having served on the Committee on Interior and Insular Affairs and developed into one of the water leaders on that committee, I did get involved in water development projects throughout the country. I was involved, to some extent, on the Garrison Project up in the Dakotas. We dealt with some of the problems on the Missouri. I was involved in the authorization of the San Angelo Project in Texas. West Texas has some irrigation problems. The Navaho Project in New Mexico, the Frying Pan Project in Colorado, the Lake Powell upper basin development—all these projects were authorized in the late 1950s and the early 1960s. After I became a member of the Rules Committee, in most cases when a bill on water or a water project came out of the Interior and Insular Affairs or Public Works committees, the committee chairman or members of the committee would talk to me about it because all important legislation had to clear the Rules Committee in order to be taken up on the floor.

AID: *How were you involved in the California-Arizona water dispute?*

SISK: The really tough part of that occurred in the 1950s when I was on the Interior and Insular Affairs Committee. Aspinall and the Colorado delegation and the Arizona delegation, joined by small delegations throughout the West from Utah, Nevada, Montana, and Wyoming, were pushing to get this upper basin. The Metropolitan Water District moved in to absolutely stop them. MWD felt that as long as there was no actual authorization by Congress making a call on Colorado River water, it ought to let that water keep coming down to Southern California where it was used, more or less, in unlimited quantities. MWD believed that once the development began in the upper basin states and once Arizona was in a position to apply its proportionate share of that water to lands or to municipal use, it was going to be much more difficult to get any extra water to Southern California. Later, of course, this is what actually happened.

In connection with the upper basin dispute, I remember John Philips from Riverside, California, who represented the Imperial Valley area. Philips was a very conservative Republican. He was on the Appropriations Committee. Harry Sheppard from Yucaipa, who was then the

President Johnson appears pensive as he signs the Tehipite bill in August 1965. The legislation withdrew Kings River Conservation District and Kings River Water Association power reservations from the Cedar Grove and Tehipite Valley areas of Kings Canyon National Park.

dean of our delegation, appointed a committee with John Philips as chairman to work with Southern California in this hassle. He appointed me to that committee along with several others. You would think that there would be no question about John Philips' position on the Colorado River because he was from Southern California. He became so thoroughly disgusted with some of the activities of the Metropolitan Water District board that one morning at a meeting in the old Congressional Hotel in Washington, he absolutely lectured them. He chewed them up and spat them out. We pleaded with the Metropolitan Water District to at least recognize there were some legitimate water rights and requirements in the upper basin, and that there was legitimate ownership up there. We pleaded with Southern California to sit down and work this out. Board members were adamant. They said, "We are going to fight them every step of the way and stop them any way that we can."

The National Reclamation Association meeting was held in Omaha, Nebraska that year. The Metropolitan Water District public relations people put what was called the "red sheet" under every delegate's hotel door. It was an inflammatory attack on the upper basin proposal, trying to justify Southern California entitlement to all the water from the Colorado River. The "red sheet" boomeranged and hurt the MWD. We had asked them not to get involved in that type of nasty action. Shortly thereafter, we had this meeting in Washington. When John Philips got through chewing out the MWD board, members got up and walked out with their tails between their legs. The committee did authorize the upper basin.

I re-established a working relationship with the Metropolitan. Bob Will, MWD's chief counsel, was a personal friend. Joe Jenson, the chairman of the Metropolitan Water District board for many years, helped get the San Luis Project approved. Although I did support the upper basin, I think it was an honest and fair position. At the same time, where I could, I helped the people from Southern California. In fact, in 1978 they invited me down to Los Angeles where the Metropolitan Water District board gave me a beautiful plaque for the work I had done for California water.

Above: House baseball squad, 1956. Standing, from left, are Reps. MacDonald, Rogers, Sisk, Rivers, Addonizio, Tumulty, McCarthy, Magmusom, Harris, Herlong, O. Teague, Natcher, Alexander, Edmonson, Forrester and Thompson. Kneeling, left to right, are Rep. Fountain, House Doorkeeper "Fishbait" Miller, Reps. Clark, Fascell, S. Udall, Hagen and Flynt.
Right: Sisk takes a cut at a curve ball in this 1957 game, held in Washington's Griffith Stadium.

Part 4:

ORDER IN THE HOUSE

Bernie Sisk truly came into his own as a man of stature and a legislator of clout upon appointment to the prestigious Rules Committee in 1961.

His selection by Rayburn, while a tribute to Sisk's growing acumen, also signified his political security. In six years, Sisk had transformed a marginal district into a safe one—thus fulfilling one of the committee's unwritten prerequisites.

Bernie was the beneficiary of a so-called "packing" arrangment, enlarging the committee by three, engineered by Rayburn and Majority Leader John McCormack and intended to lighten the heavy hand of Judge Howard Smith, Rules chairman.

The Committee on Rules—the traffic cop and key arbiter for the bulk of House legislation—gave Sisk an opportunity to deal with a plethora of issues "from shoe tacks to wagon wheels." As the panel's swing vote, he left his imprint on bills fully across that spectrum.

B. F. Sisk's weightiest assignment on Rules came with his floor management of the Legislative Reorganization Act of 1970, a massive modernization and democratization of congressional procedures. The task again called upon his penchant for doggedness and compromise; when the dust cleared, he had successfully guided the bill through the most protracted debate in House history.

Here Sisk ticks off the results of reform efforts: congressional participation in the budget process; televised proceedings, including Watergate; a stronger General Accounting Office; electronic voting; relaxation of the seniority system; and a host of parliamentary moves designed to make the House run more openly and efficiently.

Bernie then turns his discussion of House reform into a concise, understandable primer on the legislative process, steering the reader from mark-up to conference committee.

But Sisk did not live by Rules alone. In addition to his responsibilities on the Interior and space committees, both of which preceded Rules, he served on the Veterans Affairs Committee.

Again assisted by House leadership, Sisk was one of several legislators to break the "exclusive" status of the Rules Committee, gaining a seat on the District of Columbia Committee. There, he worked on behalf of home rule for the nation's capital.

He also broke with precedent in receiving a second major committee assignment, joining the Agriculture Committee when the leadership sought California representation.

As chairman of the Cotton Subcommittee, Sisk helped heal the long-standing rift between southern and western producers. A proponent of production inducements rather than direct farm subsidies, he backed legislation to aid the dairy, wine, sugar, fig and raisin industries.

On the homefront, he describes the founding of the California Agricultural Leadership Program and his work to secure federal research dollars for California State University, Fresno.

In lighthearted vein, Sisk became a vocal advocate for the retention of a major league baseball franchise in Washington, D.C. and ultimately headed up a 1976 House select committee on sports. While he couldn't keep the Senators in the nation's capital, Bernie did garner the "Mr. Sam Award" from the Washington Touchdown Club, a tribute to the ex-hurler's determination.

Presiding over the House of Representatives, 1964.

17.
The Rules Committee:
Involvement in National Politics

AID: *Let's talk about the Rules Committee.*

SISK: I think history has recorded pretty clearly what happened during the years of the 1940s and 1950s: the Committee on Rules was probably the most dominant force in Congress. It was referred to by many historians as the great roadblock to all good legislation. I suppose that is a matter of opinion. I don't necessarily agree with all of the charges that were made.

Judge Howard Smith of Virginia was, for many years, chairman of the Committee on Rules. He was a very conservative Democrat who was one of the most honest men I have ever met. He was part of the Byrd machine of Virginia. He used his position as chairman of Rules to try to guide the government in the direction he felt it should go, whether you agreed with him or not. I didn't agree with him a lot of the time, but that was a certain fact of life.

Speaker Rayburn, who had been in a leadership position for many years, had a continuous head-on battle with Judge Smith, although personally they were friends. Judge Smith made it difficult for Rayburn to put through the kind of programs he wanted.

After some of us were elected in 1954 and 1956, the Democratic Party was somewhat liberalized; the new members changed the complexion of the party. During this time, Rayburn was trying to get better control of the party machinery. Because we were continuously being shot down by a combination of conservative Democrats and Republicans, the liberal wing of the Democratic Party organized the DSG, the Democratic Study Group, of which I was a charter member. I have already talked about its origins.

AID: *Is that group still in existence?*

SISK: Yes. It is probably the single most potent Democratic organization in Washington, although it was more influential in the past. Most Democratic members are active in it.

AID: *Do you have to be invited to belong?*

SISK: If you are a Democratic member of the Congress, you automatically belong. In the last ten or fifteen years, it has become more of a research group. It puts out a daily and monthly sheet on legislative procedures, and

105

year-end reports. It has a fairly substantial staff. In the beginnning, we were just an informal group, meeting from time to time. Key people in those days were Chet Holifield, Eugene McCarthy, John Blatnik, Frank Thompson, and Lee Metcalf, who is now dead. In 1957 we decided to formalize it and I was selected as chairman of the organizing committee. We set up the bylaws and elected its first official family.

We were formed originally over Rayburn's objections because he preferred an orderly process. Once DSG was an accomplished fact, he accepted it and used us to an extent. I think we were helpful to him. DSG helped in the battle over Rules that came up in 1960-61 amid the election of John F. Kennedy. It was decided by Rayburn, along with members of the DSG and others, to finally make this fight. In the past, it was thought the coalition of conservative Democrats and Republicans could never be beaten.

The method chosen to overcome the bloc in the Rules Committee was to enlarge the committee, adding new members. This would break the stranglehold of Judge Smith and the combination of Republicans and conservative Democrats. Carl Vinson of Georgia, the oldest member of the House in point of service (more than fifty years), told me this was the most bitter fight he had experienced in his life; the pressure was put on by both sides, one group led by Smith and the other group led by Rayburn— a battle of the giants. It was one of those very impressive votes in which you could hear a pin drop in the House. If you have been in the House of Representatives, you have heard the noise that normally goes on, but on this occasion the House got very quiet. In those days, the vote was done by roll call, not with the board used now. The clerks stood up and called the name of every member. You answered "yea" or "nay." One of the most historic moments in the Congress was that vote on the Rules Committee. It meant a change in direction for years to come. Rayburn finally won by about five votes.

AID: *Were you involved in that fight?*

SISK: Not other than in my commitment to Rayburn's position. I was also a strong supporter of Jack Kennedy as president of the United States.

AID: *In that fight, was Carl Vinson the key?*

SISK: You have to realize that, at that point, I was not a senior member of Congress since I had been there for only six years. But it was my understanding that Carl Vinson, who was a long time friend of Rayburn's (although they had their philosophical differences), committed himself to go with Rayburn, although he was a vocal southerner and was greatly respected in the South. As a result, Vinson was bound to influence votes because he was a senior member of the House, carrying great weight and respect. However, a lot of southerners resented his position on this fight. It probably hurt Carl's future to some extent; he was sensitive about this issue later on. Without Vinson's help, Rayburn would not have won, in my opinion.

That vote occurred about 2:00 P.M. I don't have the exact date. About 4:00 P.M. on that day, I was back in my office working. My secretary said, "The Speaker is on the phone." When Rayburn called, you jumped. I picked up the telephone: "Yes, Mr. Speaker." He said, "Son, I want you to serve on the Rules Committee." I hadn't thought of being under consideration. It had not been mentioned to me by anybody in my delegation. The chairman of my delegation, Harry Sheppard, a former Alabaman who was considered close to Rayburn, didn't know anything about it or he would have talked to me. Mind you, I was chairman of two permanent subcommittees which were vital to my district. One was a subcommittee of the Interior and Insular Affairs Committee and the other was a subcommittee on space of the Science and Astronautics Committee. I had never dreamed about becoming a member of Rules because I knew it was a very select and small committee. I was so jarred by this phone call from the Speaker that I stammered and stuttered rather ridiculously. I finally got up enough nerve to say, "Mr. Speaker, I am deeply grateful and honored that you would think of me in connection with this position, but in view of my already existing commitments on other committees, I wonder if I could have a little time to think this over?" Normally, you didn't make that kind of a request of the Speaker. He could be very abrupt, although he had always been very nice to me. He said, "This is something that we have to move very quickly on. I will tell you what, you think this over this afternoon and you let me know by eight o'clock in the morning." This was between four and five o'clock at night. I said, "All right, Mr. Speaker, I will call you before eight in the morning—and thank you, sir." He hung up. I was in a sweat. I didn't know what in the world to do.

I immediately consulted my own staff. Then I called Harry Sheppard. By this time, Rayburn had called Sheppard and told him he had asked me to be on the committee. Everybody said, "You have to take it. The prestige involved is such that you cannot turn it down." It wasn't all that easy for me. But I did call him the next morning about 7:45 and thanked him very kindly for his appointment and told him I would gratefully accept the appointment. Carl Elliott of Alabama, a liberal southerner, and I were the two additions to the Rules Committee on the Democratic side. On the Republican side, it was up to the Republicans to make that appointment. The committee at that time included eight Democrats and four Republicans. The increase made it ten Democrats and five Republicans. The Republicans got around to making their appointment a month later, because they actually opposed enlargement of the committee and had an internal fight over this. Republican H. Allen Smith of Glendale,

California was named to the committee. Allen and I were philosophically poles apart, but we became very close friends. In matters dealing with California, we were in lock-step. I don't seek any honor out of it, but it gave California a fantastic amount of power, which we were able to use, sparingly, but I believe we used it well. The combination of Allen on the Republican and myself on the Democratic side (I operated as an independent—I was known as a swing vote—and Allen was conservative) did a lot of things for California.

That was only the beginning of my experience on the Rules Committee. First, we didn't even have chairs to sit in. There was a lot of kidding and the press played this up quite a bit. It went so far that some people in Alabama shipped up a chair to Washington. We finally got chairs. It was rough in that first Congress during the years 1961 and 1962 because Clarence J. Brown, the ranking Republican, had an acid tongue and he could be brutal. He referred to it as a packing of the Rules Committee. Later Clarence and I became good friends. His son [Clarence Brown III] is now serving in Congress representing the same Ohio district as his late father. Clarence Brown was a power in the Republican Party. I understand that he was instrumental in the nomination of Harding back in the days of the race against Cox.

Judge Smith was deeply resentful of what had happened, I am sure. Yet as far as I was concerned, he was very fair. I don't think he ever accepted Carl Elliott [who had served in the Eighty-first Congress and the next seven Congresses, through 1964] to the extent he did me because, to him, Carl had violated the unwritten code of the South in that, as a southerner, he had turned on his own. I was a different ball of wax because I came from California. Carl ran for the Senate in 1964 and lost. In 1966 he ran for governor of Alabama and lost.

I later became good friends with Judge Smith. I loved the old man. He was ninety-six years old when he died and he had a mind which was as sharp as could be. He went to his law office and practiced law to the day he died.

AID: *What about William M. Colmer?*

SISK: Bill Colmer was very resentful and needled us a great deal. You see, Smith, Colmer and the four Republicans had been able to block any liberal Democratic program that came along. Colmer was the ranking Democrat next to Smith. I became a good friend of Bill's and he and I later worked very closely together on some matters.

The new line-up on the Rules Committee was: Democrats—Howard W. Smith, Virginia; William M. Colmer, Mississippi; Ray J. Madden, Indiana; James J. Delaney, New York; Homer Thornberry, Texas; Richard Bolling, Maryland; Thomas P. O'Neill, Jr., Massachusetts; Carl Elliot, Alabama; B. F. Sisk, California; and Republicans—Clarence J.

Brown, Ohio; Katherine St. George, New York; H. Allen Smith, California; Elmer J. Hoffman, Illinois; William H. Avery, Kansas.

The Rules Committee ceased to be the bloc it had been. President Kennedy had a program of legislation which, in spite of the fact that it could get to the floor by virtue of changes in the Rules Committee, still never flowed very well. I doubt that anybody, worldwide, was more popular than Jack Kennedy. I had great admiration and love for him. Most of the Democrats did. Unfortunately, if you look back at the record, his legislative program wasn't very successful because of a number of problems in a controversial time. It was an era in which you couldn't put a civil rights bill through because of the coalition against it. President Kennedy came up with a civil rights bill. He delegated his brother, Bob, the attorney general, to handle the fight. They contacted ten or fifteen of us to sell the Congress on the bill. Once we got a bill out of committee but didn't have the floor votes, we would go on down to the "Jacqueline K" or the "Honey Fitz," the two presidential yachts down on the Potomac River. There would be six or eight Democrats along with six or eight Republicans. We would get one group today and a different group tomorrow. Sometimes we would go as often as two or three times a week. We would have a little reception on board, with a few drinks and some food, and be out for two or three hours and come back, we would hope, having convinced them they should support the bill. That's the way we put together the votes to pass that first civil rights bill under the Kennedy Administration. (The landmark 1964 bill was passed under President Johnson following the death of Kennedy.) I worked with President Kennedy very closely. Working on the civil rights bill was one basic association that I had with Bob Kennedy. I was never very fond of Bob, although I got along with him. Some people formed a kind of adoration society when he ran for president. He was a cold fish to me. The old saying goes that you have to have somebody do the dirty work in any administration. Bob Kennedy was considered to be that person for Jack Kennedy.

The Rules Committee had many important pieces of legislation which, for the first time, got action. Bills dealing with social legislation, housing, improvements in welfare, the Democratic program for agriculture, and the food stamp program were getting to the floor. They all had been locked up for years. Some later failed in the Senate. Activity developed by 1964 and 1965 into what became the first flood tide of social legislation. Some of it we frankly overdid; some of it we had to undo; for some of it, we went too far. It was a reaction to a situation during which the government had literally been locked up. The people with liberal philosophies were seeking to do something about blacks and other minorities and the poor in the ghettos. That all began to break loose and

109

President Harry S Truman, in a jovial mood, bids a hearty hello to Sisk and Rep. Dalip Saund.

move. We ended up with twenty-two different manpower programs. You had cities literally going crazy trying to figure out one program or another.

Many things did not gel for Kennedy despite his determined efforts, and those of his brother Bob and others. We did enact his program to send kids all over the world: the Peace Corps. This was one of Jack Kennedy's early dreams. Sargent Shriver, his brother-in-law, was put in charge. I was one of the first to endorse the Peace Corps. I worked with Sarge very closely and we got that bill through. We were moving in the direction of a more liberal and open approach to the problems of the world. However, there was only a limited amount of success on Kennedy Administration legislation because of some antagonism toward him and a continuing coalition between Republicans and conservative southern Democrats. They were still in a position, in many instances, to stop us on the floor of the House.

When Kennedy was killed and Johnson came into office, you immediately saw a change—Washington did a complete flip-flop. The southern bloc, to a large extent, backed away from the coalition because Johnson was one of theirs, even though Johnson was not really considered a southerner. He was just the nearest thing they had to a southern president of the United States. As a result, a flood of legislation began to move. The coalition of Republicans and conservative Democrats was broken; they were now Johnson Democrats.

There were two big, tough issues. One was civil rights and the other was federal aid to education. These became focal points and were both stalled before Rules. Bill after bill had been voted out of committee, later to die in Rules. The aid to education bill never got a ruling. This was due to a coalition of southern conservatives, Republicans, and, because of the religious schools issue, Catholics. Jim Delaney of New York was a ranking member of Rules along with Ray Madden of Indiana, both Catholic.

AID: *Madden became chairman for a time, later on.*

SISK: Yes. Tip [Thomas P.] O'Neill, on Rules, was also Catholic. Jim Delaney took his orders from Cardinal Spellman. Spellman wasn't about to let any aid for public education bill move that could in any sense be considered adverse to the parochial school system.

President Johnson, through the Education and Labor Committee, came up with the idea of a program where you help the individual student, called categorical aid. He concentrated on that to get around the battle of public versus private schools. It got before the Rules Committee and apparently Spellman wasn't happy with it. Immediately, we hung up again even though we had a liberalized Rules Committee.

Johnson called and wanted a group of us to come down. He didn't ask for Judge Smith or Bill Colmer, but the rest of the Democrats went down to the White House. There were eight of us. Johnson was proceeding to tell us how important this education bill was. Jim Delaney was sitting on the divan, swelling up like a toad. Sometimes Jim could be very tough if he wanted to be. He wasn't saying a word. Johnson was giving us a lecture on why we needed to move this bill. Madden had given him a commitment and I think O'Neill was kind of wishy-washy, but was depending on Delaney because Delaney was calling the shots for the parochial school people. Johnson blew up and used some pretty rough language. I won't quote him exactly but he said he had put a Catholic in charge of this program and that what we were doing would make it possible for Catholics to reap benefits because it would be via categorical aid for the student. We would not be giving it to the school per se. I remember seeing red come up the back of his neck. That was how you knew when Johnson was losing his temper. To make a long story short, we passed that bill out as the first education bill cleared through the Rules Committee to go before the House. It became law. It was the first time federal aid was given to secondary and primary schools. That is one example of the battles even after we had supposedly liberalized the Rules Committee.

AID: *Going back just a step, I remember vaguely that when Kennedy came in, one of the major parts of his legislative program was federal aid to education.*

SISK: That's right. We couldn't get it out of the Rules Committee because of that battle between public and private schools. The Republicans on Rules were in lock-step with Smith and Colmer against federal aid to education. All they needed to block this bill was one more vote. They had it in Delaney. O'Neill would go along with them at times. With Smith, Colmer, and Delaney—three Democrats plus the five Republicans—there was a bloc. They had the majority. They kept us blocked until the incident at the White House when Johnson, by force of his personality and strong language, broke the bottleneck and got that bill out.

During these years, there were changes in Rules Committee personnel. When I went on the committee, Leo E. Allen of Illinois was ranking Republican. Clarence Brown was second ranking. Allen passed away only a few weeks after the start of that Congress, and Hoffman replaced him. Then Clarence became ranking. Clarence passed away several years later. We had a woman on the committee named Katherine St. George, a New Yorker. She was very much a blueblood, a very conservative Republican woman. Allen Smith served as ranking Republican for several years before he retired from the committee. There have been a lot of changes on the Republican side.

AID: *Wasn't there a black woman on the committee?*

SISK: Shirley Chisholm, a Democrat, serves on the committee. She came on the committee only two or three years ago.

AID: *They also put her on Agriculture?*

SISK: They tried to but she wouldn't take a seat on it. It was the first and only case I know of where a member was assigned to a committee, but flatly refused to take the seat. She was put on the Agriculture Committee on the basis that she would serve consumer interests. It would have been a wonderful spot for her.

AID: *Even though she came from the city?*

SISK: She evidently resented it on the theory that it was being dumped on her as a throwaway because she was black and a woman. There was a period of time when she was without a committee. Carl Albert was Speaker at the time. Some members said, "To heck with her. Don't give her anything." They finally worked something out. They didn't give her Rules then but they did several years later. They gave her Veterans Affairs and she went along with it. I think she wanted the Education and Labor Committee and they wouldn't give her that. I think she ran for president in the meantime before she got on to Rules. I personally think she was able, although some people thought she was crazy and really wild. She was pretty wild when she first came up, but she calmed down a lot. I came to have a good deal of respect for Shirley. She and I worked together on some things and we voted together on some issues before the Rules Committee. She is not as wild as a lot of people think. She is more conservative and solid than a lot of the liberals. She is tough. If she doesn't like what you are doing, she will fight you.

AID: *Talking about not taking a committee assignment, didn't Jim O'Hara, who was on Education and Labor, decline a Rules assignment when it was offered in 1967?*

SISK: Between you and me, I have some doubts. I don't wish to question the integrity of any of my colleagues or ex-colleagues. I remember there had been a rumor that Jim had been offered it, but there was no verification. In fact, it was denied by certain people on the staff of the Speaker at the time. He ran for the Senate and was defeated. He ran for majority leader the same time I did. He was low man on the totem pole.

AID: *Let's go back to the telephone call from the Speaker. You hesitated, but called back the next morning, accepting the position. I believe at one time you told me one of the reasons for this appointment by the Speaker might have been that you came from a safe district and that you could take a stand on an unpopular issue. Is that right?*

SISK: That's correct. This was a statement by the leadership, by the Speaker as well as some of the others. Rayburn did not appoint a person to the Rules Committee who was from a marginal district.

AID: *What impresses me is that when you got there in 1955, he put you on Veterans Affairs because you were from a marginal district and it would help you. In six short years, you changed the district from marginal to safe.*

SISK: I don't necessarily take personal credit, but we, as a team (myself, my staff and my supporters) did a job. We served the people. When people called, we answered. When they wrote letters, they got a reply. I worked 365 days of the year for them. We got around and saw people. We did turn the marginal district around and in the years following I had little or no problem being re-elected. I was lucky I had such a good staff.

AID: *What other advantages did you get from Rules? Is it easier to get re-elected? Does it make that much of an impression on the district?*

SISK: I am not sure it does. At the time, I even had a question in the back of my mind whether it was going to hurt me. This was the problem I had when that telephone call came through at four in the afternoon. I still had water difficulties even though I had gotten the San Luis through. This is one of the things that the Speaker said: "You got that project through and you're in good shape on that. You've a good, safe district and you aren't going to have any major problems." At the same time, I represented a mainly agricultural economy. Suddenly, the appointment threw out everything I had been doing and all my interests and work. I had been out to the South Pacific as chairman of a subcommittee. I was helping set up the legisla-

113

tive procedures for the Micronesians and Polynesians throughout the South Pacific area.

AID: *What subcommittee was that?*

SISK: The subcommittee in charge of trust territories under Interior and Insular Affairs. I spent a month in Micronesia setting up legislative procedures. Today, they are developing the ability to legislate for themselves. But I just mention that in passing. The Rules Committee didn't travel. You were grounded in Washington, sitting there day in and day out and worrying about every kind of legislation.

AID: *And there were no subcommittees and you were the junior member?*

SISK: That's right. There never has been a subcommittee on Rules. So you are sitting down at the end of the Rules Committee and looking at the top where there are three or four guys in their eighties who have been there forever. It was a dismal-looking sight except for the fact that you were a member of the Rules Committee. It *did* carry prestige.

AID: *And there was also a lot of opposition within the Rules Committee.*

SISK: That's right. It wasn't a pleasant spot.

AID: *Did the prestige finally get you?*

SISK: You mean what finally convinced me? More important than anything else was that I had never turned Mr. Rayburn down (except once on natural gas deregulation). He was largely responsible for my having a safe district. He had been kind to me, doing everything I had ever requested of him. I was deeply grateful for what he had done for me because I was just a country boy who most people figured would never be re-elected for a second term. I owed him an awful lot. There were other things that entered into it, but above everything was a loyalty to Mr. Rayburn.

The Rules Committee was an interesting, never-ending challenge because you dealt with every conceivable subject in the world, from shoe tacks to wagon wheels. All major legislation had to go through Rules.

AID: *I have a note here along those lines. After Judge Smith, Bill Colmer became chairman and okayed the granting of Rules to bills in which Rules members had personal interest. This was true in all Congresses from the Eighty-eighth through the Ninety-second. If a member requested a postponement of action because of a forced absence, he would get a postponement.*

SISK: That's right. Bill respected the requests of members. He never tried to run roughshod over anybody.

AID: *Later, when Madden became chairman, he misinformed you on an occasion.*

SISK: Madden did not adhere to that rule nearly to the extent Colmer did. In spite of the fact that I, along with the middle and more liberal members of the Democratic Party, differed philosophically with Colmer and Smith, we respected their integrity. They were absolutely honest men and were totally dedicated to their particular philosophy. If they told you some-

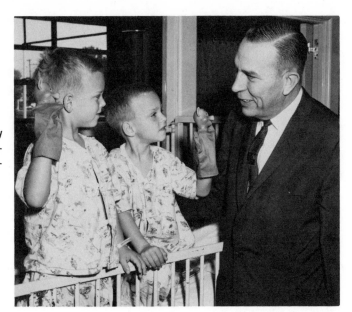

During a 1962 trip to Valley Children's Hospital in Fresno, Sisk ran across this impromptu puppet show.

thing, you could swear by it. I never met a more honest man in my life than Judge Howard Smith. He would bend over backwards to fulfill his obligations, but at the same time, he would do everything he could to beat you if he disagreed with you. But he would give you your opportunity. If you went to Bill and told him, "You have this matter scheduled, but I can't be here," he would call it off—even though you were on the opposite side. Madden didn't adhere to that same kind of rule.

AID: *You had to go to California and you had an understanding . . .*

SISK: Yes. Madden brought up a bill and I was supposed to be protected, but he didn't protect me on it. To save my life, I can't remember the issue. That was not the only incident. There were hard feelings at times with Madden. Let me say this in fairness to Ray Madden: during those latter years, I don't think Madden understood what was going on. I don't mean to be critical, but I think Ray probably should have retired before he did. He simply forgot he had told you a thing.

AID: *This is from* Rule Makers of the House *by Matsunaga and Ping-Chen. It says: "On April 11, 1973, Congressman B. F. Sisk was assured that there would be no committee meeting on the next day to take up the economic stabilization bill, HR 6168-Ninety-third, one in which he had a serious interest. With this understanding, Sisk was on his way to California on the morning of Friday, April 12, unaware upon the request of the leadership, Madden had scheduled a meeting anyway. Learning on his arrival in Los Angeles about this hastily called session, Sisk telephoned the committee in an attempt to speak to the chairman about the possibility of postponement. Madden refused to take the call. He convincingly demonstrated his preference for loyalty to leadership over accommodating committee*

115

> *members despite the long-standing tradition of protecting absent com-*
> *mittee members."*

SISK: I wasn't the only one he treated that way. I don't want the record to be too derogatory, but he did not leave the Congress with the respect that some other men had because of some of those incidents. I think he forgot. He would get lost.

AID: *What is next?*

18.
The District of Columbia Committee

SISK: By this time, we are getting into the 1960s and many interesting matters. I had some unusual experiences during the 1960s. For instance, a situation developed in the District of Columbia Committee. I got on that committee although I didn't want to. Very few members want to get on that committee. Rules was exclusive; I couldn't serve on any other committee. Let me give a little background. We had a new Congress coming in in 1965-1966. John McCormack was Speaker of the House. The *Washington Post*, as usual, was trying to name the new members of the D.C. Committee. (The *Washington Post* feels that it knows it all and is ahead of everybody. It is a most arrogant newspaper. It wants to run the District and it wants to run Congress, even the country.) It would try to name the members on the D.C. Committee. If there was a flexible Speaker, who would go along with the paper, its nominees were appointed. John McCormack did not like the *Washington Post*. He got in cahoots with Wilbur Mills, chairman of the Ways and Means Committee. In those days, the Democratic members of Ways and Means formed the Committee on Committees. (This was before the Reorganization Act of 1970.) They were not going to stand by and let the *Washington Post* run the show. There were two vacancies on the D.C. Committee. They made an exception to the rule, on this occasion, by putting me and [James William] Trimble of Arkansas on the D.C. Committee, but let us stay on Rules.

AID: *That was the first time that was ever done?*

SISK: Yes. This was all done unbeknownst to anybody because it was between the Speaker and Mills. That night, I went down to a reception at the (now) Capitol Hilton Hotel. As I walked in, the Speaker had that Irish gleam in his eyes. That meant he had something that he wanted to pull on you. He came up and said, "Hello, Bernard. By the way, congratulations, congratulations." I said, "What are you talking about?" He said, "Oh, on your ascension to the committee on the District of Columbia. Aren't you aware of your new assignment?" I said, "Not on your life." I won't repeat all I said. He said, "Oh, yes, you and your good friend, Jim Trimble from Rules, have now been nominated for D.C. Committee."

This came as quite a blow to the *Washington Post*. It was probably announced when we were at this reception. I had my mind made up, although I didn't say anything further to him, that I was just not going to take the spot. After the reception, when I got home, my wife said, "The *Washington Post* has just called." I didn't call them back, but they called me again. They wanted to know my reaction to serving on the D.C. Committee. I said, "I have been shanghaied," then added, "Don't you know what shanghaied means? I have been shanghaied and I don't like it." They wrote this up as bigger than life. Well, I served on that committee for four or six years, I don't remember exactly. I was chairman of a subcommittee and held a lot of hearings. John McMillan of South Carolina was the D.C. chairman.

During the time I was on the D.C. Committee, there was a great battle. Johnson decided to support home rule for the District of Columbia. That had been a controversial subject for years. Every Congress faced some sort of bill about granting home rule for the District of Columbia. No president had become too involved until Johnson. Abe [Abraham J.] Multer from New York, then a ranking member of Banking and Currency, also served on the D.C. Committee. He introduced a bill, which I thought was kind of far out, supported by the administration. Because I opposed it, it was one of the few times I ever teamed up with Judge Smith, who served on the D.C. Committee because he supposedly represented a substantial bloc of federal employees in Alexandria, Arlington, and the Pentagon area across the river. So Judge Smith was allowed to be on this committee even though he was chairman of Rules. (By virtue of this, McCormack and Mills finagled this deal to put me and Trimble on this commiteee.) I knew Judge Smith's position because I had talked to him. He played his part in the background. I took the lead and became author of another bill that got to the floor. (D.C. bills had preference. They didn't have to go through Rules. D.C. Day is twice a month, every other Tuesday. We sat as city council for the city of Washington, D.C. This tradition goes back a hundred years or more.) The Multer bill came to the floor. Everybody had turned out. The galleries were full of D.C. people and administration people. Meanwhile, we had been working quietly in the background putting our bill together. I had the southern Democrats and the Republicans lined up with me on this thing. When the debates had almost finished and they were about ready to move their bill (it only had to go through the amending stage), I got on the floor and offered mine as a substitute for Multer's bill. Mine was considerably different although it, too, was for home rule. Apparently they didn't realize that we had done a lot of homework. The bill was debated for an hour or so; then they called for a vote. We demanded a teller vote. We beat them by two-to-one. The *Chicago Tribune* gave me credit for whipping Johnson, for the first time, in a legislative program. The *Tribune* didn't like Johnson; it was strongly Republican. So they head-lined "Johnson Takes Tremendous Legislative Defeat" or something like that. Anyway, that is an example of one of the curious things that happened to me. I had a lot of fun with it.

The Senate never did act on our bill in the first session. Wayne Morse, who was strongly for Johnson's bill, held it up. He was very upset about my bill. I talked to Wayne about it in a friendly way, but we didn't agree at all. Alan Bible, the veteran senator from Nevada, was chairman of the D.C. Committee on the Senate side. Alan wasn't all that gung-ho for Johnson's bill. After Congress adjourned, Alan Bible and a couple of his staff flew out to Fresno and we had a conference. We reached an agree-ment, but when we went back, Wayne Morse killed it in the Senate.

AID: *Did President Johnson ever talk to you about that?*

SISK: He never did say much although he needled me a little bit. I don't think he was that upset about the bill; he had a commitment to some of the blacks in the District. I enjoyed serving on the committee, but it took time away from my district. The local press would write me up and put my picture in the paper every night. However, this was in Washington and didn't do me any good in the Fresno area. The *Washington Post* and the *Washington Star* can be very parochial when it comes to the District, even though they claim to be great national papers.

19.
The 1970 Legislative
Reorganization Act

Approaching the end of the 1960s it became evident that we were stymied on the matter of proper legislative procedures. The Legislative Reorganization Act of 1946 was much outdated. Trying to move legisla-tion was getting worse. We were bogged down with nitpicking. Com-mittees were disproportioned, subcommittees were sprouting up all over the place; there were select and special committees. There were committees which were too large. There were outdated procedures. For instance, the clerk had to call all 435 names for roll call and then repeat them for those not answering on the first call. There was every possible tactic for delay. Television and radio were not permitted in the House. We were still living in the late eighteenth century. It was evident some-thing had to be done.

There was a big hassle about what should be done. Bill Colmer, Rules chairman at that time, claimed Rules had jurisdiction. There was no question about that. Colmer immediately nominated me to chair a special committee to handle this, which created a problem because Dick Bolling resented that he was not selected. I asked Bill to put Dick on the committee since he was a very able person. It was hard for him to accept because he was ahead of me in seniority on the committee yet would be serving under my chairmanship. In recent years Dick and I had been going in opposite directions. Allen Smith, the ranking Republican, was put on the committee. Del Latta of Ohio was the other Republican. On my side was Claude Pepper from Florida and Bolling of Missouri. It was a five-man committee. We were delegated authority to start hearings and come up with recommendations. This was the initial delegation of the committee by the chairman. We had the full cooperation of the leadership (the Speaker included). There were many members of the Congress, even senators, who wanted to testify. Outside groups wanted to testify. People like John Gardner of Common Cause wanted to testify. We developed voluminous testimony on a whole variety of subjects. The whole Rule Book in essence was open for consideration. There was every conceivable kind of proposal, things that would have totally changed the whole complexion of congressional procedures. We held nearly a full year of hearings. Late in the first year, we started weeding out the proposals. We recognized the political facts of life: there are some things you can't do, even though you feel that certain changes are needed. When you are dealing with something every member of Congress has a little piece of, or a personal interest in, you have problems.

AID: *Can you give an example?*

SISK: I wanted to open up the House to television. We had a proposal pending to open not only the committees to television and radio, but the House itself. After talking to a lot of people, including the leadership, and listening to testimony, I came to the conclusion there was no way I was going to get the House open. I compromised by just opening up the committees. We had to be very careful on that. We had to provide initially that each committee became its own governing body on this matter. The only way you could open up a committee for radio and television would be for a member of the committee to make a motion that it be open on a particular date for that purpose and then have a vote of the committee with a quorum present. That is what we settled for.

AID: *The Speaker was opposed to television?*

SISK: Yes. Even to this day, I don't think [Speaker] Tip O'Neill is favorably impressed with it. At the time we were holding these hearings, McCormack was Speaker of the House, Carl Albert was majority leader, and Hale Boggs was majority whip. I could get along with McCormack on this better than with some of the others. Tip O'Neill was very much opposed to it, as were other key people in the House. Carl Albert was not a real strong leader, and it was hard to pin Carl down. McCormack had

119

Above: Carmen Warschaw, then state chairwoman of the California Democratic Council, greets the Sisks during a Valentine's Day party held in Los Angeles in 1965.
Left: Bernie and Reta Sisk pause during the Valentine's Day festivities. It was at this gathering that Sisk first met Tony Coelho, the man who succeeded him in 1979 after serving more than a decade on Sisk's staff.

some reservations, but he would have gone much farther than some other members of the House.

AID: *What was Peter Rodino's stand?*

SISK: Pete Rodino of New Jersey had some reservations. Later on, after we got the bill passed, when the proceedings came up on Nixon, his committee voted to open them up to television. After that, he was a staunch advocate because he saw what it did in connection with Nixon.

AID: *But he had opposed it?*

SISK: Initially, as I recall. This was in 1969 and 1970 when we were debating the issue. This was long before anything was heard of Watergate. Pete joined the more senior members in opposition to opening it up. Most older members felt it was going to delay procedures in the House.

Nothing in the world is more tradition-bound than the Congress of the U.S. For example, one of the decisions we made eliminated the calling of the roll by the clerks. We authorized, under the Reorganization Act, the creation of electronic voting procedures. There was a lot of opposition to that. Some said, "This is going to change the whole complexion of the House. How is the leadership going to be able to go around and check its members? The way it is now, they have time. They hear votes. They have time to go out and talk to people, do a little lobbying here and there." You should have heard some of the speeches.

AID: *Let's talk about Watergate on television. I was told by Tony Coelho that the Judiciary Committee voted to televise the hearings. Rodino was opposed—and so was the Speaker. They got the parliamentarian, Lewis Deschler, to rule that the 1970 Reorganization Act applied only to hearings, whereas Watergate was a proceeding. The committee came to you and members were indignant. Then what happened?*

SISK: I had forgotten that. Deschler, who was opposed to any television in the House, was very conservative. To him, that Rule Book was sacred material; you didn't cross one "t" or dot one "i" that wasn't crossed or dotted as it had been for a thousand years. You wouldn't believe what dyed-in-the-wool traditionalists some people are. Rodino got a ruling out of Deschler that our procedure only applied to hearings and not to proceedings. Therefore, he was going to rule that it couldn't be opened up. His committee came to me and I said, "That is ridiculous. This committee has the right to open any and all of its proceedings to the press, radio and television, if it desires, whether they be hearings or proceedings, whether it be voting or not voting, whether it be a debate on a certain issue—regardless."

AID: *What did you do about it?*

SISK: That was my position—and my position prevailed.

AID: *An amendment was put in? A privileged amendment?*

SISK: That did have high privilege. That's right. I think we moved a motion out of the Rules Committee because Rules always has privilege. The Speaker had to recognize it. I am glad you mentioned that since I had forgotten. In any event, I remember the hassle that developed. I know we went ahead and did what was necessary. We put through a simple procedural resolution out of the Rules Committee.

AID: *Most people feel that if the Nixon proceedings had not been televised, he would not have resigned.*

SISK: I think that is probably right. There is no question that television was very important. A lot of people supported the position on opening the House to television to reveal to the American people some of the inner workings of the House. In a sense, this has improved the image of the House. I think there were a lot a questions about what the House was doing and to what degree it was partisan—or to what extent it was out to destroy Nixon. Television gave people the real story. It was an excellent defense of the position we had taken in giving people the right to know what was going on.

AID: *One way of looking at it is that you were a key factor in Nixon's resignation.*

SISK: I don't know to what extent anyone wants to give me credit for that. We were interested in open proceedings and open decisions openly arrived at.

AID: *What were some of the other changes that took place after the Reorganization Act?*

SISK: I mentioned changing the voting procedure. We pushed that through. We eliminated the unrecorded teller vote and allowed individual votes on bills. Under the procedure we had before, you couldn't get a record vote. This was a key change.

This may not mean very much unless you understand the inner workings of the House. The House of Representatives acts either as the House or as the Committee of the Whole. It can be either one. You move to go into Committee of the Whole House on the State of the Union for the consideration of a given bill. In the days before the Reorganization Act, you could not have a record vote of any kind, quorum call or anything else, in the Committee of the Whole House on the State of the Union. Let's say the procedure was this: The Committee of the Whole House goes into session. You are in the House. The mace is up on the high pedestal. You proceed to discuss matters that are apropos in the House. You already have a published record of what you are going to do that day. You are going to discuss a bill on national defense having to do with authorizing certain new vessels for the navy.

In a timely fashion, the Speaker recognizes the chairman of the Armed Services Committee. Call him Mr. X. He rises and says, "Mr. Speaker, I move that the House now resolve itself into the Committee of the Whole House on the State of the Union for the consideration (or the further consideration) of HR 1234 dealing with naval vessels for the navy." The Speaker immediately puts the question, "All in favor, etc." Then the Speaker says, "The House is now in the Committee of the Whole House on the State of the Union. To preside over the committee today, I nominate Mr. X." Mr. X comes up and there is a formal exchange of the gavel. The mace is moved from the high pedestal to the low pedestal. You are now in a totally different body. You are now in the Committee of the Whole House on the State of the Union for the consideration of this particular bill. Nothing else can be considered at that point except that bill.

Until the Reorganization Act was passed and put into effect, you could not get a recorded vote of any kind while in this procedure. Someone makes the point of no quorum. Now 100 members make a quorum in the Committee of the Whole House on the State of the Union, whereas 218 members are required for a quorum in the House. So Mr. X counts and finds only eighty-two members present. The pages have already run out to get members from the lobby, the cloakroom and the benches. But there are only eighty-two in all. The quorum is not present so the Committee rises. Mr. X stands and waits because the Speaker or someone standing in for him has to get back on the floor. He takes the chair. The mace is lifted back on the high pedestal. The Speaker raps the gavel and says, "The House is now in session. A point has been made and a quorum is not present. Only eighty-two members have been counted. Therefore, a quorum is not present and a roll call is in order. The clerk will now call the roll."

The members settle back and the clerk, in a monotone, calls the roll for 435 members. This goes on and on until a quorum is established. You continue through the double call completely so everyone may have an opportunity to be there and be on record. The names of those who do not answer will be listed in the record. Once a quorum has been established and you have finished all of the procedures, the Speaker says, "The names shall be published on the basis of the record." Then he raps the gavel and says, "The committee will resume its sitting." He gets off the stand and Mr. X comes back on and resumes the gavel. The mace is removed to the low pedestal. If you have ever sat in there you would understand how bound up we were in customs established between 1793 and 1801. You can read those adopted procedures right out of the book. All the books on my first shelf contain rules of the House.

How are we going to change all this if there are traditionalists in the House who don't want anything touched? Some of them have been in Congress for twenty or thirty years. They like the old procedure because it gives them plenty of time to get to the floor. They can even call the hotel downtown and the member can get up there in time to answer. It takes about thirty minutes to get through the roll call. Then they can wind up in the well because you have the right to go there after they have gone through the roll call twice. You can stand in the well and be recognized and answer and get on the record. Voting consumes about forty-five minutes. If you have a half-dozen roll calls during a day, you have used up most of the day. The greatest number of roll calls, under the old procedure, that I remember, was fourteen in one day. We didn't do anything else that day.

Years ago we had a big battle over an appropriations bill. The conservatives and the Republicans had lined up and were determined to cut and slice the bill. Believe me, they were doing it. They were beating us at every turn. This was under Johnson, I think. We were in the Committee (of the Whole) during all of this. You could have either voice votes or teller votes. If it was a teller vote, it wasn't on record. You go down the aisle and count all those who were voting "aye" and then count all those voting "no"—but there was no record of it.

If an amendment carried, then when you went back into the House (let's say I moved an amendment to cut fifty million dollars out of that appropriation), you debate the issue. You finally get an agreement to cut-off time. You can't move the previous question in the Committee; you can't even cut the debate off. That's another difference from being in the House; it cuts off all debate and requires a vote. You can't do that in the Committee, but you finally get an agreement on a cut-off time.

After you cut off time, the question goes to a vote. The chairman of the

Committee of the Whole, sitting in the Speaker's chair, asks for a vote. If he rules the "ayes" have it, then you demand a teller's list. This is done if you don't like the amendment. The amendment still carries, let's say. If the amendment carries, then you debate the bill (as much as a week sometimes). You may have adopted twenty amendments in the Committee procedure.

On a certain date, you complete the debate and the Committee rises and goes back into the House. The Speaker rises and says, "The Committee of the Whole House on the State of the Union has completed its work on HR 1234 and reports the bill back (with sundry amendments) with the recommendation the bill be passed. Are there separate votes demanded on any amendment?" At that point, you rise and say, "Mr. Speaker, I demand a separate vote on so and so . . . " You can demand a separate vote and get a roll call on each separate amendment. (If an amendment didn't pass, you can't get a vote.)

I was insistent on eliminating this business of having to go back into the House every time you call a quorum. It's one thing I take credit for as author, even though a lot of people were disgruntled about it despite its time-saving feature. Under the reorganized procedure, when you debate an issue on the Committee of the Whole House and you arise and say, "I make a point of order that a quorum is not present; there are only fifty-two members," a roll call is automatic. The clerk will call the roll. On the answering of 100 members, further calling of the roll is suspended and the House reverts back to business. The committee chairman simply sits there. You turn on the electric equipment. (We authorized this, too.) When the bells ring, it notifies the members that that particular type of quorum call is going on. Members then come in. As quickly as you reach one hundred, you rap the gavel and say, "Further proceedings under this call are dispensed with." You go about your business. You don't even record who was there and who wasn't.

Every one of those changes I had to wring out of Deschler, almost forcing him. I would go to Carl Albert or the Speaker and say, "Let's try this at least." Deschler would fight every step of the way. The Reorganization Act marked the longest period in total debate in the last fifty years. We started debate on the bill approximately the first of July. We concluded and passed that bill in late September, I believe. We would go on the floor and debate it for a few days until we were taken off by virtue of other legislation. We would be on and off, on and off. We had a recess in part of August. It was an unusual procedure; once you started on a bill, you usually stayed with it. Because of the nature and importance of this bill, we used the time procedure I've outlined. I was on and off the floor because I handled the debate. I managed the bill, being chairman of the committee. There wasn't really that much sweeping change because you had to modify and compromise a great deal.

For example, we got an agreement that required so many members to stand in order to get a roll call vote in the Committee (of the Whole). To try to reduce the number of roll calls, we authorized actual roll record votes in Committee. This eliminated the business of not only having to go back to the House for a quorum, but also made it possible to vote on an issue in the Committee at the time. Let's say you move an amendment, you debate it and get it to a vote. If you aren't satisfied with the "yea" and "nay" vote, you could ask for a standing vote. If you still aren't satisfied, you could ask for a roll call vote, but you would have to get twenty members to stand. (We later tried to raise that to forty to cut down on it.) If you can't get twenty members to stand, you can't get a record vote. There are all types of ways to delay things. This business of demanding roll calls in many cases results in a substantial filibuster. I originally authored an amendment to ask for forty members to stand, not twenty. It didn't quite make it.

We opened up the House committees to radio and television under certain conditions, as I have said. We opened up the House in the last Congress. I am not entirely satisfied with the way it has been handled: the Speaker insisted it be done by the House, while I maintained the media should be allowed to do it. I think there is a question of integrity in the way television cameras are handled. In a sense, the present agreement leaves the House in control of what is filmed and what isn't. I don't think the public should be subjected to any type of censorship. That is what I am afraid of.

The Reorganization Act changed the rules in as many as one hundred instances. In many cases, these were minor changes. We changed the rules in the handling of conference reports. I authored privileged resolutions on three or four different occasions, trying to straighten out the conference procedure between the House and Senate in order to stop the Senate from doing some things we felt were not in the best interests of good legislation. The House has had a stiff rule governing germaneness for at least 150 years. When we bring out a bill dealing, say, with armed services, a water project, or a banking bill, we hassle over it and pass it. Then we send it to the Senate. There some guy would come along and put his water project on the banking and currency bill. They would send the bill back to conference, where there would be another big hassle. Then they would send it down to the floor and we would get into a big fight over it. Frankly, under our rules, it was not fair to force it down our throats. We dealt with that complicated subject.

The Senate rebuffed the language we used, and we had to go back over it three or four times. But we worked out this procedure: when a non-germane Senate amendment attached to a House-passed bill comes back to the floor of the House (if the committee having jurisdiction has been in conference and brings it back), the chairman must stand up and state that the conference adopted certain amendments. At that point, any member who desires to do so can rise and make a point of order against that non-germane amendment. That automatically brings into play a procedure whereby you debate the issue and then have a vote on whether you are going to consider it. At least it gives each side in the House twenty minutes to have the right to act on it. In the old days, you couldn't even get a separate vote on the non-germane Senate amendment. To me, as a legislator, this is vital. I am not sure how the public might interpret it. It gets very complicated.

A vast amount of work was done by that committee. One of the most important things we did was to create the Congressional Research Service. We changed the procedures of the Library of Congress. We also set up a Government Operations Committee, headed by Jack Brooks of Texas. The Congressional Research Service is set up under a separate director. We supply ample resources for the service. What it does, in an objective manner and without partisanship, is deal with the great issues that face the country. It has specialists come into the research service branch of the library. Research in great depth concerns issues like inflation and energy, for example. CRS takes recommendations from individual standing committees. The chairman of a committee, at the end of a congressional session, submits a request for information on matters affecting the country, relating to his committee's jurisdiction. The service amasses voluminous amounts of information on these subjects and will make recommendations; it will answer questions or work with staff members. Often, it will assign its people, who will work under and for you, in the event your staff needs expertise along certain lines. This service, which was one of the more important things we accomplished, was a vast improvement because it furnishes detailed, researched information to the Congress.

We eliminated some committees, e.g. a whole library committee, which didn't function much anyway. We even changed some of the committee names.

There has been follow-up since then with the Hansen Committee in 1975 or 1976. So there have been further modifications, although we opened the door to a whole slew of revisions and eliminations.

We also required the parliamentarian to bring up to date the precedents of the House, which are just as important as the Rule Book itself, since the precedents become controlling. Let's say you are in the chair presiding over the Committee of the Whole House on the State of the Union which is debating an important issue such as foreign relations, and a question comes up about offering an amendment.

I rise and say, "Mr. Chairman, I make a point of order on this amendment on the basis that it is non-germane" (or whatever my justification may be). The people offering the amendment will defend their

Above left: Sisk's 1968 campaign gets a boost—and a tasty send-off—from the Fresno Asian-American Forum. Joining Bernie and Reta is dinner chairman Frank Tuck. Above right: Sisk welcomes backers at a campaign fund-raising dinner in Fresno.

position. Sometimes you can argue a question on a point of order indefinitely. Normally, it doesn't take too long. At some point, the chairman has to rule on that point of order. You, the committee chairman, must do it because you—not the Speaker—are running the show at the time. That can be vital because once you rule, it goes into the book of precedents.

Ten years later I am sitting in the chair when a point of order is made on a question and debate ensues on the point of order. At my request for information, an assistant parliamentarian will say to me, the chairman, "Ten years ago, Congressman Dickman ruled so-and-so and here is the precedent and here is how he justified it." This solves the situation for me, the chairman. I then recognize everyone who wants to debate. After listening, then I say, "I find this amendment to be in accord with the amendment offered by Congressman X on the occasion when Chairman Dickman ruled thus-and-so. Therefore, I sustain that position." The precedents are voluminous. They issue from the past two hundred years.

The last time the precedents were brought up to date was around the 1920s. Deschler, who had been a parliamentarian or an assistant parliamentarian for the last forty years, never brought the precedents up to date. He was fiddling with the idea. He wanted to do work he would receive credit for, which was fine. Lew was probably one of the greatest parliamentarians ever to sit in the House of Representatives. But he was a stickler; every word in the rule book was sacred writ to him and you couldn't change it. That was his great trouble. We forced him to change. We built a fire underneath him. We required, within a limited period of time, that he bring the precedents up to date. Lew has since passed away, I believe eighteen months to two years ago.

127

There is no question the rules of the House of Representatives are the most complex devised by the mind of man. No legislative body in the world has a set of such complex rules and precedents as those that govern the House. If you had all the precedents of the House here, they would fill this room.

AID: *Please discuss the conference procedure whereby the House and the Senate get together.*

SISK: When a bill passes the House of Representatives, by the time it has run the gamut through the subcommittee, full committee, the floor, and the amending stage there, the same legislation may be enacted simultaneously on the Senate side. Or it may go over there and the Senate then takes it up. But in either case, almost invariably there are some differences; they will amend a bill one way and we will amend it another way. The body which sends it to the other body first picks up the legislation and amends it to suit itself. Then it is passed and sent back.

At this point the conference comes into being. A request for a conference between the two bodies to iron out the differences between the two bills is made by the last body passing the legislation. With the concurrence of the leadership on both sides, members are appointed by both the House and Senate and a time certain is agreed for meeting. At the meeting, they discuss the differences on articles and titles. This is done article by article and title by title until both sides reach an agreement— sometimes it takes a good long while. Sometimes a bill will lie in conference for as long as a year. Sometimes bills die in conference.

The normal procedure is to reasonably amend, reading the bill together to work out an agreement, or to compromise. The bill comes back to the House and the Senate and then is passed by a very brief action which takes place by motion on both floors. At that point, the bill is engrossed and signed by the proper officials, the Speaker and the president of the Senate, and is sent to the president. With the president's signature, it becomes law.

AID: *When you say engrossed, you mean it has been passed by both houses?*

SISK: Yes. We say the bill has been engrossed—read a third time—and has passed. It is a procedure; all the legal qualifications have been met. That is the final act before it is hand-delivered to the president. The president has so many days to sign it or return it.

AID: *What about the input of the agency which will administer the bill? Or of scientists and experts—is that input all at the hearings?*

SISK: That input comes during the hearings. After a bill has been introduced it is referred to a committee. Let's say I am the author of a bill and have just introduced it. It has been referred to the Committee on Interstate and Foreign Commerce. I immediately write a letter to the chairman of that committee saying I have just introduced a bill, which has been referred to your committee and I would appreciate it if you would institute a request for departmental reports on this legislation. Various agencies of government may be involved in this. Sometimes you are dealing with a number of agencies, depending on how comprehensive the bill is. On the other hand, there may be only one department involved.

At any rate, you ask the chairman to seek agency positions. Nine times out of ten, if it is anything controversial, you will find that after a month or so they will not have reported. Then you get on the phone and call the departments involved and say that they've got a letter requesting their position regarding the bill. "We have to move this bill because a lot of people are interested in it," you would say. They would say, "Okay, let's see what we can do." You may have to push pretty hard, but finally you get a report. Once the report or reports are in, the chairman will set a date for hearings on your bill.

That report is the first input from the executive branch. Ordinarily, the report will say, "Yes, we support this bill" or "No, we do not support this bill because we do not think it is in the best interests of the country" or "We would support this if it was amended in such and such a way." At that point, the chairman sets a hearing during the following week, for example. He will ask you to appear on behalf of your legislation. He will have department witnesses there. This usually takes all morning. You make a brief statement and are asked questions. Then they call the department or departments involved and they testify, as do any public witnesses. If the department supports the bill, you are in good shape; if it is in opposition, you have a battle. Then it is up to the committee.

After all the differences have been worked out on a bill in the Congress and it has been sent to the president and signed into law, the importance of the department comes into play. The bill is referred to the relevant department to set up regulations and implement the law. How it regulates and implements the bill is very important.

We have been putting provisos in a number of bills. The administration is furious about it, but we have been doing it consistently for the last couple of years. Before the implementation of the law, we required that the department report back to the committee having jurisdiction regarding the regulations it is proposing. This gives the committee the opportunity to pass judgment on whether the proposed regulations meet the intent of Congress when it passed the bill. I think this is absolutely important. We have seen legislation destroyed so many times. So the input of the department(s) becomes important when the bill is implemented.

AID: *I have one more question on that. The Environmental Protection Agency, for example, has an advisory committee composed of scientists. Emil Mrak, a chancellor emeritus of the University of California, Davis, has been its chairman. I was curious about its input. Where would you get the benefit of that kind of information? Is it up to them to seek you out or is it up to you or your staff to seek them out?*

129

SISK: The committee would request reports from the agency. The agency would express its position, subject to the advice that it had received from these scientists. In turn, the members of the committee who are knowledgeable in this area are going to know about that committee of scientists.

For example, one member might say, "I know Dr. Joe Blow over there. I know he is involved with this. I would like the chairman to call him before the committee for information on this matter." The committee chairman asks him to appear. If he doesn't want to appear, it can subpoena him, because all committees have that power.

In many cases, committee members and departments depend on information supplied by scientists. This information is made available to a department by means of reports. If a member of a committee gets an inkling that a department is following the advice of a report representing the majority opinion of a group of scientists in a certain field, nine times out of ten this member will ask the chairman to call in experts to testify. Committees reserve the right to make the final decision. They are powers unto themselves.

20.
More House Reform

AID: *May we talk a bit more about the Reorganization Act of 1970? I understand this Act provided for a new procedure for Congress to oversee budget control.*

SISK: Correct. A portion of that reform led to the setting up of the Budget Committee. One of our national weaknesses was the inadequate control of expenditures; the national debt was continuing to increase. We were trying to control expenditures viz-a-viz revenue. Congress felt this situation was out of hand and that there should be some better way to do it. There is always fear, particularly by the more liberal bloc, that budget control would be used to destroy what it felt were good social programs (state programs, housing for the poor, food stamps, etc.). Liberals felt budget control might go so far as to say you cannot use deficit spending.

Some counties, states, or local jurisdictions have provisions in their constitutions forbidding them from exceeding revenues. In other words, if they set up a budget for fifty million dollars and their revenues do not come up with that, then they cannot spend the total fifty million. Therefore, there has been a traditional battle over this. It has long been recognized by responsible people that Congress needed to get a better handle on expenditures so we could have more control over the budget process, rather than accepting what administration after administration tossed out.

For many years the normal procedure allowed for the president to designate certain of his people (a combination of his cabinet and various groups) to put together a budget. These budget processes always start two years ahead of time. The twenty-first of January is the deadline for the president to submit his budget to Congress.

For a long time we had felt that we just sat there and accepted it. Of course, we would hold hearings on the president's budget, but you can imagine the problems of understanding that would be involved with a massive document dealing with tens of thousands of different items.

Because of all this, there were numerous recommendations that we do something about it. Congress had to take a greater hand, be in a better position of knowing about the budget, so the Congress could set the budget and not necessarily yield to the administration—Democratic or Republican. As a result, we created the Budget Committee, with a budget director, and gave it substantial authority to set up a budget process. This was done by concurrence of the House and the Senate.

A firmly set sequence of events was created. It was essential that each Congress not put off to the last minute (usually along about November) passing an emergency resolution of some kind, because it had not completed its actions in connection with appropriations. So we do the same things we did the year before, and we call it a continuing resolution. This is a gimmick most people don't understand. All it means is that the department can only spend the same amount it spent last year and cannot spend anything in excess until there is further authorization.

So we set up the sequence of events that had to occur. Certain things had to be done in February, March, or April, etc. I think a resolution had to be passed by the middle of May. This resolution would be the first one—suggesting the maximum budget. Along with that, we changed the fiscal year in order to give this process an opportunity to work through both this series of events and the resolution that had to pass in the House and Senate.

Places on the Budget Committee are much sought-after because they are considered to be prestigious. Conservative members seek spots on it, giving them the opportunity to torpedo programs they don't like. In the final analysis, the Budget Committee does have to come to the House for approval or disapproval. Sometimes the Budget Committee submits a budget and the House turns it down. These are hard-fought issues.

For the first time, the Congress has a method to formulate a budget which will correspond to revenues after it receives reports on income from the Ways and Means Committee and the Internal Revenue Service.

In the final analysis, the Congress approves and passes a resolution from the Budget Committee which says, for example, in the year 1980, we will not exceed deficit expenditures of more than twenty-two billion dollars. If it wants to go further, it can say expenditures will not exceed what is now predicted to be total revenues of $480 billion. That, in essence, will balance the budget.

AID: *This is a clear signal to the executive?*

SISK: That becomes binding on the executive. So for the first time, while the executive will continue to submit the budget, the Congress has seized control; it will dictate what the budget will be and what the deficit expenditures will be—or, we hope, what surplus has been attained.

AID: *Was there White House opposition to this?*

SISK: There were real questions raised by the administration that this proposed measure might create economic anarchy. But people were greatly concerned about the size of the national debt. To give you an idea, when I went to Congress in 1954 (and I am citing these figures right off the top of my head, so they may be wrong), the total national debt was about $270 billion. Most of this debt was incurred during and after World War II. Today, twenty-five years later, this debt is more like $800 billion. These are the figures about which people are concerned. Most of the increase came after 1967 or 1968. In the last ten years there have been fantastic jumps in the budget and the size of the national debt! The only way you are going to cut that down is to reduce expenditures below revenues and have a surplus. We have not had a surplus for a number of years.

AID: *The reform act also gave the General Accounting Office the power to investigate, did it not?*

SISK: Yes. It gave the GAO vast new powers. Many people may not realize that GAO is not an agency of the executive, even though the comptroller general is appointed by the president of the United States. The GAO is an arm of Congress. (I and many others have proposed legislation to do this differently, although we have never been able to pass it.) Despite the fact that the president appoints the comptroller general, the latter is responsible only to Congress.

There was some resistance on the part of GAO, which is a very responsible agency. Very frankly, the comptroller general and others were very much concerned that it was going to become overloaded. GAO was fearful of being put into the position of literally not being able to police the executive branch. In other words, we were requesting that the GAO obtain certain information from the executive, but the executive may proclaim executive privilege, refusing GAO the right to go into an agency and check its books. However, we insisted. And today GAO has broad new powers and can investigate any agency of the government if it is deemed necessary. The reform act has increased its size and responsibility, but the General Accounting Office is an independent agency composed of able people. Its responsibility is accounting to the public just how taxpayers' money is being handled.

AID: *You also abolished the Internal Security Committee?*

SISK: That's right. That was a controversial issue for years—even before I went

Sisk flanks Education and Labor Committee Chairman Carl Perkins during congressional hearings on the federal food stamp program. Also on the panel is Fresno County welfare director Reed Clegg, left.

to Congress in 1954. This goes way back to what was called the old Walters Committee. The committee was called all sorts of names. Liberals generally opposed it. It was an arm which investigated alleged communist activity.

AID: *Is this the same as the Un-American Activities Committee?*

SISK: It was basically the same, just a new name for it. The Un-American Activities Committee started back in the 1930s. Martin Dies was the head of it. By the way, I served with Congressman Martin Dies later on. He was a very unusual character in a lot of ways. Tad Walters was very active and the committee was almost renamed the Walters Committee. I served with Tad Walters, too.

In order to clean up some of the stigma of the Un-American Activities Committee, we changed the name of the committee, updated it, increased its membership, and broadened it—putting on more liberal members to balance the committee philosophically. We called it the Internal Security Committee.

Don't misunderstand me. I was very critical of this committee, but on the other hand I generally supported its basic aims. Clyde Doyle was a Democratic congressman from Long Beach, California, going back to the 1940s. He was a liberal Democrat and was respected by both liberals and conservatives generally; he was pretty much in the middle-of-the-road. He served for many years on this committee and basically defended it, but at all times attempted to correct its procedures. He was very much opposed to some of the things Dies had done and even some of the things Walters had done. There was abuse or mistreatment of witnesses, etc.

Doyle spent a great deal of time and effort through the early years of my service in Congress attempting to clean up the committee. He amended and changed most of the procedures and revised the name.

Although it was a considerably different committee, it still had the old stigma. It still had those files, which some of the more left-wing people in the country opposed. This was because names in those files could lead to a type of McCarthyism. It came to the point that we discontinued the committee.

AID: *Briefly, what were some of the characteristics of Martin Dies?*

SISK: Martin Dies was truly an unusual character. He was probably among the last of what might be called the old-time southern orators. Dies could take the floor and have them standing in the aisles screaming. He had that knack. He was truly the old-time orator type; he could influence people.

One incident was most revealing of Dies; I say this thoughtfully and without any particular criticism. During the early days of my service I once heard him go on the floor and make a rip-roaring speech in support of an issue. Then he came back to the cloakroom and frankly admitted he had put on a show. He was a demagogue from the word go. However, he was honest enough to admit he was not all that sincere.

AID: *You also required written rules for committees as part of the reform act?*

SISK: That's right, because in the old days a chairman could act like a czar, if he wanted to. He had broad powers including hiring and firing at will— virtually without consultation from anyone else. (In most cases a chairman did not do this, but these were powers inherent in the office of chairman.) The chairman could call or not call meetings. As the committee chairman went, so went the committee.

As new members began coming in, they would ask, "What are the rules?" The truth of the matter was that there were no rules; the rules were the chairman's wishes. Younger members especially were a little frightened of the chairman's power because he could stop your legislation or make you look bad.

To standardize the procedures, we said every committee must have written rules and must make these rules by democratic process. In addition, the rules must be submitted to the *Congressional Record*.

AID: *You were talking about younger members. Is this the group referred to as the "Young Turks"?*

SISK: The term "Young Turk" is an old term that has been around for years. It applies generally to new members of the legislative body because they seek changes. To some extent this action (of standardizing procedures for rules in committees) was taken by younger members. In reference to this, to call them "Young Turks" is correct. I would have been classified as a "Young Turk," although I wasn't all that young. I basically supported reform in this area, however. I had seen too much abuse by chairmen, in some cases men for whom I had great respect.

Let me cite an example. One such man is Carl Vinson of Georgia, who served in the Congress for more than fifty years. He was chairman of the Armed Services Committee. Carl was a total dictator in that committee in the old days, under the old procedure. He said he came to Washington to fill in a spot temporarily and after fifty years, he felt that was long enough for a temporary job. I remember an incident which illustrates Vinson's czar-like procedures.

Clair Engle and I were very much interested in a bill. We appeared before Vinson's committee to testify on an important matter in which we Californians were very much interested. Vinson looked at a brief statement we had submitted and said frankly, "I think the two gentlemen have submitted adequate statements." With that, he just rapped the gavel and cut us both right off. He had done this to Engle, the chairman of the Interior and Insular Affairs Committee! It was said that Vinson normally allowed freshman members one question a year.

Vinson used to appear before the Rules Committee. There was always a unanimous position on the bills from his committee, never any opposition. Yet Vinson dealt in an area which could be very controversial. He dealt with authorizations for billions of dollars for guns, tanks, planes, and ships. But Carl would come before Rules with a unanimous position from his committee. One day, one of the members said, "Chairman Vinson, you always seem to come here with unanimous positions. Don't you ever have any opposition?" He had a glint in his eye when he replied, "Once in a while we have some young fellows who have various opinions, but we have ways of working out reasonable agreements."

Another member of the Rules Committee spoke up. "Is it possible that you find opposing members other things to do?" Carl, with a little grin on his face, said, "Well, yes. We have three men right now flying to Paris." In other words, there wasn't any opposition because these three men weren't there. Anyway, he was a great man and a great legislator. It was a real honor to serve with those kinds of people. Carl Vinson was, I always thought, a benevolent dictator. He didn't cut you to pieces.

AID: *The Ways and Means Committee lost the right to be the Committee on Committees and that went to the Steering and Policy Committee, composed of the Speaker, majority leader, and the chairman of the Democratic caucus?*

SISK: Yes. That is one area of reform I did not support. I had some reservations about the way that matter was handled. Let me make clear that that action was not part of the 1970 Reorganization Act, but was taken up later on by the Hansen committee; we will talk about that shortly. After passage of the 1970 Reorganization Act, there was a demand by the "Young Turks"— the newer members of Congress—for even more reform. Dick Bolling headed a supposedly bipartisan reform committee. The Bolling committee came up with a program opposed by a considerable bloc of Congress, particularly the leadership of the House, which did not want known its opposition to some portions of this program.

Certain provisions in the Bolling program were also opposed by

135

moderate and liberal blocs within the Democratic Party. So the Democratic caucus became active. During the old days under Rayburn, the caucus met once every two years and that was about it. Rayburn didn't believe in getting many extraneous groups formed because they might cause problems. An action was taken by the Democratic caucus to appoint a committee with Julia Butler Hansen as chairwoman. In a head-on conflict in the Democratic caucus, the Hansen forces overwhelmed the Bolling forces. The Hansen report was adopted and was later incorporated into the rules for procedures of the House. That is where the change was made in the Committee on Committees; the Ways and Means Committee was stripped of its jurisdiction. Hence, the steering committee was created. In our original Reorganization Act, we tended toward the steering committee procedures to enhance the leadership's position, but we didn't go nearly as far as the Hansen committee did.

AID: *What was Philip Burton's role in the Hansen committee?*

SISK: He did not agree with some of the things being done. On the other hand, Philip Burton is a master technician at figuring out where the wind is blowing and how to go with it. This is not said because I am critical of Phil; he is simply a sharp politician. He has had years of experience at it. He was active in the Hansen group, although there were things he would have done differently.

AID: *Could you talk about some of the reform that has taken place which you haven't already discussed? For example, more staff was allowed for subcommittees.*

SISK: That broke down more of the authority of the chairmen by giving subcommittee chairmen the right to make some personnel selections. This was in the 1970 Act. There have been other reforms on that issue, too.

AID: *Does the Speaker nominate the Rules Committee?*

SISK: Yes. There had been one attempt some years before to provide direct appointment to the Rules Committee by the Speaker alone. I fought this—and so did other members of the Rules Committee. We beat it easily two or four years before. All of a sudden, this came up just as Tip O'Neill took over as Speaker. In the 1975 organizing caucus, Bolling arose and offered a resolution to change the method of appointing members to the Rules Committee; they would be subject to appointment by the Speaker. I didn't think there would be much support. But Tip O'Neill, the nominee for Speaker (which meant he would be elected since the Democrats had nominated him), got up and supported it, and it passed.

There was a saving clause in this resolution—and I think this is the only reason it did pass—that the Speaker's appointments can be voted down. Let's say the Speaker attempted to take a member off Rules—which he never has—because he didn't like this person. In this eventuality, the full caucus would have to ratify it. So this was the saving grace. In spite of the fact I and many members don't like it, it is not really as serious as it seems on the surface.

AID: *Who appoints the minority members of Rules?*

SISK: The minority members are appointed by the Republican conference. The Republicans operate in somewhat the same way as the Democrats. When Jerry Ford was minority leader, he would appoint people to fill vacancies on Rules and then these appointments would be submitted to the Republican conference, which is the equivalent to the Democratic caucus. John Anderson of Illinois has been chairman of the Republican conference. If the conference disapproves the appointments, the minority leader comes up with somebody else.

AID: *Were executive sessions reduced in frequency?*

SISK: Are you referring to the Rules Committee?

AID: *Yes, and in general.*

SISK: The number of executive sessions in all committees was substantially reduced after the reform act of 1970. In that bill we provided that you needed a majority vote to have executive sessions and there weren't to be any automatic executive sessions. This was at a time when all Rules Committee actions were taken in executive session, just automatically, although the hearings would be open. For example, the chairman and the ranking minority member of the committee would ask for a rule on a given bill. There could be a lot of open testimony—the press and others would be there. Once the hearings were over, the chairman would rap his gavel and say, "The committee will now go into executive session." Then everybody left. That is when we would have our fight, debate, vote, and decide.

AID: *Now all of that is done in open session?*

SISK: Yes, unless someone moves to close it. Then it takes a majority vote to close it. As a result, Rules rarely has a closed session. The same thing is true of all other committees.

AID: *Were bill-drafting sessions opened?*

SISK: In the normal procedures in the legislative committees, prior to reform, practically all mark-up sessions of all subcommittees were closed. (Mark-up sessions are generally done in subcommittees.)

AID: *Please explain mark-up sessions.*

SISK: After all the hearings, testimony is printed and the staff does its analytical work, which is then submitted and is scheduled on a date certain for a mark-up session. A subcommittee will then go into session. If I had amendments for a bill, I would have them ready to be offered. We would start reading the bill for amendment. It is marked up section by section and paragraph by paragraph. It is amended, changed, and finally adopted. (This was always done in executive session.) Then you would report to the full committee. The only things open in those days were public hearings. Now that has been changed; almost everything is done in open session.

AID: *What were the specific ways in which the seniority system was changed by the reforms?*

SISK: Many things we did affected the seniority system, which is still very much part of Congress. A variety of things are done according to seniority. You move up on committees according to seniority; your office allocation is by seniority. In other words, as a freshman you don't move into the [newer] Rayburn building. Each class draws, of course, for rooms and a number of things. Even in parking, seniority is considered.

What is important about the reforms is that they broke the strangle hold that three to five people on a committee could have. By this I mean these people would gobble up all (subcommittee) chairmanships. For example, just before I got on the Rules Committee, I was chairman of three subcommittees. We stopped, by way of reform, this business of one or two people or the chairman of the full committee serving as chairmen of several subcommittees. We limited the number of chairmanships a person could hold. A person can be chairman of only one subcommittee. The full committee chairman is limited to service on his/her committee and one subcommittee. These reforms broke down the control of small, senior groups within the committee system, giving more people a chance to operate. This widened the opportunities and responsibilities of newer, younger members.

AID: *Do you recall the vote tally for the 1970 Reorganization Act?*

SISK: After we ironed out some differences, it was passed by a rather substantial vote. It was not close. I have said that it was considered the longest-debated bill in history, but it wasn't a continuous debate; it was a periodic debate. As we moved through the debate, it had a number of titles with many, many sections. As we amended, changed, and perfected a section, we would move on. Anyway, it finally passed. I have a picture, which is on a signed copy of the legislation, showing all the members of the committee and giving the date the bill was enacted.

AID: *Tony Coelho and Jackson Carle say—and they may be a little preju-diced—that the only person who could have gotten the 1970 Act through was you, because of your ability to work out differences.*

SISK: We were given a good deal of credit, although I am not sure if we warranted all that credit. The House, as it always is, is a very sensitive group of people which reacts in strange ways at times; along with this business of reform, you had the anti-reformers. There was always a strong bloc which said, "Oh, that is just a bunch of nonsense." They were strong traditionalists. Do you remember the famous play, "Fiddler on the Roof," where the old man sings, "Tradition, tradition"? When I saw that show, I said, "There is nothing in the world more tradition-bound than the House of Representatives." Some people felt that since I had a reputation for working rather closely with Sam Rayburn (although he was gone at this time) and the Texas delegation and even Joe Waggoner, the leader of the conservatives from the South, and with some Georgia people and some of the middle-of-the-road Republicans, etc., maybe they had a little more confidence that I was not going to go off the deep end in this reform.

The reform was a delicate, sensitive situation that had to be carefully handled. People did not wish to destroy the traditions of Congress. It was not an easy task. In fact, I think I spent more time on that than any other single thing, outside of water, during the years I was in Congress. But saying that I was the only one who could have won passage of the 1970 reform bill is a little overdoing it. It was a matter of keeping the confidence of these people and sitting down and talking with them, compromising here and there, that finally got the legislation through.

AID: *The reform that has taken place since the 1970 Act (such as the Hansen committee) deserves further discussion. For example, you have said the caucus has been rejuvenated.*

SISK: Right. It became more active. The pendulum swings from one extreme to the other in every organization. The caucus had very little importance when Rayburn was there. During Speaker McCormack's time, it was not too active, although it met a little more often. During the period when I was working on the 1970 reform bill, and later on, when Carl Albert came along as Speaker, the caucus became more active. It peaked with the Phil Burton period, when the caucus kind of took over. I think this was intended; it was part of a program, right or wrong. I had some strong feelings about what was happening. I was one of those who, after the 1972 election, helped organize the UDC, United Democrats of Congress, which became the moderate Democratic group. We numbered about 120. I was the first chairman. By creating a bloc and taking certain positions, we warded off things we thought were bad in reference to the caucus. Gillis Long of Louisiana was very active in UDC. We had a broad cross-section of Democrats, from all over the country, including some Californians. It began to offset some of the power asserted within the Democratic caucus under the Burton crowd. Once Burton was out, the caucus resumed its traditional position.

AID: *At the height of the caucus's power, if it so ruled, could it overturn a decision of a committee chairman?*

SISK: Technically, no. A committee chairman is only responsible to the House. You have to keep in mind that in those shelves of rules, the responsibility of each individual member and his chairman was to the House, not just to a party line. There was no question that because of the huge Democratic majority, if the caucus majority took certain positions, they almost became rulings. The Democratic majority asserted great power—power which I think was sometimes abused.

~

139

George Mahon, senior member of Congress and chairman of the Appropriations Committee, testifies before the Rules Committee during this 1978 hearing. Sisk, second from right, queries Mahon on his testimony.

21.
Functions and Powers
of the Rules Committee

AID: *Let me check on a few more things on Rules before we wind up this section. Being on Rules means that you have extraordinary importance. Were you lobbied by other members of the House?*

SISK: I was regularly lobbied by my colleagues. Naturally, they had bills pending before Rules and they were anxious to talk to me.

AID: *So you can exchange favors?*

SISK: Let's say you have been waiting months for a hearing on a certain bill, as I did with my good friend, Paul Rogers. There was a bill that I had before him dealing with hospitalization for illegal aliens, in which we had some interest. Paul kept stalling. Finally, Paul wanted something out of the Rules Committee. Of course, that was nice and convenient. I would say, "By the way, Paul, I appreciate your call and I am going to try to help you, but how soon can we get a hearing for that bill I'm interested in?" It's the old idea of tit-for-tat.

An oft-debated observation holds that when you serve on Rules, you serve as the voice of the Speaker or the leadership and therefore surrender your independence. I have said that I was not asked to surrender my independence to Mr. Rayburn. I still had integrity. I still maintained my own feelings on positions and issues. I was willing to go along with unpopular issues or do that which in the final analysis would provide an opportunity for the House to have a voice. I voted my conscience on all bills, in the final analysis.

AID: *Regarding the general control the Rules Committee has over legislation, what is your stand?*

SISK: The Rules Committee has a very definite responsibility for orderly procedure. I don't think any of us has a right to block or destroy the rights of others to cast a vote or state a position on an issue. Yet when the chips are down and you have an issue about which you feel very strongly and believe would be harmful to your country, state or district, you are going to use any and all ethical methods to stop this disastrous legislation. A person can say that you are varying from your responsibility as the Rules Committee for orderly procedure. You are, in essence, setting yourself up as the final determinant and you are denying me the right to cast a vote. This is where the going gets real sticky. I have voted for rules to send legislation to the floor—bills that I have later voted against on the floor. I felt the action of a committee which had given the subject much study over months or years entitled the House to work its will. This was in spite of the fact I thought the given bill wasn't good legislation; I would bow to the theory that with all the studies and hearings, the members had a right to make their decisions publicly known.

I have also voted to kill bills in the Rules Committee, preventing them from going to the floor for a variety of reasons. I didn't think they had the necessary kind of understanding in the hearings, or the public did not have knowledge of the issue at that time, or they were not timely. Often, a committee comes up with something suddenly. It gets a bill before the Rules Committee and boom, boom, it wants you to go with it. You take a look at the legislation. There has been no publicity on it. There are a lot of people in areas of influence—whether in education, veterans affairs, agriculture or law—who don't know about the proposed legislation because of this lack of publicity. In these cases, I would vote to delay, postpone, or vote against a rule on this legislation. There are very fine lines of demarcation. Lord knows, it is difficult to advise a new member of Rules on what he should do, but I maintain that he should keep his integrity and independence. He should cooperate with the leadership to the extent possible for orderly procedure, but at the same time, retain his own judgment and conscience. Otherwise, he becomes a eunuch.

AID: *Doesn't it take a majority of the members to block?*

SISK: It has to be a vote by the majority; no one member can block, unless it's the chairman, who refuses to schedule a bill. Now there is a way to overcome that. In the Reorganization Act we included certain provisions dealing with obstreperous chairmen, even dealing with a refusal to call a committee meeting. An example of that occurred when a barn burned down on Judge Smith's farm and he was gone for nearly a month. If that situation happened under our reorganization proceedings, a notice would be sent to the chairman that within five days, unless otherwise notified, the next ranking member would call a caucus of the committee. If the majority of the caucus saw fit, it would set up a hearing and go ahead. In the old days, a chairman could just disappear and the committee had no legal right to act. I think about some of the rules in effect when I first went to Congress and wonder how anything got done.

AID: *In 1972 you used Rules to get a bill to the floor to end a west coast dock strike.*

SISK: I did. This has been considered an abuse of power by many people, and I admit that to a certain extent it was. It was used because raisin growers and others had suffered substantial losses. Raisins were literally rotting on the west coast. It was hurting my district terribly. It cost millions of dollars. It was hurting California—and the nation—because we couldn't deliver farm goods. I tried everything in the world to get Frank Thompson and his committee to move. I pleaded with them, to no avail. Finally, I said, "I will use any ethical method." It was ethical because it didn't violate any rules. I used the rules of the House and of the committee to my district's benefit. It was deeply resented by some people because they felt it was an abuse of power. I defend my action because at times you have to meet power with power.

AID: *So Rules can not only control flow of legislation, but can create legislation?*

SISK: The Rules Committee has great power; it can reach into a committee and pick out legislation that has been buried there for twenty years and send it to the floor.

AID: *Would you describe further how the Rules Committee works? My information is, in the Eighty-eighth Congress, Rules had 134 full committee meetings. That seems like a lot, but I am curious how many bills are moved by Rules every year.*

SISK: The Rules Committee in the House is not a legislative committee, you know. It does not normally hold public hearings or hear outside witnesses. I say normally, because it very rarely hears an outside witness or seeks a governmental witness other than a member of Congress. The legislation that the committee handles deals with rules or is limited to the area over which it has exclusive jurisdiction.

AID: *Please give an example.*

SISK: Let's go back to something we have discussed before: a piece of water legislation which has originated in California by a California member. It has been introduced in the Interior and Insular Affairs Committee and hearings have been held in the subcommittee and then the full committee. After long deliberation (which may go on for weeks or years), it ultimately reaches a conclusion. The subcommittee acts favorably on it and reports to the full committee, which also acts favorably on it after having it amended, corrected, and changed; then the chairman of the Interior and Insular Affairs Committee is directed by law (and by the committee in its vote to secure a rule) to go to the Rules Committee so that it may go to the floor of the House to be voted upon. The chairman of the Interior and Insular Affairs Committee sends a letter to the chairman of the Rules Committee saying that his committee has recently reported favorably on bill so-and-so dealing with a certain subject in which he seeks a rule at the chairman of Rules' convenience.

The Committee on Rules reviews its schedule (since it has received similar communications from eighteen or nineteen legislative committees), then proceeds to send a letter back to the chairman. In many cases, there are discussions on the telephone and in person. It is decided that a hearing will be held on a date certain for that particular bill by that committee. If the bill happens to concern a very controversial matter, the hearing before the Committee on Rules could be rather extensive. On the other hand, if it is not particularly controversial, it could be a very brief hearing, in which the chairman and the ranking minority member (the minority opinion is always represented in these hearings) would appear and address the committee—explaining what the legislation does and requesting the kind of rule he (the chairman) wants. How many hours of debate does he feel are adequate? Does he want an open or closed rule (that is, whether he wants to permit amendments on the House floor or not)?

AID: *Open means you can have amendments?*

SISK: If the Rules Committee voted to grant an open rule and the bill goes to the floor, the House has to adopt by resolution the act of the Rules Committee. In the final analysis, the House, in total, always has to approve anything any committee does. If we saw fit to vote for a resolution which said so many hours of debate shall be provided and equally divided between the majority and minority, etc., it would go on to stipulate that these matters shall be open for amendment at any point. It is spelled out because there are various ways of ruling: sometimes part of a bill can be open for amendment and other parts can be closed, which is particularly true in tax bills. Once it is taken to the House floor by either the chairman or a member of the Rules Committee, the House votes up or down on the rule. Once in a while it defeats a rule, although most are automatically adopted. During debates, if it is an open rule, it is subject to amendments at any point.

Assuming that this is a noncontroversial bill, the chairman of the committee introducing the bill may address the Rules Committee for only ten or fifteen minutes, explaining the bill briefly. The chairman will then give members of the Rules Committee an opportunity to question him. If it is noncontroversial, it is likely that there will be few questions. Then the minority is given its opportunity to voice support or objections.

143

If the minority is in support, usually it's a very short hearing. Keeping in mind that a quorum has to be present at all times, a motion is made that a rule be granted in line with the request of the full committee chairman introducing the bill. The staff immediately prepares the rules in the appropriate language and the bill is scheduled by leadership for calling up on the floor.

On the other hand, if it is a controversial measure, there can be days of hearings before the Rules Committee on a single piece of legislation. Let's say it is a banking bill dealing with housing, which brings out strong partisan differences. You can hear dozens of witnesses. On a highly controversial piece of legislation, stalling tactics are often used by the opposition. This is done by scheduling a great number of witnesses—as many as twenty or thirty. All of these witnesses are members of Congress.

During the nearly twenty years that I served on the Committee on Rules, we heard outside witnesses less than half a dozen times. One outside witness was the former president of the Philippines testifying about the concerns of the Philippine Islands. At the most five times, we called in cabinet secretaries. In these instances, questions had arisen amid charges and countercharges that seemed to indicate a conflict in statements. As I say, most of the time the only witnesses to appear before the Committee on Rules were members of the committee or other members of Congress. That procedure provides about 80 percent of the work of the Committee on Rules.

AID: *You said that after a rule is passed by the Committee on Rules and the staff gets it, then the leadership schedules the date certain. The chairman of Rules, alone, doesn't determine the date certain?*

SISK: I have already said that the House of Representatives has the most complicated set of rules ever devised by the mind of man. There are all kinds of safeguards. If everything works smoothly, and there is cooperation between the Rules Committee and the leadership (the Speaker and the majority leader), there is generally concurrence. The Rules Committee then tries to cooperate with the leadership in scheduling legislation. At least weekly, the leadership meets with the Rules Committee and a schedule is outlined. Here is what they might say: "Fellows, we've got so many days left in this session. How much do you have before you? What is your situation?" You work together.

After you have granted a rule, normally you report that rule immediately to the House. There is a procedure for this, which I and other members of the Rules Committee followed many times. After we had adjourned the Rules Committee, if the House is in the Whole instead of being in Committee, you tell the Speaker that we have some rules we wish to get printed. He recognizes you and you say, "Mr. Speaker, I offer a privileged resolution for printing under the rules." (All resolutions out of Rules are privileged.) The difference between privileged and nonprivileged resolutions is that the Speaker cannot refuse to recognize you if you have a privileged resolution. A privileged resolution is a safeguard against a leadership that would refuse to schedule a bill which the Rules Committee wants reported. To protect the minority of the Committee on Rules, neither the chairman nor any single member of the Rules Committee can pocket a resolution.

Let's say that after we have passed a resolution on this water bill, it would be given to me and because of my position on this bill I put it in my pocket and say, "Well, I just won't call it up." I have actually taken this position a few times—and so have other members. The truth of the matter is that you can only do that for a limited time because the rules say that seven legislative days from the date the committee voted it out, any member of the Rules Committee can call this bill up. The Speaker has to recognize him. Even a minority member can call it up. That's a protection, although it is usually not needed. Once in a while it is—when antagonism develops and partisanship gets in. The important thing is that all resolutions from the Rules Committee are privileged matters and normally you have cooperation in scheduling legislation. On the other hand, if there is a fight and it is a tough bill, the Rules Committee is almost in a position to force the matter to the floor if it desires to do so.

To further answer your question of whether the chairman of the Rules Committee alone schedules legislation—the answer, as I have said, is that the leadership and the chairman work together to schedule it. Every Friday—or if we have adjourned on Thursday over to the following Monday, it will occur on Thursday afternoon at the conclusion of business—the majority leader will arise and you will find a great many members of the floor listening because it is important to them. He will arise and say, "Mr. Speaker, I would like consent to address the House for one minute and to revise and extend my remarks." At this point, the Speaker recognizes him.

He says, "Mr. Speaker, I take this time to advise the House of the program for next week," so he will have before him a list of bills. His counterpart on the Republican side will have a copy. They will have already conferred. He will read off the bills. He will say, "On next Monday, we have scheduled bill so-and-so dealing with taxes. Following that we have bill so-and-so dealing with veterans' problems." So he will read this long list. From time to time, the minority will interrupt and say, "Will the gentleman yield and let me ask a question on this particular bill?" or "Why hasn't a certain bill been scheduled?" They have a colloquy which may go on for several minutes.

But this is informative to the House. It tells me, as a member of Congress, what I am going to be faced with next week so I can make plans to go out to my district for the weekend, for example. In many cases the majority leader will say, "Let me say to my colleague, the minority leader,

145

that we would hope to schedule a bill out of the Interstate and Foreign Commerce Committee dealing with the FCC, subject to a rule being granted. It is the understanding of the majority leader that the matter is now pending before the Committee on Rules. I have been informed by the chairman of the Rules Committee that it will probably hold a meeting on this bill Monday or Tuesday. If it grants a rule, we will schedule it on Thursday." These are the kinds of exchanges of information that occur and are very important to the members. This is where cooperation between the leadership and the Rules Committee is very important. The Rules Committee has always been considered an arm of the leadership. If everything works well, you have an even flow of legislation.

AID: *What was the effect of the 1970 Reorganization Act on this procedure?*

SISK: It makes it possible for the majority of the Rules Committee members to override or take control if you have an obstreperous chairman or individual member who is trying to block a rule.

AID: *So it can be blocked in the committee by the chairman for how long?*

SISK: Seven days is the normal procedure. There is a two-step arrangement: If after seven days the chairman or a member does not act (you can go on for about three weeks or longer sometimes—it depends on the issue—before action is taken), you serve notice by letter to the chairman (or other obstreperous member) that within five days you are going to ask for a meeting. That notice has to be delivered to him. Three days after the arrival of the notice in the chairman's hands, the next ranking member can call the meeting to order. Some of this may sound confusing.

AID: *You have already said that Washington, D.C. matters do not go through Rules. Every other Tuesday is District Day. Are there any other bills that don't need Rules to get to the floor?*

SISK: Yes. Appropriations bills, which are vital, do not go through Rules, although they can go through Rules for a very specific reason. The normal appropriations bill does not have to come before the Committee on Rules unless a waiver of a point of order is sought or legislation on an appropriations bill is asked (which is not permitted under the rules of the House, except by a waiver granted by the Rules Committee resolution). "Normal" would be an appropriations bill with no legislation involved and no question of special issues or authorization. At all times, all monies appropriated by the Appropriations Committee must be previously authorized by the authorizing committee and signed into law by the president.

The reason many appropriations bills come before Rules is that the authorizing committee has been delinquent in its duties or for some other reason has not passed the authorizing legislation and it is not signed into law. Therefore, this legislation comes before Rules which says that in spite of the fact that this matter has not been authorized by law (even though this bill has gone through a committee of the House and has been

*Congressional leaders and friends gather for a California Congressional Recogni-
tion dinner honoring Sisk. Chatting, left to right, are W. T. O'Rear, Rep. (and
future Speaker) Carl Albert, Sisk, and Russell Giffen.*

passed by the House, but is now pending in the Senate), we waive a point
of order against it, so that it cannot be stricken out by a point of order on
the floor. That's the reason it is done.

Another instance is veterans' legislation, which normally goes through
Rules because it is easier to set procedures (that is, certain number of
hours of debate and open and closed rulings), yet is privileged legislation and could go directly to the floor. This is a long-standing matter
which goes back to the early days with the American Legion after World
War I.

AID: *A device to get around Rules is Calendar Wednesday. Is that used very
often?*

SISK: Very rarely. I think two or three times in the twenty-four years I served
I actually saw it used, although attempts or threats were made from time
to time by members saying they would use Calendar Wednesday. There
are so many ways to demagogue the issue, to delay the issue, to filibuster,
and all sorts of gimmicks. When you go to Calendar Wednesday, you're
wide open; you are out there being shot at from every direction without
any set procedure such as limits on debate. It is just not a good way to
legislate.

It was proved in the rules many years ago that some way is needed to
get to the floor if everything else has failed. Normally these procedures

are used when the leadership is opposed to the bill. It is a way of forcing leadership to move. There are so many ways to stop bills. We had a situation with Adam Clayton Powell one time. We had some civil rights legislation involved on the Calendar Wednesday deal. You have the same type of thing when you have 218 members sign a petition. If it is brought under that procedure, you are wide open because you don't have rules on debate and there is every possibility of delay. The petition method has rarely proved successful.

AID: *What is the twenty-one day rule?*

SISK: That rule goes back many years. At first, it was adopted temporarily, but it simply stayed. As far as my terms in Congress, it survived only one Congress. At the organizing meeting of the Eighty-ninth Congress, a motion was made to invoke the twenty-one day rule. This rule provided that any bill referred to the Committee on Rules from a legislative committee—which had not been acted on or had been acted on adversely—could be called up on the House floor after the expiration of twenty-one days. This was an attempt to circumvent Judge Smith; even though the Rules Committee had been enlarged, there was still a touch-and-go situation with controversial legislation. Some of the liberals moved this twenty-one day rule and it was adopted. Now this was just for the Eighty-ninth Congress. During the following Ninetieth Congress a motion was made to strike this rule and it was stricken. It is not in effect now. This rule was first used when Joe Cannon—as "Czar of the House" in his day—was practically the Rules Committee unto himself.

You have three calendars: the general calendar, including all bills; the private calendar—called on the first and third Monday—which is different from the consent calendar, the third calendar, but it requires unanimous consent to get it through. For example, there may be an immigration case in which you ask, in spite of law so-and-so, that this person be permitted to enter this country. Or it may be a case dealing with payment of funds because the immigrant has been put upon by his government. These are private bills, dealing with individuals. The consent calendar is called on the first and third Tuesday of each month. (They may have changed the days now.) The day before voting on bills on the consent calendar, a congressman receives the list of them for review. Nine times out of ten he will have a bill on there, too, so a congressman doesn't go around indiscriminately objecting to someone else's bill.

AID: *Consent calendar bills don't go to Rules?*

SISK: None of these "special calendar" bills goes to Rules. This is because the bills on the consent calendar come out of committee unanimously, although this is not always the case, in which event there may be an objection.

If a person calls me telling me how my bill would tend to discriminate against one of his interests, what I might do is raise a question. "Mr.

148

Speaker, I ask unanimous consent that this bill be skipped without preju-ice." This simply means to the House and to the Speaker that I have suddenly heard something about this bill and I want it delayed. Normally, nobody would object to that.

There are certain people to whom the responsibility of handling the consent calendar is delegated. The person offering the consent bill or a person handling the consent calendar may object. If a person handling the consent calendar objects, with several members to stand up with me, I could knock the bill clear off the calendar. Usually, there aren't any objections. Consequently, when I ask for unanimous consent that a bill be passed without prejudice, the bill is going to stay on the consent calendar and it will be called up the next consent day, which is every two weeks. All I have asked for is delay of action. This immediately signals the people who have the bill that Sisk has some questions about it. So they come to me and ask me what the problem is. We have an official Objectors Committee (for each party).

AID: *Does the Speaker appoint them?*

SISK: Yes, they are generally appointed by the Speaker. However, many times the Speaker will leave this up to the majority leader. Ed Boland of Massa-chusetts was chairman of that during my last Congress. Wayne Aspinall was also on that committee. I never wanted to get on the committee because you always had to be there and it was a mean job. The official objectors had to study all these things, in addition to all their other work. Usually you have about four or five people on the committee, and when they parcel out the work there are probably about ten bills for each person.

The official objector has to know about the bills because he has to recognize anything that is going to cause problems for his party so the party can be in a position to object. If someone wants to object to your request for a unanimous consent, you can get two people to stand up with you and you can get the bill knocked off the calendar. So the objectors are going to let it pass over without prejudice and they are going to come to you and talk about it. There are hundreds of these small bills and there is no way the Rules Committee could go through all of them.

AID: *I was wondering if the consent calendar was a way of circumventing Rules?*

SISK: There are all kinds of ways. Members try to get matters called up by unan-imous consent. The Rules Committee has to be constantly on the alert for committees which are trying to circumvent Rules. However, the Objectors Committee is so well organized that it would be difficult to get around it on the consent calendar bills.

~

22.
Agriculture

AID: *In 1970 you went on the Agriculture Committee because exceptions had been made permitting members of Rules to be on other committees. Did that stem from the fact that the chairman of Rules himself was on the D.C. Committee and later you were put on that committee? Or did it stem from some other reason?*

SISK: The exception that permitted me to go on Agriculture was entirely different from the one that permitted me to serve on D.C. District of Columbia is a minor committee. There was a hard rule that you couldn't serve on two major committees. Let's say if you were on Armed Services, you couldn't serve on Agriculture; both of them are major committees. You could serve on one major committee like Armed Services and then on a minor one like Veterans Affairs, District of Columbia or House Administration. If you are on an exclusive committee—and there are only three of those (Appropriations, Ways and Means, and Rules)—you couldn't serve on any other committee, major or minor.

When it came down to my being on the Committee on Agriculture, it was a matter of serving on an exclusive committee plus serving on a major committee, which is prohibited. That decision was made by Speaker McCormack and Ways and Means Chairman Wilbur Mills on the basis of my having the largest agricultural district in America, which included Fresno County, the number one agricultural county in the nation. California did not have a Democrat on Agriculture. They had checked around but there was no qualified Californian to serve on the committee. Previously, at the start of that Congress, I had gone to Mills and the Speaker and said, "We need a Californian on Agriculture. I recognize that I am on Rules and therefore I am ineligible. But we simply must have a California Democrat on the Committee on Agriculture. California is the number one state in the nation in agriculture. The San Joaquin Valley, of course, is the predominant area, but the important idea is to have a Californian. You have to figure out a way to get California on there."

I suggested several people, but did not expect to go on myself because I thought there was no way they were going to make that kind of an exception. What they did then, apparently at my request, was to look at and talk to every Democratic member from California. None was willing to give up his other committee assignments. McCormack and Mills told me there was no way they could get a Californian on Agriculture without making an exception. They said, "If we are going to make an exception, we are going to make it for you, because you have the largest agricultural district." That's how it happened. That conversation occurred in January

150

or February of 1969. The first session of the Ninety-first Congress in 1970 was when I went on Agriculture.

AID: *Later on, I understand that Spark Matsunaga (of Hawaii) was also on Agriculture and Rules.*

SISK: A precedent had been set for me, you see. I had sympathy for Matsunaga. When he was first elected, he was put on Agriculture because he came from the islands and was concerned with sugar legislation in particular and other agricultural legislation as well. Later, when Matsunaga was appointed to Rules, they immediately took him off Agriculture. After they had made this exception for me, Sparky said, "Wait a minute, you took me off Agriculture, but you let Sisk serve on Agriculture as well as Rules." I don't blame Sparky for this. He was justified. (I think he had been off Agriculture for some time. I think they kept him off for that session, too.) Anyway, a vacancy occurred later on. Because of his unusual situation and the fact that it would be politically helpful, they put him back on Agriculture, while I was still on there. So there were two of us at that point who served on an exclusive committee and a major committee at the same time.

AID: *When you were on the Agriculture Committee, what were the highlights of your service, as you recall?*

SISK: In January of 1955, when I first went to Congress, I had sought a spot on Agriculture because the then-Twelfth Congressional District, which is the general Fresno area, was one of the largest agriculture producing areas in the world. Congressman Harlan Hagen from the then-Fourteenth Congressional District at that time—which included Kern, Tulare, and Kings counties—had one term seniority on me. He had not been able to get on Agriculture earlier, so he sought it the year I was elected. Because of his seniority, he received first preference as a Californian. Therefore, I took Interior and Insular Affairs because of my interest in the San Luis Project. I did not make a particular effort to get on Agriculture because I was fully loaded up with other committees like space, Veterans Affairs, etc.

AID: *Incidentally, was Oakley Hunter on Agriculture?*

SISK: No. During the years Hunter was in Congress, he was on the Appropriations Committee.

Congressman Hagen was defeated in 1966, which was after I had joined the Rules Committee. That left California without any representation on Agriculture, as far as the Democratic side was concerned. It was about the Ninetieth Congress when I went to the leadership and was placed on the committee, as I have related.

I enjoyed my service on the Agriculture Committee, although it was a demanding situation because members of the Rules Committee were subject to meetings at any particular day or time, at a moment's notice. This was so even though we had regular meeting days. On Agriculture I served on several subcommittees (cotton, etc.).

AID: *You were chairman of that subcommittee?*

SISK: I was not chairman of that subcommittee the first year. Congressman W. R. Poage of Texas, who was chairman of the full committee at that time, called me around January 1971. He asked me if I would be interested in serving as chairman of the Cotton Subcommittee. Tom Abernathy of Mississippi, who had been the chairman of the Cotton Subcommittee, had retired. I told Poage I would be interested. Poage knew my district was a big cotton producer. In fact, the congressional district here in the western part of Fresno and Merced counties produces more cotton in volume than all states in the union except two—Texas and Mississippi.

AID: *Your district's cotton productivity per acre was also far ahead of other cotton-growing areas.*

SISK: Fantastic production! In 1974, California produced more cotton than any other state in the Union. That was the only time California outdid Texas in the production of cotton. Anyway, I said "Yes" to the chairman, but I realized there would be problems because the only chairmen to serve on that subcommittee came from the deep South—Alabama, Mississippi, South Carolina, and that area. Despite this fact, the chairman said he still would like me to take a run at it. I left it up to him. He made the appointment and it was accepted.

It was among the most interesting experiences of my career. I met with the various leaders of cotton-growing segments throughout the United States. Cotton is a big industry in this country. I believe people do not realize the peripheral industries related to the cotton industry. This represents employment of hundreds of thousands of people. For example, the textile industry is a huge industry—and again it is strictly deep South. There was a time when the textile industry was New England-based. But it has all moved South, as we all know, for very specific reasons—labor problems and possibly other reasons.

My position as chairman meant not only getting acquainted with and being acceptable to thousands of cotton growers throughout the South and Southwest, but also working with the textile industry which has a fantastic amount of influence in Congress; the "textile caucus," as it is called, is a substantial caucus composed of members from South Carolina, North Carolina, Tennessee, Kentucky, Alabama, Mississippi, Louisiana, Texas, Arkansas, and Missouri. I later became a member of the textile caucus, too. In addition, there is the transportation industry and the warehouse industry in cotton, which is big. It takes a lot of transportation to move cotton across this country and to the various shipping points.

AID: *Just as an aside, are there other industrial caucuses like the textile caucus?*

SISK: Yes. There is a steel caucus, composed of members from Pennsylvania, Ohio, and other states which are heavily engaged in steel production. This group meets from time to time so it can discuss common problems. Several of these types of caucuses do operate.

Farm legislation is the topic as Sisk confers with Secretary of Agriculture Clifford Hardin, center, and Agriculture Committee Chairman W. R. Poage.

There are also hundreds of thousands of people employed in cotton processing, starting with the mechanics of cotton gathering. Today, all cotton is mechanically harvested, then goes to the ginning process, separating the seed from the lint. It then goes through the various cleaning processes. Then the cotton goes into very compressed bales for shipping purposes. Finally, it goes to the textile mills. So you have a great processing industry, as well as transportation and textiles, which form the cotton production industry. Texas is one of the larger producers of cotton. It has many large co-ops, which is typical of this industry. We have Calcot in California, one of the largest in the world. Working and getting acquainted with these people, I felt I got along with them well.

AID: *What part of Texas was Poage from?*

SISK: Waco—somewhat central Texas.

AID: *The ranking Republican on the committee was Page Belcher, I think.*

SISK: Yes, Page Belcher from Oklahoma.

AID: *And twelve of eighteen Democrats were from the South; and probably most of those twelve were from the deep South . . .*

SISK: Southern states were always represented. A lot of times there would be two from the same southern state.

AID: *And you had Republican Congressman Bob Mathias from California.*

SISK: He had defeated Congressman Hagen in the Tulare and Kern counties district.

AID: *My point is that you found yourself facing a formidable bloc of people who were opposed to California agricultural interests.*

SISK: There was a time during the late 1930s and particularly the 1940s when a

153

very deep bitterness had grown between the southern and western cotton producers. It literally revolved around the right to grow cotton. The southerners had very deep feelings about it. One of them once said to me, "You know, after all, the South has the God-given right to produce the cotton in this country; we have the people, the land, the climate, and we know how to grow it—and you Californians don't have any business being in this industry in the first place."

Cotton was a southern tradition. It became a very hot issue. What heated up this issue further was that as cotton and some other commodities got into financial trouble and we went for agricultural programs in which subsidies were involved (acreage control and allocations), the South and the West really had a confrontation. The South, because of the power it had through a union with the midwestern Republican bloc, controlled agriculture in Congress. When laws were written about acreage allocations, it was amazing how discriminatory they were, protecting all the acreage in existence in South Carolina, North Carolina, Mississippi, Alabama, Texas, and so on—to the detriment of California. The laws used historical acreage and California, of course, was a fairly new producer, bringing in lands without historical acreage.

Toward the end of World War II, when the government was pleading for more cotton and more everything, California farmers increased their cotton acreage. We got more water on the land on the west side, growing more cotton. The way the cotton bloc had these laws written, California was cut right out of acreage allocations, because it (the South) historically had all the acreage—and it wasn't about to give it up. That is how the bitterness started.

This is what I faced when I went on the Committee on Agriculture. There were reasonable heads in both camps, though. There is an organization called the Western Cotton Growers, which is made up of Californians, Arizonans, a few New Mexicans, and even a few growers from the El Paso area, the extreme western part of Texas. (The El Paso growers joined because of some common problems.) Essentially, the Western Cotton Growers were from California and Arizona. There were some level-headed people in this group who realized the cotton industry in the 1950s was getting into some problems and that we desperately needed to develop a common front. There were those in the South (Mississippi, South Carolina, Alabama) who also recognized the same thing; this business of fighting each other was non-productive.

Despite the fact there was still a lot of bitterness when I came along as chairman, many people recognized that we had to try to get along. I will have to say, in all fairness to the southerners, that they treated me very kindly. I talked frankly with them. "We have a common problem and I'm not interested in anything that is going to split us up; I think what is good for the cotton industry is good for California and it is good for all the

As chairman of the Cotton Subcommittee, Sisk toured Arkansas cotton fields, attempting to heal the rift between western producers and farmers from Dixie.

cotton states and this business of fighting over a little acreage here and there is a little ridiculous." The truth of the matter is that a lot of level-headed people had come to the conclusion that the soil formation in the South was better suited to the cultivation of soybeans than to cotton. The movement began in the Carolinas and much of the South went into soybeans, cattle, and pasture lands and moved away from total dependence on cotton, which had been traditional for over a hundred years.

These things modified the opinions of many so that it was clear, in many national conventions and national association meetings where I met with the cotton industry people (e.g. Charleston, South Carolina; Memphis, Tennessee; Lubbock, Texas), that feelings had begun to change. I don't claim a lot of credit for it, although I did hammer away at my philosophy, which I felt was important. I give the credit to the leaders in the cotton industry and the peripheral industries for recognizing that they had to join together and that fighting each other was letting some other commodity outgun them.

It was a very interesting challenge and one I enjoyed. I helped write the farm bills of the late 1960s, the 1970 farm bill, and the 1973 farm bill. I sat across the table from some pretty tough negotiators, old-timers from Mississippi like Senator Jim Eastland and from Georgia, Senator Herman Talmadge, who is in trouble now. Senator Allen Ellender from Louisiana was a tough customer. (He is now dead.) He never lost his antagonism for California. I tried everything I could to get along with him. We went away from our first conference as friends; he at least recognized my right to take my position. We had some tough fights, and I take pride in what has happened in agricultural legislation in recent years.

AID: *Before you got on the Agriculture Committee, in 1958 there was a westerners' bloc to kill the South's agricultural bill. Did that leave any scars?*

SISK: There is no question about it. There were still some scars present when I went on Agriculture. Harlan Hagen, who got on the committee in 1954, had made enemies of some southerners because he hadn't been very sympathetic to some of their positions. This was one of the problems we had to overcome.

AID: *Will you talk a little about your position on farm subsidies, particularly cotton subsidies? But first, regarding general farm subsidies, wasn't there a $50,000 limitation which eliminated loopholes that permitted collecting excessive amounts of money?*

SISK: Yes, this was one of the big fights of the 1950s and the 1960s over direct farm subsidies in which a grower would be guaranteed a set price. Let's say he was guaranteed thirty-five cents a pound and if his cotton sold below that figure, the government made up the difference. The grower was guaranteed this whether he grew five or five hundred bales of cotton. Any limitation on this was tough on the West because we did have a number of big growers in Fresno and Merced and particularly in Kings County. The west side was developed by larger farmers for the reasons already mentioned. To have a farm there required having or borrowing a lot of money. In the Mississippi Delta, there were also a number of large growers so this was not an exclusively western issue.

In the 1950s, rules on limitations were written, but none was successful until 1970. Various approaches were made. I opposed those limitations because I opposed direct subsidies; that was not my kind of a farm bill. My approach finally won out because more and more people thought the government could not justify payment of direct farm subsidies—and that there should be a better way to do it. Instead we developed programs in which there would be inducements to maintain production in line with consumption. In other words, let the market set the price normally. There would also be a loan program for growers, giving them a more orderly way of selling their commodities, so the entire cotton crop wouldn't have to be sold when it was harvested in the fall. The growers could put the cotton in a loan and then sell it throughout the year. Not only did it make for more orderly marketing, it also provided for allocation, not acreage control, by the farmers' willingness to do certain things to enjoy certain privileges if they cut back on their acreage. This would get us away from direct price subsidies.

AID: *What was your position on cotton imports?*

SISK: I opposed cotton imports. We produce plenty of cotton; we are a big exporting country of cotton. We ship cotton to Japan, Hong Kong, Korea, China, and throughout the Southeast Asian area. The problem was that these Southeast Asian countries would buy the cotton and then weave it into material. This is why the textile caucus organized. It wanted to stop the flow of textiles into the United States from other countries. Labor got involved, too. Let's say we shipped 100,000 bales of cotton to Korea; Korea, a cheap labor area, would spin that cotton into textile forms and ship it back to this country. Hence, American labor was losing a huge number of labor hours.

My position was that we had to work out a reasonable approach to this. I didn't feel we could arbitrarily cut off all imports because if you are going to sell, you are going to buy something. I took a balanced position in connection with this problem. I wanted to stop unlimited importations. Otherwise, competing nations could literally destroy the textile industry in this country. And, as I have said, this would hurt labor. For example, we permitted the importation of glass, which ruined the glass industry in this country. There is no watchmaking industry in this country because we buy watches which are cheaply made elsewhere. Take shoes as another example. The importation of shoes has crushed the shoe industry in this country. These are matters of serious concern—and they have to be a concern of Congress. That is why the New England shoe caucus or "leather caucus" was formed. The U.S. shoe industry was centered in New England, especially in Massachusetts.

AID: *ACP, is that cross-compliance?*

SISK: Yes. I don't know if I am an expert on cross-compliance. I always interpreted this in connection with farm legislation where you have more than one commodity involved. For example, in our farm bills we had what we called small grains—feed grain, which is milo, and so forth; also wheat, corn, and cotton. Those were the basic commodities. Cross-compliance was the way in which a farmer conducted his farming arrangements to comply with various programs in which he would "cross over" from one commodity to another. Many diversified farmers found this cross-compliance to their advantage, of course.

AID: *You were in Congress during the last part of the bracero program?*

SISK: Yes, I was the author of one of the last two or three extension bills. We extended it year by year and it got to be a very tough fight. It was agreed, in order to get the last extension, that I would not seek any further extensions.

AID: *What is your feeling about the bracero program? Wasn't it killed by a combination of organized religion and organized labor?*

SISK: Frankly, it is my feeling that there was only one thing that killed it: the influence and power of organized labor. The record will show that I was a staunch supporter of labor, but this is one case where I split the blanket with the AFL-CIO. The AFL-CIO lobbyists understood what I was going to do and the reasons I was doing it. I never lost any friends over it, but I fought them on that issue. Until the very closing days of Public Law-78 [bracero authorization], the top lobbyists of the AFL-CIO would come in and say, "You have to understand that we have a doctrine and we are going to maintian that position." I understood that, yet they didn't go out and beat anybody on the head, insisting that members vote with them on that issue or making it into a big issue. The truth was that they told you, off the record, they couldn't furnish labor for the farms. They agreed that in order to get harvesting done, we had to have labor from somewhere.

Pressure began to build from labor. The AFL-CIO decided to organize farm labor and sent in labor organizers, starting around Stockton, which is where I first knew of it. This was long before Cesar Chavez was known. But it was never very successful. The farm labor organizing movement never had deep-seated support from the powers of organized labor. I am talking about the building trades, the Teamsters Union, the steelworkers, United Mine Workers, and so forth. Organized labor gave lip service to it and that was about it. Friends of mine in the labor movement said there was no way to organize farm labor successfully, because there were all kinds or organizational and administrative problems. They were never too sold on it until Chavez came along. Now the UAW was the real mainstay of Chavez; Walter Reuther, then head of the United Auto Workers, and the Butchers International got involved. However, the UAW furnished more money.

AID: *What was its interest?*

SISK: I never understood why it was involved. To me, the whole Chavez movement was a quasi-religious and racial, as well as a labor, issue. It was pushed by the more liberal wing of the Catholic hierarchy, as I saw it. I do not speak critically because I have friends among Catholic priests involved in the movement. Mexico, of course, is a Catholic nation. In many rural areas of Mexico, the only government or conformity is through the Catholic church, so that was a very strong part of it. The other was the racial situation. I think Chavez and his cohorts used this issue. They took advantage of the labor movement to ride this three-headed program.

AID: *When did Chavez first come into the picture?*

SISK: As far as I know, he became really effective around 1967 or 1968—around ten years ago. It was after the bracero program had ended.

AID: *Did Chavez have any influence in killing that?*

SISK: If my memory serves me correctly, Chavez was not a particular force to end it. During the middle 1960s, unemployment began to develop and the Viet Nam War, which was unpopular, was going on. There was a combination of things. It was at this time labor decided to really get active, instead of just having a doctrine. I said this (and it's in the records if you want to look it up): "When we stop Public Law-78 (the bracero program), we will be up to our necks in wetbacks." We would have people over here in a totally disorganized way—and in my opinion it would be worse than the bracero program. Mexico supported and wanted to continue the

Victory proved as sweet for Sisk's ninth term as for the preceding eight. Clockwise from Sisk's left are daughters Marilyn Pittenger and Bobbye Temple; Eric, Lisa, Gretchen and Karin Temple; Reta Sisk, and Randy and Alenne Pittenger. Sisk beat Phillip V. Sanchez.

bracero program. There was a treaty between the United States and Mexico; it was a controlled program.

Organized labor fought it on this theory: The bracero program was indentured or slave labor since agricultural associations asked members how many workers they could use and then brought that number north. Let's say three thousand people were brought to the United States to do a certain job for a certain period of time, whether one month, six weeks, or several months; they would then return home to Mexico. But labor's theory—and I don't know how practical it was—held that the workers were not free to do as they pleased. The fact was that the workers brought to the United States were protected by very strict laws governing housing, transportation, health insurance coverage, and wages.

AID: *Furthermore, these workers were brought to the United States only after it was proved that no domestic labor was available; the employer had to scour the area first for domestic labor.*

SISK: Not only this area, but as far away as Texas. To me, this bracero program provided all the protection in the world for the workers.

Today, when I talk to people who opposed the program and are now retired, they admit there are a lot of problems associated with the millions of illegal aliens and that they were wrong. I don't like to say "I told you so," but many of us predicted exactly what was going to happen—and

159

that is what has happened. I don't know what the future holds. Chavez, of course, has made some headway. Last year, I was told, he was at the end of his rope, but he has since signed some more contracts. They called a strike the other day and I don't know what the outcome will be.

The serious problem is that we are overrun by people who are not legal residents of this country. As the law reads now, the Border Patrol and the Immigration and Naturalization Service have an obligation to try to pick these people up and return them to Mexico. This creates all kinds of problems.

AID: *As soon as the aliens are returned, I am told, they are back in this country because they use the money they have been paid to get on a plane and fly back to the border.*

SISK: There are organized groups bringing them here. The tragedy is that this leaves illegal aliens vulnerable to employers who may maltreat them or discriminate against them. The employer knows that if the illegals don't do as he says, all he has to do is pick up the phone and call the INS or the Border Patrol. They talked about indentured labor under Public Law-78!

AID: *Just for the record, agriculture does not use the bulk of the wetback flow.*

SISK: If you go down to Los Angeles to hotels, restaurants, laundries, etc.—

AID: *Consumerism was important both because it influenced the composition of the Agriculture Committee and affected legislation. Could you discuss this?*

SISK: Consumer representatives are very important on the Committee on Agriculture. I think back to the election of Shirley Chisholm of New York, which I have already discussed. She was put on Agriculture despite the fact she sought another committee. How wonderful it would have been if she would have taken a consumer position on Agriculture. That's the point I am trying to make. Later on, New Yorkers and other easterners got on the committee, some of whom served as consumer representatives. The Agriculture Committee is no longer dominated by the southern Democrats and the midwestern Republicans. As of the early 1970s there was a broad cross-section on the committee: New Yorkers, Illinois people, midwesterners, southerners, westerners, and a representative from Hawaii—Sparky Matsunaga [now a member of the Senate]. This cross-section was interested in all aspects of agriculture as it affects American life. This made others who essentially represented agricultural food and fiber (like myself) aware of the problems of consumers and city people.

I appeared, from time to time, on a television program with a friend of mine who represented the Queens borough of New York City, Congressman Lester Wolff. Congressman Wolff represented a totally urban district. We would discuss where the food his people ate came from. The eggs were not laid in the back of the store; they had to come from a poultry farm. The beef had to be raised. The cereal was grown on a wheat farm out in Minnesota, South Dakota, or Montana. The cotton in the clothing they wore came from a cotton farm. It was very elementary, but Wolff encouraged this. He was a moderate, for a New Yorker, a pretty solid guy. He was trying to say, "Yes, I know from time to time you criticize me because I support a farm bill for Texas or California, but I have to do this because I need their help for New York City in connection with loans for water, sewage development, housing, and many things. What other states produce has an effect on what you pay for food." Wolff's program was a logical idea. I think consumer representatives are good for the Committee on Agriculture.

AID: *One of Cesar Chavez's great tools has been the consumer (or secondary) boycott. What is your position on the issue? Former Senator George Murphy wanted to prohibit all consumer boycotts and you opposed that.*

SISK: I oppose consumer boycotts because I don't think anyone wins with that strategy. I was irate over some of the distortions, misconceptions, and propaganda spread by the Chavez people in their fight against the grape growers, lettuce growers, etc. You wouldn't believe some of the lies that were printed. Chavez people would leave these (sheets of propaganda) on product counters in major markets. My wife would pick them up and get furious. In fact, she came home with produce we didn't need because this propaganda made her mad. Finally I told her, "We can't eat all those grapes." I resented consumer boycotts deeply. On the other hand, to pass a law saying there can't be consumer boycotts is probably unconstitutional. Despite the fact I had a great deal of sympathy for the position Senator Murphy took, I simply couldn't support what he was proposing. There was a time when those boycotts did hurt because of what I call the "do-good" crowd—the idle rich or the Cape Cod group. The Kennedys would have a big blow-out and invite Chavez. But these groups found other interests later; there is always a group running around looking for some cause to pursue. Recently, I don't think these boycotts have had much effect.

AID: *Let's get into an area in agriculture dealing with government regulation and how it has proliferated. Exemplifying this is a case you entered on behalf of California Canners and Growers in the matter of cyclamates.*

SISK: That, of course, illustrates the problems agriculture faced in connection with the increasing regulatory powers of the federal and state governments. In many cases there are overlapping and conflicting regulations, which make compliance almost impossible. This is true regarding pesticides, insecticides, rodenticides, and fungicides. The federal government pre-empted some state legislation, leaving growers frustrated and without protection to maintain the quality of the fruits and vegetables they produce. It has been very unfortunate. We passed OSHA for example. On the surface, the Occupational Safety and Health Act was good. You always want to protect workers. Unfortunately, when you pass a law, you can't deal with every potential nut in the business. You have to write a general law and hope the regulatory agencies will set up common-sense regulations. But administrators went completely off the deep end. It finally became such a mess that legislators, in a single swoop, eliminated eleven hundred regulations.

There is also environmental protection, which is fine; we all want clean air to breathe and clean water to drink. With the combination of EPA, OSHA, the pesticide acts, and the Food and Drug Administration, the number of conflicting regulations has almost produced anarchy in the production of food and fiber.

The cyclamates affair was a demonstration of how utterly unfair a government can be, and how it can shatter an industry. Because a few people made some bad judgments, a ruling almost bankrupted a very large co-op here in California. It also disrupted substantially other institutions here.

Scientists and others dealing with this subject initiated a variety of tests in this country and in Europe researching potential hazards. There was no basis for the FDA ruling to ban cyclamates; it was without any justification. We attempted to recoup the losses of California Canners and Growers on the grounds of unfair governmental action, and tried to sue the government in our attempts to recover, but were not successful.

I often stressed that we have become an over-regulated society. In our anxiety to meet problems, particularly during the wave of emotionalism in the middle 1960s, caused by the Viet Nam War and issues dealing with the environment, we went to extremes. We left too much to the agencies setting up regulations. We severely impaired our ability to produce.

AID: *There was an important farm marketing bill in 1972 called the National Marketing and Bargaining Act. Why did you introduce that legislation?*

SISK: I introduced that legislation on behalf of the North American Farm Bureau Federation, various farm groups, bargaining groups, and co-operatives. It dealt with some assurances for producers. This legislation came about after a great deal of study and investigation into the treatment of growers. I recall vividly how arbitrarily some tomato processors treated the producers. In this district we have one of the few successful bargaining operations in the country—known as the Raisin Bargaining Association—headed up by friends of mine. Talking about walking the picket line! I well remember when I joined with the growers down here in picketing Bonner Packing. It was a symbolic type of thing. This bargaining association has been very successful, but there were times when I cautioned my friends that in their bargaining they were going a little far.

Last year, because of the shortage of raisins, they set a price of $1,950 per ton. I called up the executive of the association and said, "I have always supported you; I know the beatings raisin growers take." (One year they are broke and the next year they might make a little.) "But," I said, "it seems to me that in spite of the shortage of raisins and the

162

problems growers have, don't destroy the goose that laid the golden egg. If you get the price so high that people are paying $1.50 for a little twelve-ounce package, poor people can't buy raisins." I was talking about the black mother who goes to the market to buy food. I said that if you get your price too high, you destroy your market for the following year. This year it looks like we are going to have a big crop, unless we have some bad weather. I still believe in the bargaining association, though.

One of the most tragic situations concerns the poultry group. In Maryland, Georgia, Arkansas, and many places in the South, there was a time when there were a lot of independent poultry producers, thousands of growers, producing fryers or broilers for market. Four or five feed companies organized and moved in to take over. First thing you knew, they controlled the poultry industry. The feed companies fought me harder than any other single group in the United States. They spent money on all sorts of propaganda because we were after them. You wouldn't believe the testimony on how they abused and bankrupted the poultry growers who wouldn't join them. They did this by refusing them a market; they had no place to send their chickens. The poultry growers industry is now dominated by three or four major feed companies.

AID: *Does that apply to turkeys, too?*

SISK: They haven't gained the control they sought. There was a time when turkeys were big in this area. Turkey growers were among my early supporters. They overproduced and couldn't sell their product. They weren't doing effective merchandising. To a large extent, feed companies control turkey production, too, as far as I know. They were hell-bent that we shouldn't legislate in this area.

AID: *When you got into this legislation, which required processors to bargain with growers, was the dairy industry included?*

SISK: The national milk cooperative and the milk industry was very much involved. Some of the things that occurred, particularly in the large co-operatives, were unfortunate. Serious charges developed over activities of large co-ops in the Midwest and Texas. There was a Department of Justice investigation into the amount of money a big dairy co-op in the Midwest invested in political campaigns. It ran into the millions of dollars. This struck a sour note and hurt the dairy industry. We have a big dairy industry in California, particularly in this area. It was difficult to help them for a time because of the Department of Justice investigation.

AID: *You saw the elimination of tax shelter loopholes used by farm syndicates back in 1972.*

SISK: Quite a little investigation had gone on. I was on the Agriculture Committee at that time. In some of the hearings and investigative reports that came out, it was found that syndicates were being used to launder underworld money. We attempted to come up with legislation to correct that situation. I don't think we were very successful, although there were some changes made . . . I don't remember the details, but I think the situation was cleaned up some. However, the legislation you were referring to didn't get out of the committee at that time.

AID: *You mentioned earlier that the National Labor Relations Board did not include agriculture. In 1973 you sponsored a bill to put the National Labor Relations Act into the farm picture and to pay workers' compensation—and it failed.*

SISK: At that point, we were wrestling with some of the problems of farm labor. The fact I supported Public Law-78 and opposed some of the things Chavez was doing made it appear that I was not sympathetic to farm labor. Yet having been a farm laborer myself and knowing farm workers, I have great respect for them. I felt there were certain benefits farm labor should be granted. If you are going to treat one group of workers one way, then every group should be treated the same way. In most cases, workers' compensation was run at the state level. In connection with farm labor, the states had failed to take care of the issue. To make workers' compensation uniform nationwide and to avoid discrimination, I felt it should be administered by the federal government, rather than by the individual states. I still feel the bill I supported was right. But it is like so many other things, you take a run and you do the best you can—sometimes you win and sometimes you lose. In this case, we simply did not have enough muscle to get it out of committee. There are substantial numbers of states' rights groups in this country. Whenever you ask the federal government to assert pre-emptive legislative or regulatory powers over the states, you have your hand in their cookie jar and you are going to get in trouble. I think that is the simplest explanation of why this particular legislation did not get off the ground in the Committee on Agriculture.

AID: *You were the author of about twenty farm bills. We have talked about a number of them. Do you recall any specifics about the Dairymen's Bargaining Act?*

SISK: Yes, but vaguely since it has been quite some time. If I am not mistaken, I introduced that long before I was ever on Agriculture. Even early on, when I first went to Congress, I was very sensitive about the dairy industry. While campaigning in this district for the 1954 election, I became aware of a situation I hadn't known of—and of which a lot of other people weren't aware. In our district, we had literally hundreds of class B dairymen, many of whom were Portuguese. (There were also Swiss, Italian, and German dairymen, and so forth.) In particular, around Riverdale and Fresno County and all through that area (including Merced County) there were hundreds of small-time dairymen—I am talking about dairies of less than fifty cows. These dairymen were struggling for their lives. You talk about hard work. They didn't have modern equipment because they couldn't afford it. The processors would say, "We will buy only so much."

Getting a first-hand look at the problems of west side San Joaquin Valley farmers, Sisk, center, discusses the area's needs with Agriculture Secretary Bob Bergland, right, and field station superintendent Burt Hoyle in this 1977 photo.

Courtesy Fresno Bee

Processors would arbitrarily cut them off, saying, "We can't take your milk any more."

AID: *The dairymen were at their mercy.*

SISK: The poor farmer had his twenty-five cows and no market; it was all he had. As pressure developed about the quality of milk (Lord knows, I can't object to cleanliness), these people couldn't meet the standards so they had to go class B at a lower price. I became well aware of this problem and one of my first efforts in Washington was to see what could be done to help these people. I tried to develop a financing program to help them clean up their facilities so they could become self-sustaining. This financing would have been through long-term loans. I met with dairymen in all parts of my district. We fought hard, getting increases in dairy price supports and being helpful in other cases, but I have always been unhappy because we couldn't come up with something better.

The truth is that most of these people went broke or sold out, or went to growing crops. They just couldn't make it. As a result, although there were hundreds of small class B dairies in the past, most of them are gone today. Where you had twelve small dairies, today you have one larger one. I have no criticism of dairies with hundreds of cows. They are doing a good job. What we were trying to do was preserve the small family farm. The disappearance of these small dairies by the dozens was the tragic end of small dairy farms. The old houses and barns are still there— falling down in some cases.

AID: *This is interesting because you have talked about two industries in agriculture which have either been greatly diminished or wiped out, one being the small dairy farm and the other the small, independent poultry producer.*

165

SISK: That is exactly what happened. It is politically expedient for a politician to defend the family farm, but it is a cliche. Farming is like any other business—you either operate as a business or you are out of business. The old way of doing things has gone by the boards.

AID: *Pertaining to dairymen, if you don't belong to a Dairy Herd Improvement Association, you don't know which cows are profitable producers, you can't cull your herd properly, and you have difficulty with profitable herd management. Of course, California is great grape-growing country for wine, table grapes and raisin production. Pertaining to California wine legislation—including the aspects of selling it abroad—how were you involved?*

SISK: There was a delegation meeting shortly after I arrived in Washington in January 1955. Harry Sheppard said, "You come from Fresno. You have a lot of wine up there and I understand that you used to work for a winery, so I am going to make you chairman of the wine committee of our delegation." From then on, for twenty-four years, I served as chairman of the wine committee of the full California delegation, including Democrats and Republicans. I always used a Republican member as my cohort. Recently it was Don Clausen from the north country, First Congressional District. I have enjoyed my association with the wine people. I spoke at least annually to the San Joaquin Wine Growers or to the Wine Institute in San Francisco, with whom I worked closely.

When you look at the total tonnage of grapes produced in California, the largest end of the tonnage by far goes into wine. The rest of the grape tonnage goes into fresh pack and raisins. Naturally, the health of the wine industry is vital to the well-being of California because packing grapes for wine, raisins, and fresh pack is one of the largest industries in the state. Sometimes cotton has superseded it, but in most cases grapes and wine form one of the largest agricultural commodities in the state.

For many years, as chairman of the wine committee, I sponsored wine-tasting in Washington. Our first one was in 1955. We had about one hundred people attending in the old Congressional Hotel. Wine-tasting grew until we had about two thousand people tasting in a huge, underground Metro station in Washington, D.C. These wine-tasting events got so big that we couldn't find a building spacious enough to house them. The various wineries would furnish wine in large quantities. Wine-tasting was so popular we made it black-tie in our attempt to reduce the size of the crowds. All members of Congress were invited with their spouses, as were the top people in the three branches of government, as well as embassy people, diplomats, and so forth. We had some wonderful parties through the years.

AID: *That took care of half the year's wine production.* [Laughter]

SISK: One of the things we constantly faced was how to meet the competition from certain countries. We were fighting what we generally refer to as

166

Above: Sisk and members of the California Wine Institute meet with President Johnson in the Oval Office in 1967.

Right: Joined by Sen. Thomas Kuchel, right, and Rep. George Miller, Sisk plays host to a 1963 Washington wine-tasting—with California vintners featured exclusively.

dumping. Under the law, certain actions can be taken if a commodity is being dumped by foreign governments—certain limitations and restrictions will automatically come into play. This applies not only to wine but to many other commodities. It is called the Anti-Dumping Law. The French were one of the biggest violators in many instances.

The attitude of the California Wine Institute and the San Joaquin Valley Wine Growers was that they didn't mind competition from the premium wines—whether from France, Germany, Spain, or wherever. They were having problems with what is called the "ordinaires." After testing over a few years, it was found that the average California wine we were selling

167

here for three or four dollars a bottle was so superior to the European "ordinaires" that no comparison could be made.

We couldn't beg, borrow or steal a way to get a bottle of California wine on a shelf in France. We finally got a little in England. The Common Market had us blocked. Yet here we were importing these "ordinaires." We discussed quality standards, markings on the bottles, the size of bottles, the way the wine was made. This has been one of the key jobs of the Agriculture Committee because grapes and the California wine industry are vital to California, and in particular to the San Joaquin Valley. Incidentally, more and more varietals are being grown here. When I worked in a winery forty years ago, we didn't produce any varietals. Today, companies like Gallo, Italian Swiss Colony, and others are producing varietals all over this valley.

AID: *What about the Rural Development Act of 1971?*

SISK: That was a bill out of the Committee on Agriculture of which I was co-sponsor. There were a lot of hearings in which Bob Poage and I were very much interested. It passed in our committee by a substantial vote. It passed in the House and became law. It was signed by Richard Nixon.

To get the Department of Agriculture to act upon it was like pulling teeth. Yet this law held a tremendous amount of promise. There is as much poverty in rural areas as there is in the cities. Many rural areas need a lot of help, guidance, and seed money as inducement to do things on their own. Demonstration projects have shown how the quality of rural life can be markedly improved. The Rural Development Act was a multi-faceted approach in which seed money would become available as loans and assistance in housing would be provided.

That program for some reason didn't receive adequate funding and was never pushed by the USDA. Even now, under the Carter Administration (I talked to Agriculture Secretary Bob Bergland about it), I am still of the opinion nothing has been done with it.

AID: *The Rural Telephone and Bank Act?*

SISK: There was quite a bit of controversy on that. In some cases, the rural co-ops did an outstanding job; others were criticized. Private businesses felt the co-ops were unfair and that the federal government was actually in competition with them. I was very much sold on the goals of this bill.

Had it not been for the Rural Telephone and Bank Act, there would have been thousands of rural homes in this country without telephone service. Very simply put, the Bell System and other companies were not prepared to go out to rural areas and spend the kind of money needed to string the lines.

The same is true of the Rural Electrification Act, which did amazing things for this country. That is the way a good part of the country was electrified. I am not being critical of Pacific Gas and Electric or Southern California Edison or Con Edison, or any other utility company, but none could see the economic justification of stringing lines when farms were miles apart. At one time I was living in a little town that had no power because the utility company had not seen fit to run a line down there. If I am not mistaken, fifty years ago my father (with some other people) raised several thousand dollars so that the company would run a line into that little community.

The Rural Telephone Act and the Rural Electrification Act came in with Franklin D. Roosevelt. These acts have done a vast amount of good for rural areas.

AID: *Incidentally, the rural electrification program was supported in California by P.G. & E. and it recently celebrated its fiftieth year of sponsorship. It has provided a lot of money to the University of California for research.*

SISK: Even though there was a lot of doubt by the private utility companies at the start, this has proved to be a boon to them. In the final analysis, the utility companies furnished the power and—as it worked out—finally took over and operated in the normal procedure, coming under the Public Utilities Commission.

AID: *The Sugar Act?*

SISK: We had our ups and downs with sugar acts. I have authored, co-authored, and sponsored sugar acts, since I represented a substantial beet sugar industry. John Duncan, who was undersecretary of agriculture when Orville Freeman was secretary of agriculture under Kennedy in the early 1960s, came out to California to dedicate a sugar plant in Mendota. Guy Manuel is still heading up that factory. He has always been a friend of mine.

The sugar industry people never needed to come to Washington to see me because I always worked closely with them out here. We fought the battles of sugar. Sugar beets were an alternative when cotton was bad or if there were problems with other crops—for instance, when seed alfalfa went haywire. Beet sugar is a big item; there is a lot of money involved. It's a big fight because the sugar acts in Washington were unbelievable. If someone were to write the history of sugar acts, you would think it was fiction.

From time to time, the Agriculture Committee passed an extension of the Sugar Act, in which we allocated sugar to foreign countries. We would argue, usually in executive session, "Are we going to sell the Philippines 200,000 tons, are we going to sell South Africa 500,000 tons, are we going to sell Cuba a million and a half tons, or, what are we going to do now with the Cuban quota since Castro has come into power?" We had a million and a half tons to distribute, but we weren't going to sell Cuba any more sugar.

Consequently, every foreign Tom, Dick, and Harry started making bids. I was sitting in my office one day when my secretary said the French embassy was on the line. A gentleman proceeded to tell me he and his agricultural representatives felt there could be a change of policy regarding some California citrus shipments into France, if we could work out some reasonable kind of exchange.

This was a complete reversal of what had been the previous French position; they had turned down our citrus—cold. (The French, in recent years, haven't been friendly in more ways than one, particularly since the formation of the Common Market.) I was curious about what was going on, so I thanked the French representative very kindly for the call, told him I thought our people would be interested, and that I would be contacting him soon. The next day I learned there was a French island that wanted a sugar quota. The French were trying to give that island an amount of our sugar quota.

I cite this as an example of how representatives from all over the world come to Washington to call on members of the Agriculture Committee. They invite you to visit them as their guests. Brazil and other Latin American countries want to show you how they load sugar and ship it up here in enormous barges and how high the quality of their sugar is. I haven't been down there, but others have. Sugar is a big business in this world.

For some reason, in every session of Congress, our last battle would be over the Sugar Act. About two in the morning during the last day of the session (when you are trying to close up the Congress and go home for Christmas), you would have to fight the sugar battle and get some agreement between the House and the Senate, then have it run down to the president.

AID: *What percentage of sugar consumed in the U.S. is domestically produced?*

SISK: Close to 50 percent.

AID: *The Sugar Act dealt with how much sugar you were going to import and from where, and then all the pressures generated from that?*

SISK: Yes. Because of this, you pretty well controlled the price. This was not really price control, but it had the effect of maintaining a price level on sugar. Finally, in 1975 or thereabouts, we let the Sugar Act expire. We have no Sugar Act at the present time. It's a wide open deal. It's on a roller coaster. Dropping the Act was, to an extent, led by one of the New York members who maintained this would save the American consumer a lot of money. I don't believe it. In the long run, it could cost consumers money.

Since the Sugar Act expired, there have been great ups and downs in sugar prices. On a ten-pound bag of sugar, you see as much as two or three dollars difference this month against six months ago. I understand in Washington, the American sugar industry might go by the boards unless it can get another decent Sugar Act. It has a temporary agreement to stabilize prices. This fluctuation has hurt the domestic sugar industry and particularly the Hawaiian sugar industry. There is a lot of cane sugar in

Hawaii. This green sugar is shipped over here and processed in the Bay Area, where there are several sugar plants. Spreckels has a plant in Mendota which processes a lot of that sugar.

The history of the sugar industry and sugar pressure in diplomatic circles world-wide is an interesting story. You would be amazed at the implications of it.

AID: *The California Agricultural Leadership Program?*

SISK: I was aware of the program and had been thoroughly sold on the idea of inducing continued interest in agriculture and, in particular, having places for graduates from agricultural schools. I have a great deal of pride in California State University at Fresno. I know you are from Davis and I know that UC Davis has a great agricultural school. But we think we have a better one at Fresno State.

AID: *I have talked to George Ilg, Fresno State assistant dean of agriculture, emeritus.*

SISK: What George and some of these guys have done here in connection with the wineries! Fresno State has offered a course in enology for a great many years.

Getting back to the farm management program, I was interested because these agricultural schools need help for both men and women, coming from Fresno State, Cal Poly, UC Davis, and throughout the state. Agriculture has been in trouble in that the average age of farmers has been increasing at a rapid clip. In 1972 the average age of the American farmer was fifty-six. There was no question about an urgent need to interest younger people in agriculture.

A group of farmers, together with the University of California, Fresno State, and Cal Poly, got their heads together and came up with this idea of travel for a selected and qualified group of agricultural leaders. There were a couple of foundations which had commitments of $150,000 to $250,000 for this activity, but they were not ready to donate the money without certain tax-exempt status. They phoned me in Washington and asked if I could help out. I was right in the middle of trying to get an IRS processing center for Fresno and I was competing with San Diego, Tucson, Arizona, Portland, Oregon, and a few other places for it. I had friends in the IRS. We got quick approval of the tax-exempt status for the foundation.

I was invited to participate in the leadership program and attended the opening meeting of the first class of thirty people. I went up to Sacramento and Davis to observe the program. Our office has generally handled the arrangements for the Washington visits, usually a couple of times a year. We made the reservations, arranged for people to talk to the group, and arranged for them to meet with members of the Department of Agriculture and Department of State.

It is quite an extensive program. We are now into our eighth or ninth class. I am just thoroughly sold on it and the quality of these thirty to thirty-five young men, who are usually from twenty-seven to thirty-seven years old. They make substantial contributions on their own. On the other hand, they get their travel paid. They go overseas. They might go to Russia. I have spoken to class after class. Tony Coelho, our present congressman, is also very much involved. We have always had several members of the class from our district.

AID: *Were you the author?*

SISK: There was no particular author; it was not that type of program. It was a program that was put together here. As far as I know, there wasn't any state or federal authorization. It was simply the University of California, George Ilg of Fresno State, and a group of farmers like Jack Harris, Russell Giffen, and other farm leaders throughout the state who got together and said, "We have got to have better management; we need graduates from the agricultural colleges running these farms."

AID: *You were lucky that George Ilg graduated from a fine university.*

SISK: Really?

AID: *Yes, from UC Davis. [Laughter] What about the Foreign Agricultural Service? You got a half million dollars for raisins one year and a million dollars another year on a matching basis through Jamie L. Whitten, chairman of the Subcommittee on Agricultural Appropriations, even though his committee was angry at the Foreign Agricultural Service.*

SISK: Whitten of Mississippi had been chairman of the Agricultural Appropriations Subcommittee for many years. He was a tough customer and was opinionated. I went to his office and visited with him because there were times when he had to come before the Rules Committee. I don't wish to overemphasize this, but my being on the Rules Committee opened doors for me. I don't kid anybody about this; it wasn't just my own personality that did it. It didn't hurt when you were a member of the Rules Committee. You just asked for a little favor here and there. That's the way the ball bounces.

Anyway, this money was totally justifiable. We needed it to encourage production of raisins, particularly overseas sales, handling of raisins, meeting with other raisin-producing countries, and working out international agreements which were vital to our well-being. As a result of the expenditures, our market ran up to thirty, forty thousand tons of raisins to Japan, for example. Our sale of California raisins to Japan has been high. Our raisin industry has increased sales to Scandinavia, Germany, England, and the Far East. It has done a great job. At times, though, the industry has been its own worst enemy. After a couple of bad rains where the raisin crop was lost—like last year—the industry let the price get out of hand and then didn't have the raisins to supply to foreigners. When foreign customers go to Greece, Turkey, or Israel to buy, they might stay there.

Stumping for "raisin power," Sisk makes a presentation before the Fresno County Board of Supervisors on behalf of the raisin industry.

The change in the foreign market for raisins required other action on my part. I deserve no credit for initiating this because the raisin industry had pointed out the problem to me and had asked me for relief. Prior to World War I, raisin plantings were based upon a healthy foreign market. The two world wars practically destroyed that market. The domestic market was unfavorably changed because the shift to prepared mixes and baked goods meant that the average baker no longer used raisins as much as before. Raisins couldn't be added to prepared mix because they didn't mix well with it due to a moisture barrier.

To try to correct this problem, I was able to get some funds earmarked for research. The Martinez lab of USDA quickly came up with the solution—the use of hot beeswax. The packers had some trouble with it, however, and a better solution was found that satisfied everyone.

The raisin people tell me that my help in opening the raisin market got the ball rolling and with the use of television commercials and other advertising, the market has vastly increased. To indicate the importance of that, in 1960 I asked my administrative assistant, Jackson Carle, to take a survey of the economic situation of the raisin growers. He found that 40 percent of them were receiving less than $3,000 a year in income from growing raisins. They were not eligible for welfare only because of the value of their land. Currently, grower returns have increased from one hundred dollars a ton, or less, to about one thousand dollars in normal years. The short crop of 1978 because of the rain at the time of harvest increased that price, as I have said.

The Foreign Agricultural Service, in my opinion, has generally done a good job. The subcommittee on appropriations, for some reason, has had bitter differences with FAS. FAS has occasionally taken positions opposing the subcommittee. FAS has been part of an administration which has opposed increased duties and high tariffs. It has to live with foreign countries and is subject to day-in and day-out diplomatic relationships. If you have to deal with somebody who you've just kicked in the teeth by setting a high tariff on what they are trying to sell, you can understand their attitude.

I have always felt that we in California—and particularly in the valley—have been discriminated against concerning many of our fruits and vegetables. We have very strict requirements—limitations on the types of pesticides, fungicides, rodenticides, etc. that we can spray on our raisins, olives, and all of our fruits and vegetables. Countries importing olives, for example, don't follow our practices. The sprays others use on trees and the way those commodities are handled certainly wouldn't be permitted in the U.S.A.

One of the battles I had early in my career dealt with ways to preserve the fig industry in this area. Virtually all the figs grown on the North American continent come from my district—and the growers were fighting for their lives. They were being cut to ribbons by Greeks and Turks shipping in figs. I fought with the Department of Agriculture. I fought with the State Department. A Dr. Miller with the Department of Agriculture came to see me one day during my second or third term. He told me in a nice way: "Mr. Sisk, I want to explain this to you carefully. I know how unhappy you are about the way things have been handled concerning the fig industry, but let me tell you the attitude of the administration. Your fig people can grow something else. Our State Department people feel we just have to buy something from the Turks, the Greeks, the Italians, and the Spanish. You only have about thirty thousand acres of figs and you can pull those fig trees up and grow something else." I said, "Dr. Miller, do you want to go there and tell those people that?"

After that conversation, I didn't let up. I appeared before the Tariff Commission three times on behalf of the fig industry. On several occasions, the Tariff Commission recommended that something be done about it, but the Eisenhower Administration wouldn't take any action. To them, the fig industry in California wasn't that important. The industry finally got a process developed, with some help from the Agriculture Department, which tested incoming fig paste and counted the insect segments (bodies and legs, etc.). We turned back a thousand tons of Turkish figs at the New York docks and that shook the whole international fig industry. One thousand tons of figs aren't many, but it made the Turks take notice. They had to clean up their operations. When they started cleaning up their operations, it cost them more.

AID: *Was it your idea to go to the Food and Drug Administration and get that inspection?*

SISK: We talked about it with fig industry representatives. It is a demonstration of the fact there are more ways to choke a dog to death than on butter; if you can't get it done one way, try another. I give this fig industry a lot of credit for pulling itself up by its own bootstraps. I was helpful in terms of getting some governmental aid. Interestingly, many of the larger fig growers, including the Roberts, the Forkners, and Monty Montgomery of Merced, were Republicans. They became my supporters.

AID: *Why did you leave the Agriculture Committee?*

SISK: This goes back to how I got on it in the first place. I have said that an arrangement was made permitting an exception to the exclusive committee rule, subject to the fact no other Californian who represented agriculture could serve. The understanding between Wilbur Mills and John McCormack was that if and when there was a Californian from an agricultural area who was interested in going on the Agriculture Committee, we would then revert back. When John Krebs was elected in 1974 from the Seventeenth District, representing Kings and parts of Fresno and Tulare counties, he wanted Agriculture. I stepped off. That was the end of the line for me on Agriculture.

23.
Additional Sisk-Directed Bills

AID: *I want to ask you about some of the bills you authored, co-authored, or sponsored that we haven't discussed. What about the Tax Reform Act of 1978?*

SISK: I was a co-author of that. The bill is still pending before the Ways and Means Committee. When you feel strongly about the provisions of a law and are attempting to amend or change it, as a member you solicit support for the legislation. Because of this activity, I don't know all the details of this bill, although I was in favor of it, which is why I co-sponsored it.

AID: *Several of your district people told me about some of your other legislative accomplishments: amendments to the Social Security Act; a Health Security Act; new medical schools to specialize in veterans' illnesses, among others.*

SISK: These are matters that I believed in and fought for. I was involved in a number of Social Security amendments. The way the original Social Security Act was written, women were discriminated against. I just don't think we should have discriminatory laws—men and women ought to be treated the same. I have tried to improve the Social Security Act to help widows. Gwen Luty and Christine Clary, members of my Washington office, became experts on Social Security.

AID: *What other important legislation did you introduce or sponsor?*

SISK: I don't think I can supply an adequate answer to that question—there were just so many bills. It was said that my congressional district got involved in practically every conceivable problem or controversy. My colleagues kidded me when I was on the Committee on Agriculture. Most agricultural districts in this country are single-shot districts; they grow mainly wheat or corn, or beef cattle, or pigs. They would say, "Here comes Sisk—he has a piece of it. He has cotton, grapes, citrus fruits, dairy cattle, pigs, beef cattle, and chickens." Maybe we got involved in too much; maybe we should have concentrated on fewer things.

Promoting the state's agricultural output is very much a part of a California congressman's job. Here, the subject is olives—and joining Sisk, at right, are, from left, Rep. John McFall, Water Commission Chairman Jack Chrisman, Rep. Harlan Hagen, Sen. Clair Engle, Rep. Dalip Saund, and Rep. Bizz Johnson. Woman and child are unidentified.

AID: *We have talked about victories and defeats. What were the most important defeats you suffered?*

SISK: I have felt very crushed sometimes, although you have to roll with the punches. You can't get too emotionally tied up in these things. I have never felt particularly crushed over a bill I authored and put a lot of work into and which then lost. But as part of a group of Democrats who try to put together a program and then go to the floor and find it losing by two or three votes, I felt the inequity of it. You can really feel down. However,

An Amtrak passenger train linking Bakersfield and Oakland pulls into the Fresno depot. Sisk was instrumental in retaining service along the valley route.

Courtesy Fresno Bee

the people who took defeats too personally would find themselves in trouble emotionally. Every time you vote, you win or lose. You have to learn to take the bad with the good.

There was a time when I wanted amendments to pass to S109—the Farmers' Bargaining Rights Act—which recognized certain rights of producers to bargain. It supposedly required processors to do some bargaining. I was particularly wrapped up in this bill. Because of the emotionalism which developed over some of the testimony (stemming from Maryland poultry producers), it got in committee and couldn't get out. I felt bad about it.

Shortly after action had been completed on the San Luis, about fifteen or twenty years ago, and we were beginning construction on it, we started the east side project. I've mentioned that in detail. There was a lot of interest in and support for it. I spent a lot of time introducing legislation on it and at one point we felt there was a possibility of putting it together, but it started falling apart. It ultimately lost and proved a great economic loss to this state. Something has to be done about the desperate situation that put us in.

I fought very hard for transportation systems here, to keep the trains running. Some people give me credit for being instrumental in getting Amtrak back here. We may still lose this, though. John McFall, who was on the Appropriations Committee, and I didn't see eye to eye on that— even though Amtrak came right down his district. I put pressure on him to support Amtrak. I did an enormous amount of work on that. I was very disappointed after I thought I had this thing going, when the Amtrak people claimed they couldn't run trains over the track they felt was the most appropriate and served the most people. (I felt they had the power to do this.) They let Southern Pacific push them out of shape on it.

177

For example, when that train comes out of the San Francisco-Oakland area, it should leave Oakland on the Santa Fe tracks and arrive in Stockton because Santa Fe is the only line that goes through Stockton. From Stockton, the train should use the Southern Pacific tracks, which go right through Modesto, Merced, and Madera. The Southern Pacific was able to block that, forcing Amtrak to stay on the Santa Fe, putting them clear out to River Bank, missing Modesto. The Santa Fe does come back through the eastern edge of Merced, but it completely misses Madera. It goes through Fresno and then to Corcoran down the west side rather than going down the center of the valley like the S.P. If we could force Southern Pacific to cooperate, we could have a much better chance of keeping Amtrak here.

Talking about things I worked hard for, I tried to get a medical school here. You mentioned this indirectly. I was a co-sponsor of legislation which provided for eight pilot schools in connection with veterans hospitals on a national basis. I worked with Olin Teague of Texas, who was chairman of the Veterans Affairs subcommittee on that.

AID: *Was this when you were on Veterans Affairs?*

SISK: This was when I was on the Rules Committee, but I kept an interest in veterans' affairs. Fresno had one of the few VA hospitals in the nation which didn't have a medical school. Harry Truman decreed by executive order in 1949 that from then on no veterans hospital would be built without a medical school. That was about the time the Fresno VA hospital was finished. Since then, all VA hospitals are adjacent to or near a medical school.

AID: *What about the one in Martinez?*

SISK: I was on the committee when it authorized the construction of the veterans hospital at Martinez. Martinez was built on the premise that the San Francisco medical school was close enough for the government to not oppose its construction. The VA, under the executive order, did not like the Martinez site; it would have preferred a hospital somewhere else. John Baldwin from Martinez and I had been elected at the same time and we were friends, although he was a Republican. (John died of cancer some years ago.) I helped John get that hospital there. I attended hearings. I walked that site when it was just an open pasture. Finally, we got the administration to go along on the basis that it was in the vicinity of the University of California, San Francisco, medical school.

AID: *I believe that the Martinez VA hospital also is connected with the medical school at UC Davis.*

SISK: Fresno was one of the ideal places for a medical school. We had a VA hospital and the problem of staffing it was greater because we were not near a medical school. So we went all-out to get a medical school. With the participation of local people, we did make considerable headway. Milo Rowell was a name to be reckoned with here in Fresno. At one time, he

178

might have been called "Mr. Republican." The Rowells were a famous old family here. Milo Rowell's father was a judge, I believe; Milo was an attorney. There is a Rowell building downtown on the corner of Van Ness and Tulare. Milo went all-out on this. He had served at one time as a regent of the University of California. He knew of the Kearney offer of years before, in connection with locating a branch of the University of California here. He was particularly knowledgeable in the field of medicine.

It came down to getting the University of California involved. We couldn't go this alone. We had to get a school which was prepared to issue medical degrees. As much as Fresno State College (now California State University, Fresno) would have liked to have seen a medical school connected with it, it was not in a position to handle one. Under pressure from various groups, we began to consult with the University of California. We had many meetings with persons who represented the university and with Milo and the VA people. We worked on this thing months and years. We finally got authorization for a building on the grounds of the hospital here to house facilities for medical teaching and training. Students from the University of California medical school in San Francisco will be brought here for additional training and will do certain types of work within the veterans hospital.

There was a time when I dreamed much bigger dreams. We dreamed of a massive VA complex including a new VA hospital and a new medical school connected with it. Basically, we wanted a whole veterans' center. This probably was a pipe dream to start with. We had the American Legion, the Veterans of Foreign Wars, the Disabled American Veterans, and the AMVets—all the various groups were involved. There were many meetings and much enthusiasm. There was a lot of money involved. It never really developed. We were dreaming too big for the time. You have to walk before you can run.

AID: *The San Francisco medical students, according to my notes, include forty upper class medical students who will come to the veterans hospital to serve medical clerkships.*

SISK: That's right.

AID: *Chances are that your veterans hospital is a "dean's hospital," supervised by the San Francisco medical school.*

SISK: They are working together. You understand that the VA is very careful not to turn over the control of the hospital to the university, as perhaps the university would have liked. This was a conflict that we had to resolve. There is dual control, but the VA—in the final analysis—is in the saddle when it come to the last word on the hospital.

AID: *However, it has to be accredited and if it is not, then the VA cannot run its hospital.*

SISK: Of course, that's right. This was a touchy area. We had meeting after

179

meeting. The veterans affairs directors back in Washington would say "no." The university would get upset and say "no." It drove us crazy. I remember getting on the telephone dozens of times with Milo Rowell, who was carrying the ball out here.

AID: *I am going to mention various bills you were interested in. In 1957, there was a bill to protect Indian lands, for which you voted.*

SISK: I was very active in Indian affairs at that time. There were five rancherias in my district up in the foothills.

AID: *What is a rancheria?*

SISK: A small Indian reservation. In some cases, rancherias are only 160 acres. There's one in North Fork. There was one near Auberry. We had the Table Mountain Rancheria. We had Big Sandy Rancheria. These were small Indian groups on small areas of land. This is after California took the areas over from the national Bureau of Indian Affairs. The Californians said they wanted to run their own show.

AID: *When did that happen?*

SISK: Back in the early 1900s. As a result, the Indians in California had a rough time.

AID: *I remember one study reported that California had 7.2 percent of U.S. rural Indians, but receives only 1.4 percent of the BIA budget. In 1965, you supported a proposal (you might have been the author) to settle 29.1 million dollars with California Indians.*

SISK: I was the author of the bill. I tried to get more, since the Indians were not satisfied with that settlement. That matter came before the Indian Claims Commission.

In my opinion, Indians should have been made full citizens a long time ago. I was looking at what we were doing for some of the eastern and midwestern tribes like the Sioux, the Ogallala Sioux, the Cheyennes, and the Navahos, etc., and I felt the California Indians were getting a raw deal.

I had served on the Indian Affairs Subcommittee and worked with Jim Haley of Florida, the chairman. I helped to get the settlement for the Mission Indians in Palm Springs. We made all of them wealthy down there. It got to the point where the Indian Claims Commission said, "Brother, this is it." They tried to appeal, but that was the end of the line. I said, "Let's give them some money." There was a little carry-over from previous settlements. So we got that added to make the total amount thirty-three or thirty-four million. I had to get authorization from the committee for Congress to appropriate the twenty-nine million. I got it approved and it was signed into law by President Eisenhower.

Once I got the thing through, the Indians were upset—and to some extent, with me—because they said they should have more money. I told them I had done everything in the world that I could. "You had your lawyers work with the Indian Claims Commission. I was trying to get you the money. I am not saying it is enough. You probably should have four times that much."

I think they were asking for $150 million or some such figure. Anyway, we got the bill passed and the money appropriated to pay on it. Then we had a ruckus that went on for two or three years over the Indian head count, who was and was not going to be paid. It was an unbelievable problem to try to figure out which Indians were eligible.

AID: *In 1959, you wanted all armed forces in one uniform. You were against waste in the Pentagon. (This was part of that.) You also charged waste in arms research. Is there anything more that you want to say about that?*

SISK: I don't know if there is anything I need to add to that.

AID: *The* Sacramento Bee *said you switched on the Viet Nam pullout. You joined the doves in October 1971 and then you turned hawk on November 18, 1971, according to a news article.*

SISK: I disagree with that. That is a newspaper reporter's opinion, depending upon how he or she wants to interpret a given vote. My interpretation of votes does not necessarily agree with some reporter's. For example, during a recent situation I suddenly got a bunch of calls. People were upset with Tony Coelho because he had voted against a constitutional amendment dealing with school busing. I was in support of school desegregation. On the other hand, I had reservations about forced busing because I think it has hurt our educational system. Tony has basically the same position that I have. But you don't tear the Constitution apart every time you want to settle some issue. For another example, trying to amend the Constitution on abortion, or on busing—that's not the way to do it. These people screamed, "Haven't you got some influence with your successor?" I said, "Wait a minute. We are talking about amending the Constitution."

I just want to cite that as an example of misinterpretation. I probably could have been classified as pretty hawkish on Viet Nam. At least I supported Lyndon Johnson in his attempt to solve that situation—in fact, I stayed with him until the last. I finally recognized that we had to disengage ourselves in some way. In 1971, I might have voted a certain way, but I don't think I changed my position one iota.

AID: *You were talking about discrimination against women. I don't have the date, but you either authored or sponsored a bill that provided that all armed services jobs would be open to women, including combat.*

SISK: That's right. I am not saying that women should be in combat, but if they want to volunteer—all right. I took a position that the National Organization for Women supported, although I don't agree with all of the stuff that is going on now. There should be no discrimination. If a woman is qualified for a particular spot in the military and desires that spot, she should be given an equal opportunity, if in fact she can deliver.

AID: *Do you remember when the ADA misrepresented your vote? The group said you had voted against civil rights.*

SISK: Yes, Americans for Democratic Action. It totally misrepresented me. I don't know what happened there. In my opinion, ADA got so far out in left field, it went haywire. In the early days of Hubert Humphrey there was some stability in the organization, but the group now contains a bunch of kooks. It got to the point where I wouldn't even let ADA officials into my office. The group published an erroneous list, showing that I had voted against bills when I had voted for them or had voted the opposite of how I really did. I lost all respect for the ADA. It no longer has standing in the Democratic Party, in my opinion.

AID: *Let's talk about a few more things you accomplished for your district. Again, some of them affected California State University, Fresno. George Ilg, the assistant dean of agriculture, emeritus, mentioned that you sponsored legislation which got the Agricultural Research Service office on campus.*

SISK: I give a lot of credit to George and other people, along with the local institution. The truth of the matter is that a member of Congress can only operate where a known problem or activity exists. You depend on constituents for the facts to back up your position. Then you go to the agencies which have jurisdiction in that field and fight the battle for your constituents. Again, you can only fight the battle based on the information and arguments they give you. George was always very informative. I am not sure of this particular case, though, because we were involved in a whole variety of discussions and meetings year after year with the Appropriations Committee, getting research funds for Fresno State.

AID: *Before we leave the subject, according to my information, the ARS in Fresno is now a regional office. It covers California and Arizona. The Berkeley office covers the rest of the United States.*

SISK: Right.

AID: *You got a research grant for variety testing with sesame seeds. This was a cooperative project with the University of California at Riverside.*

SISK: That's right. I think it was a mutuality of interest and that over the years we developed a very fine relationship with the University of California. The university felt at times that I was taking positions adverse to its interests, but it really wasn't that. I was just fighting to get research money for Fresno State. I felt our agricultural school was doing a good job and was entitled to consideration. What came out of it (not because of me necessarily, but because of mutuality of interest) was that these groups sat down, worked together, and put together programs. I think the University of California recognized, as time went on, that Fresno State and other similar schools could make contributions to the overall ends they sought through research.

AID: *For example, Dick Eide, who is a farm advisor in Fresno in farm director Bill Hambleton's office, told me that Fresno State University is one of the best cooperators the Fresno cooperative extension office has. (A cooperator is a person or institution that cooperates on research projects, lending land, cattle, and other resources.)*

You helped secure an ARS grant, regarding mechanical harvesting of grapes for raisins drying on the vine. It was a three-year grant in excess of $150,000. Do you remember that?

SISK: Yes. That was one on which we worked a long time. It was important and the logical place for it was here. We are in the very heart of raisin country. Fresno State has gone a long way in raisin research. It has done a fantastic job with raisins.

AID: *Last year raisin growers suffered high losses because it rained. Ilg told me that with the new drying methods, many thousands of dollars worth of raisins were saved because they dried so much more quickly.*

SISK: Yes, I do understand that there were some savings from that.

AID: *You also sponsored a move to get the U.S. Forest Service research lab on the Fresno campus.*

SISK: Yes, that's also one we worked on a long time. We finally got the Forest Service with us. I was very proud of the work done there. When John Krebs was elected, Fresno State was in his district. (The university was shifted from my district four years ago.) We continued to work together, during the four years he served, to get funding for that project.

AID: *It became the Pacific Southwest Forest and Range Experiment Station.*

SISK: With that we combined some solar energy projects. We put in a solar heating plant. We got a little extra money for it.

AID: *My notes say that California State University, Fresno deeded ten acres of land to the Forest Service. Your bill provided the financing. Students work there part-time.*

SISK: Yes.

AID: *You were on Title XII Study Committee, Freedom from Hunger bill, sponsored by Hubert Humphrey to provide funds to enable land grant-type universities to do research in foreign countries toward improved food production. What do you remember about that?*

SISK: Well, a group of us got interested in the program. Hubert Humphrey was very active in that. Among the things you're confronted with when you sit in Congress and deal with foreign aid, foreign assistance and overseas problems—and it's constantly thrown in your face—are the millions of people who go hungry, the thousands who die of starvation every year. The answer is to make these countries more food-efficient in protein production. That is what we had in mind in this situation.

AID: *This may be one of the things you were talking about when you said the University of California probably thought you opposed it. The original bill called for only state land grant universities to sponsor this work. You said, "Over my dead body," and you amended it to include like or similar universities.*

SISK: That's right. [Laughter] Now that wasn't a shot at the university; it was

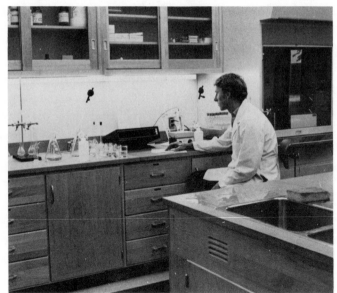

Robert Austerman, a biological technician for the Pacific Southwest Forest and Range Experiment Station, uses equipment at Fresno State University's Forestry Sciences Laboratory to test the nutrient content of forest and range soil plant samples. The station, a division of the Forest Service of the U.S. Department of Agriculture, conducts its research at the FSU facility.

Courtesy California State University, Fresno

simply saying, "Let's make this available to any university qualified to participate." The Land Grant Act goes way back. That's in the old tradition. Every state had land grant colleges. They were there first, so naturally they get the "mostest." Naturally, they hate to lose anything. I remember Paul Findley, Republican of Illinois, joined me in that because he had a similar situation.

AID: *Anything else along similar lines that you can recall?*

SISK: I can recall many telephone calls and discussion groups concerning specialty legislation. I guess a day never passed without a letter or telephone conversation seeking help for some group via special consideration or appropriations or acts of a private legislative nature.

24.
Baseball and Sports in the Nation's Capital

AID: *You and Mrs. Sisk and Tony Coelho and his wife used to attend, whenever you could, the Washington Senators home baseball games. I think it was your wife who taught everybody how to keep score.*

SISK: Yes, she got to be quite a scorekeeper. I was a great lover of baseball. Earlier I said that I played baseball in high school and college. I did a little sandlot ball afterwards. I was never good enough for the pros.

AID: *When did Washington lose the Senators?*

SISK: 1971.

AID: *You tried to get them back?*

SISK: Yes.

AID: *Why don't you tell that story?*

SISK: Calvin Griffith's father, Clark Griffith, the head of the Senators baseball team, was a real mainstay in the American League. When he passed away, his son Calvin took over. The team played in Griffith Stadium Park on the corner of Georgia and Florida avenues. After Congress decided to support building a new stadium for Washington (the old stadium was in poor condition and was owned privately by the Griffiths), we built the 55,000-seat RFK Stadium. Naturally, the pro football Redskins were looking forward to playing in it, too. We had no problem getting a contract with them right away, but Calvin Griffith bucked on the question of rentals. That was one of the principal reasons why he moved the team to Minnesota. The Washington Senators went to Minnesota and became the Minnesota Twins in the early sixties. At that point, because of the ruckus it raised, the American League expanded and put an expansion club in Washington. That would have occurred in the middle sixties or thereabouts. (I hope this history is straight as I am reviewing it.)

I had season tickets from the time that we built the new stadium. The new owner of the expansion club was abused for being the one who moved the club to Texas in 1971. When he first came, he started out well, although he didn't have much money and was operating on a shoestring. He hired Ted Williams as manager. Ted built up the club pretty well. For the first time in years he had the team over five hundred, which was in 1969.

Because of the financial situation and a variety of other things, the owner made a deal with a fellow in Texas and moved the team there, renaming it the Texas Rangers. At that point I really got aggravated. I had season tickets, as I said, and was very much a fan. I thought Washington was being abused. Other members of Congress felt the same way. We came up with a baseball committee and I wound up as chairman. Fifty to seventy-five members of Congress were at the first meeting. Congressman Frank Horton of Rochester, New York (former executive vice president of International Baseball League) was very active and supported us. Congressman Mel [Charles Melvin] Price from East Saint Louis, Illinois (former sports editor and member of the National Baseball Writers Association) was an active baseball man. We had a great group of people. We struggled with that thing for years, trying to get our team back. We were never successful, although I got very well acquainted with the baseball people. I attended a lot of meetings. It was an interesting activity, although it was a sideline.

Baseball owners are a peculiar breed of cat. Walter O'Malley, the owner of the Dodgers who passed away recently, and Gene Autry of the Angels were fantastic men. Some owners were great and some were

185

selfish. I guess Washington will finally get a baseball team because Edward Bennett Williams, the famous D.C. attorney, is 14 percent owner of the Redskins. For years he has been president of the Redskins, although Jack Kent Cooke from Los Angeles owns 86 percent of the team. Williams recently bought the Baltimore Orioles. I knew about the deal. We had worked on it sporadically for years, trying to move that team to Washington because of the team's dissatisfaction with the old Baltimore stadium. I predict that team is going to wind up in RFK Stadium in Washington someday.

AID: *As a result of your interest in athletics, in 1973 you received the "Mr. Sam Award" from the Washington Touchdown Club.*

SISK: Yes. [Sisk points to the award behind him.] I was as surprised as anyone else about this award. The Touchdown Club of Washington is one of the major athletic clubs in the world. They have a big dinner affair once a year, one of the biggest sporting events in the country. Big sports personalities attend. At this dinner, which usually occurs in late January or early February, awards are made to the top football, basketball, and baseball players, and there is a whole string of awards for other top players and coaches. Also given is the "Mr. Sam Award." This goes to the individual in government who has made the greatest contribution that year to sports.

AID: *Will you read what the award says?*

SISK: "The Touchdown Club of Washington, D.C., 'Mr. Sam Award' to the Honorable B. F. Sisk, a governmental figure who has fostered and contributed to sports."

An accompanying booklet gives a list of the people who have received it. In most cases it has gone to presidents of the U.S. and one senator, I think. It is a rather select group of people. I was deeply honored to receive the award. I am not sure I warranted it, but I appreciated it.

AID: *In 1976 weren't you on a select committee to investigate the need for legislation to regulate professional sports?*

SISK: I was chairman of the select committee on professional sports. I appointed Frank Horton my vice-chairman. It was a bipartisan committee, an effort to deal with various problems in professional sports. We had a series of hearings dealing with football, basketball, and ice hockey, because of charges and counter-charges made about violence in those sports. There was interesting testimony taken and we have some valuable records.

Part 5:

CONGRESSIONAL PERSPECTIVE

B. F. Sisk's feeling for the political center elevated him to the first chairmanship of the United Democrats of Congress, an alliance of moderate Democrats.

The UDC post, in turn, honed his leadership skills, priming the Fresno congressman for his energetic run for House majority leader in 1972.

Although unsuccessful in a three-way race, Sisk's try for the position confirmed his standing as a de facto House leader. With candor and commendable detachment, he details the strategies and personalities behind that contest and others, then offers his analysis of the six presidents and four Speakers with whom he served.

He covers the gamut: from Dwight Eisenhower and White House protocol to Lyndon Johnson and civil rights, from Gerald Ford's pardon of Richard Nixon to Jimmy Carter and his relationship with Congress. Sisk retains special feeling for John Kennedy and recalls their association. Speaker Tip O'Neill is seen as a man who grew into the job, Carl Albert as one who confronted problems in a time of change and trial. Sam Rayburn, "a giant," stands alone.

Sisk recounts the fallout from his personally trying stance in support of the Supreme Court's decision on school prayer, and takes the reader with him through a hypothetical "typical day" on Capitol Hill.

The "tour" completed, he handles with dispatch his involvement in a potpourri of issues—patronage practices, the influence of lobbyists, the impact of reapportionment, Nixon's China policy, the status of the state's congressional delegation, Viet Nam.

Bernie than shifts gears, focusing on a less visible yet uniquely satisfying facet of his tenure. Says Sisk: "The greatest gratification as a member of Congress is being able to help an individual who may feel totally helpless in a bureaucratic world." A large portion of the time and work of a congressman and his staff is absorbed by activities which are non-legislative, or only indirectly legislative, in nature. These tasks, which have increased greatly through the years, are known collectively as "case work." Case work consists of assistance provided to constituents who are confounded by the tremendous increase and complexity of federal programs.

People have difficulty finding their way among bureaus and agencies administering programs which may directly affect their lives and well-being.

Their congressman, the only federal official directly elected to serve a district and its people, has become their refuge and spokesman—their ombudsman.

Culled from his office's voluminous case work files are a half dozen examples of constituents in need—constituents whose needs spurred Sisk and his staff into action.

In a surprising percentage of cases, including those cited, a congressman who tries is able to assist individuals and groups in attaining rights or benefits to which they are entitled, sometimes because all the facts were not earlier presented, or because original applications were mis-directed or were not addressed to the applicable law or program.

In some instances appeals from individuals reveal that operation of a general law may unjustly and adversely affect a single citizen to whom it was never intended to apply. In such cases a congressman may introduce a "private bill" which operates only to adjust the rights of a named person.

In other instances general laws may be unfair to an entire group throughout the nation, but the discrimination comes to the congressman's attention only through a plea for help received from a single constituent.

In such cases, the congressman may seek an appropriate amendment to a general law to relieve the injustice imposed on all those similarly affected. Thus, the plight of a single citizen may alter and improve the welfare of thousands.

It is estimated that 75 percent of the time of a congressional staff is occupied in case work contacts with executive branch agencies and that in an equal percentage of cases, results benefit citizens.

The Sisk memoir nears its close with a look at Tony Coelho, the Loyola University graduate whom Bernie hired fresh out of college, eventually promoted to administrative assistant, and who ultimately succeeded him in 1979.

A status report on B. F. Sisk in retirement rounds out "Congressional Perspective"—a section that appropriately encompasses Kennedys and constituents alike—and the book.

25.
Inside the House
of Representatives

AID: *Tell me about patronage. Are the chairmen of the Democratic or Republican national committees in charge of patronage, primarily?*

SISK: No, not in Congress. As a matter of fact, I served for many years on the patronage committee of the Democratic Party. The matter of patronage is handled by each party. Neither gets involved in cross-party issues. For all practical purposes, the party in power has real patronage. For example, the Speaker of the House will sit down with the minority leader; let's say Tip O'Neill sits down with Jerry Ford. O'Neill might say, "Jerry, it looks like we are going to need sixty pages on the House floor. I have been hearing complaints from your people that you haven't been getting enough consideration. We have been giving you eight pages. We have talked this matter over and we are willing to increase it to ten. So out of sixty, we are going to give you ten."

This is how the situation would develop. There is a similar pattern of dealing with elevator operators and the people who work on the hill.

Through reform acts and other changes in the law, we have eliminated a great number of so-called patronage spots. I took Harry Sheppard's place on the patronage committee, because he was retiring. This was a three-man committee appointed by the Speaker. I served with Joe Evans and Dr. Thomas Morgan of Pennsylvania. Joe Evans became chairman when Sheppard retired. I was the junior member. After Evans, Morgan took over the chairmanship. The whole police department was patronage when I first went on the committee. Today we have a 1,200-member police department on the hill; that is, for the House and Senate, there's the Capitol Hill Police Department. There are about twenty or so police departments in Washington, D.C. It's a very complicated arrangement. You have the Secret Service, the White House police, the National Park Service, the Metropolitan Police, the Capitol Hill police, and so forth.

AID: *Is it patronage and not civil service?*

SISK: We discontinued patronage in connection with the police. We needed professionals and security became important. Patronage is not as significant as it used to be.

189

AID: *I was wondering if your recommendation was sought regarding federal patronage, including jobs in the executive branch?*

SISK: You are talking about an entirely different type of patronage—patronage which comes out of the executive branch. This is the appointment of judges and heads of agencies, regional directors, and those people who are GS-17 and above.

AID: *How much input did you have on these?*

SISK: We, as members of Congress, had some input, but certainly not the final say. The members of Congress have always tried to assert as much influence as possible. Let's say the matter came up about appointing a regional director of the Department of Housing and Urban Development in San Francisco. Our delegation would get together and discuss the matter: "Here is Tom Smith. We think he has done a good job and we are going to recommend him if we get a unanimous agreement." We would submit this recommendation to the new administration. With the Carter Administration, frankly, we didn't get very far. In fact, this was one of the first differences that arose between the California delegation and the present administration. The White House staff almost totally ignored congressional recommendations. This was one of the bitter things that developed early on. This and other things caused the situation that exists today. This is why Hamilton Jordan is not liked by members of Congress, generally. Most administrations do cooperate with members of Congress on this—not fully, but to whatever extent they can. In the final analysis, those decisions are made by the key people of the White House staff. The president gives certain members of the staff authority to make appointments within a given area.

Take the secretary of agriculture, for example. He will make recommendations which, in many cases, are accepted for appointments of the secretary's regional people or people at the higher levels throughout the country. This is true of other departments, too.

There is a loosely-operated committee system which handles this. If an appointment is of congressional interest, it is routed in such a way that it gets to the proper people for consideration. They will consider the agency which has jurisdiction in that field plus the problems of the White House, so there is a three-fold evaluation of it.

AID: *If an agency selects a person from your district, either with or without your knowledge, are you the one who announces it?*

SISK: Normally. That was the case before the Carter Administration. Whether it was Democratic or Republican, invariably you were done the courtesy of being told that the president had appointed so-and-so. If this person was someone you had been interested in, they would lean over backwards in order to tell you they were doing you a big favor.

AID: *I want to talk to you about leadership. The Speaker, the majority leader, the whip, his assistants, and the party caucus chairman make up the so-called priesthood?*

SISK: Yes, basically. And the steering committee, which has now become very important in this whole set-up.

AID: *What about the policy committee?*

SISK: The steering committee and the policy committee are really one and the same. We don't have a policy committee in the Democratic Party, separate and apart from the leadership or hierarchy (the Speaker, the majority leader, and the whip). The committee is represented by regions within its group. Today the steering committee has become very powerful. If it wants to get rough, it can give a Speaker some problems under the rules of the game. It can make recommendations if they have to do with policy or an appointment of an individual. Let's say it has to do with the Ways and Means Committee. The issue must be brought back to caucus and the caucus can decide to get rebellious, as it has in a few cases. The Speaker today does not have the power that previous Speakers have had. He is in somewhat the same situation as the chairmen of the committees; his wings have been clipped. But he still has a lot of power by virtue of prestige. You don't want to cross the Speaker and get him mad at you.

AID: *He can allocate extra office space and other little privileges?*

SISK: Yes. He can do a lot of nice things for you, if he wants to.

AID: *And he can help you get on a desired committee?*

SISK: Yes, that's right. That is where his power lies today. The Speaker has to maneuver much differently than he did in the old days.

AID: *He can help you get a private bill through?*

SISK: He can, but normally he doesn't get involved in that sort of thing. On the other hand, he will help you get your bill scheduled, which is of help in trying to get the bill passed. If he is opposed to the bill, you are in trouble.

AID: *He can also appoint you to various public boards, commissions, delegations, etc.?*

SISK: Yes.

AID: *How does one get to be majority whip?*

SISK: Generally, whip is the personal choice of the Speaker and majority leader. It's not an elective post. We tried a number of times to make it elective, but never succeeded. I have never supported making it elective because the Speaker and majority leader working together will usually select the whip to satisfy both. He is picked to do the job of assisting, so to speak.

AID: *John Brademas hasn't been discussed yet.*

SISK: John Brademas is today the whip and remains an unknown quantity, not very spectacular, who fits into the gray area; he's around but never quite a leader. He does a fairly good job. He represents South Bend, Indiana. Brademas was a surprise, a compromise choice. It is the general understanding that he was not [Majority Leader] Jim Wright's choice. I think the Speaker, too, had another person in mind. Differences developed over certain people. Anyway, Brademas was selected.

John is a hard worker. I never had any personal differences with him, although at times I have opposed him. John represents the Greek lobby, largely. I was one of those who felt at the time of the Greek-Turkish confrontation over Cyprus that we had to try to settle it. John got himself in trouble with the leadership in those days because it opposed his position. What his future is I don't know; most people don't believe he will go much farther.

AID: *You mentioned a number of informal clubs, the United Democrats of Congress and the Democratic Study Group. Were there others that were important? For example, Rayburn had a "Board of Education."*

SISK: The Board of Education was a very small, select group. It was made up of a few old and close political friends on whom Rayburn depended to carry out things he thought were an essential part of Congress.

There is a Board of Education Room. I know it very well and have been there for lunch many times. It has historical significance. It was in that room that Truman was informed of the death of F.D.R. Truman was a member of the Board of Education and was down there that afternoon. I guess they were having a bit of a toddy; they kept certain libations handy. It was there that McCormack was first informed of the Manhattan Project to develop the atomic bomb. It was because of the importance of total secrecy to the Manhattan Project that Congress was asked to buy hook, line, and sinker certain requests without knowing how the money was being used. Members didn't even know what the term "Manhattan" meant—except for a very select group of people—and McCormack was one of those people whom Roosevelt trusted. He was the voice of the president in Congress for getting appropriations to keep the Manhattan Project going.

The Board of Education was composed generally of Mr. Rayburn, Harry Truman, Lyndon Johnson, and John McCormack. This group formed Rayburn's old friends and cronies. It was an informal group of people. Today, there might be six or eight. Tomorrow there would be another number of people there.

AID: *In other words, you drop in and have a drink.*

SISK: That's right. That was where a lot of the world's problems were discussed. Very important decisions were made there.

AID: *What about the Buckwheat Club, the S.O.S. Club, the Marching and Chowder Club?*

SISK: Most of those were Republican clubs. The Marching and Chowder sounds Irish. This was a group that got together when Mike Kirwan was alive. Mike Kirwan, an old Irishman from Youngstown, Ohio, was chairman of the subcommittee on Appropriations dealing with public works. Since he dealt with reclamation appropriations, he was the first

Representatives and staff members turn out for one in a monthly series of Church of Christ breakfasts, held in the Speaker's dining room on Capitol Hill. Sisk is seated, third from left, in this 1976 photo.

man I had to work with to get money for the San Luis Project. He, at one time, was head of the congressional campaign committee. He raised the money for Democratic congressional campaigns. He was an influential character. He always had a big party on St. Patrick's Day with the "Irish Mafia," as we called them. This included all of the Massachusetts delegation—McCormack, O'Neill, Burke, plus Jim Delaney of New York, and so forth. There were quite a few Irish people.

AID: *Clem Miller (deceased former California representative) in his book, quoted a question he had received from one of his constituents: "How do you develop your ideas on legislation; how do you develop knowledge about an issue?" He said this queston indicated a presumption that there is an intellectual, contemplative approach to political problems and that this does not exist.*

SISK: I wouldn't be surprised if he were right. Yet you have to vote and make intelligent choices. We cast about a thousand votes a session, so we do a lot of thinking about these bills. You have to consider how legislation is going to affect your district and what its importance is to the nation.

I had a great deal of respect for Clem Miller. He was very deep and, in fact, difficult to understand sometimes. His wife, a member of the DuPont family from Wilmington, Delaware, was heiress to the DuPont fortune.

AID: *To put the question another way, let's say that these figures, representing legislative traffic during one two-year Congress, are reasonably accurate: My records say 20,500 bills were referred to a committee, 1,319 were reported out, and 1,133 were enacted into law. How do you inform yourself sufficiently on those 1,319 bills?*

SISK: You have to make a mature judgment in every case. Out of 1,300 votes, there will be about fifty gut issues—issues of outstanding importance.

193

Like, "What are you going to do about energy? What are you going to do about natural gas deregulation? What is your vote going to be on a housing bill that will cost eight billion dollars? What are you going to do on a multi-million dollar farm bill, which will create a new program?" These are big issues before you and you have read about them in the press. People are interested in these issues; they have written to you about them. These are the toughest decisions you are going to have to make because they are controversial. You have to spend a lot of time on them. You can't help but be somewhat knowledgeable on some of them.

Now let's take the other 1,300. You might vote on fifteen or twenty of them in one day on the floor. A portion of these 1,300 affect California directly, so you will have picked up some information on them. A lot of your information comes from lobbyists.

A lobbyist is a very important person. Lobbyists are basically legislative representatives. They support special interests, but everyone belongs to a special interest group. Many times a congressman does not talk directly to lobbyists. Many people think you are constantly being hammered over the head by lobbyists, but that really is not true. In the U.S. Congress, you are removed from that sort of thing—unlike state legislators. Lobbyists at the federal level are sharp, shrewd people who are knowledgeable about their business. The ones who aren't lose their credibility and are cast aside. The same is true of lobbyists who lie to congressmen—they are found out. So much of a congressman's information comes from credible lobbyists. A lot of people denigrate lobbyists, but doing so is not necessarily right.

AID: *I would like to get your opinion on various lobbies: American Medical Association, railroads, labor, Farm Bureau, American Legion, U.S. Chamber of Commerce, and so forth.*

SISK: Traditionally, newspaper cartoonists have pictured lobbyists as weighing 300 pounds and smoking big cigars. In some cases, this depiction was justifiable. In the old days, it was said the Southern Pacific owned California. Today's lobbyists are great sources of information, with integrity. If they didn't have integrity, they would be discounted, because congressmen are not a bunch of dummies. I have seen a few bad lobbyists, men who were prone to overpaint their picture and underpaint the opposition's, so you couldn't depend on their information.

Most lobbyists find out very quickly who your administrative assistant is and who your secretaries are. They come in and talk to your staff. They would like to make a personal contact occasionally, but they don't normally come in and try to bother you.

AID: *Would the A.M.A. ever use your personal physician to lobby you, for example?*

SISK: I have never experienced pressure from my personal physician in Fresno or in Washington. There is a lot of criticism that the American Medical

194

Association is a very powerful lobbying group. It does have a substantial office in Washington and does a certain amount of lobbying for its cause. From time to time, the A.M.A. calls on your administrative assistant and staff. Usually, bulletins are sent.

Most large national organizations have their own trade publications. These come across your desk. Sometimes you get thousands of pieces of mail per day—just voluminous amounts. A lot of that mail has to be sorted out. Let's say a situation comes up where members are seeking basic information on what certain legislation really means. What about this proposal from our friend in Florida? How is it going to affect California's programs? You try to get the best information you can. Good legislative representatives will give you this information, even though it may work against them temporarily. I have had this happen several times. Let me cite an example.

The National Savings and Loan League is a substantial organization, generally involved in banking legislation. Often banks line up on one side and savings and loans on the other side viz-a-viz tax provisions. If I needed information, I could call up either side and ask them—and I felt each told me the truth. I have had some fine friends of absolute integrity— men like Lew Eaton, who headed Guarantee Savings. His business was started by his father and was one of the first savings and loans in this valley. He is a highly respected man. At one time he was president of the National Savings and Loan League. Lew would just tell me the facts: "Bernie, I am not sure that our position is correct on this issue when you look at the broad-base picture."

This is the kind of integrity which you learn to appreciate. The same type of people can be found, for example, in the agriculture industry, the national Farm Bureau, or the National Farmers Union. Labor representatives generally are high types; the old types who did arm-twisting don't operate much at the federal level any more.

AID: *How about the Library of Congress? Would you get someone on your staff to go to the library for research or would you have someone from the library do research for you?*

SISK: We have the Congressional Research Service which came about as the result of the 1970 Reorganization Act, as I have mentioned. It is always there to assist you.

On Monday morning or Friday afternoon you have a list of all the bills to be voted upon. You go through the list deciding what you will do. You make up your mind pretty fast. Certain people on your staff deal with legislation all the time and they assist you in making decisions. (Others are case workers.) Your administrative assistant should know the key issues that are moving at all times. He goes over the bills with you. Maybe he says Congressman X called you last week and needs your help on this bill. If nothing is wrong with the bill, you vote for it. So, in this way, you can help a friend out as long as the bill isn't detrimental to your district or the nation.

A lot of decisions are made this way; you depend on your staff and legislative representatives. You rush on to the floor and the bells are ringing. You have ten minutes to vote.

"Gee whiz, what's that issue? I've never heard of that bill. Wait a minute, that is from Bizz Johnson's committee." Then I would rush over to Bizz Johnson and ask his advice on it.

"Bernie, that's a good bill. This is why we need it . . . "

"Good, fine—and thank you."

So this is how it is done.

26.
The Influence of a Constituent

AID: *Many people feel that a single vote doesn't count. Can a single letter make a difference?*

SISK: Sometimes one person can have a great deal of influence. You were asking about those 1,300 votes a congressman is going to cast. We have gone over the procedures which help in making a determination. I may be looking over the list of bills and everything looks to be in pretty good shape. But then the telephone rings and a fellow on the other end of the line says, "Bernie, you got a bill on so and so?"

"Yes."

"Listen, do you know how that will affect a certain thing?"

"Well no, that bill came out of committee and didn't go before Rules because it was a lesser bill, being called up under a consent calendar here. What's the problem?"

He explains it to you, citing chapter and verse. You take a look at it and sure enough, he's right. In this particular situation it will tend to discriminate against a particular interest he has (company, individual, area, and so forth). If he is correct, I am inclined to raise it as a question. Generally, these are the kinds of bills where a single objection will stop it, as I've already explained. An enormous number of bills that are passed go by the consent calendar. A consent calendar might have fifty bills on it. So a single letter or phone call from one person can make a difference.

AID: *This probably goes to the matter of what a citizen should know. I suppose you received late protests or suggestions about bills. Maybe it was too late; maybe the bill had gotten a rule, which already determined the number of amendments if it was an open bill.*

SISK: That happened very often. It was always a problem trying to let the public know what the Congress was doing. I maintained that the Rules

Committee had an obligation to be open. (I got on the nerves of some to the point that members would get a little irritated with me.) I thought one of the most important responsibilities of Rules was to make sure they weren't slipping a bill by the people of this country; the committee should not approve a rule on a bill which would be voted on before the affected parties knew what was happening to them. In examining a witness—and the witness was usually the chairman of the committee—the questions would be, "When was the bill introduced? How long were hearings held? To what extent has there been publicity on this matter? Is there anything new or unusual in the legislation that has recently been adopted, since public information has been disseminated?" There were a few cases when legislation was slipped through too fast—and the affected people informed too late. Normally that didn't happen, but it did once in a while. It wasn't unusual to get a telephone call or a letter about certain legislation which had already passed in the House. A person might not have heard of it or might not have read the newspapers. It's a never-ending problem.

AID: *If I, as a private citizen, have an interest in a bill and I want to find exactly where that bill is right now, whom do I call? The congressman's office? Would your Fresno office have had knowledge of this?*

SISK: They would have gotten you the information. They had a leased wire and could save you time and money. The best thing to do is go through the local office. If you are in a big hurry, you may want to call Washington and maybe they can get you an answer a little bit quicker. With some of our recent reforms, we are acquiring a computerized system which will make it possible to push a button and get the status of any given bill at any moment, exactly what has happened to it, and what hearings have been held. This is an essential thing that Congress has not had in the past. It's not yet in operation, but will be very shortly.

27.
In-Fighting

AID: *May we talk about your race for majority leader?*

SISK: Sure. It was a rather peculiar series of events. This was back in the days of John McCormack when Hale Boggs was still alive, the year Carl Albert became Speaker. When Albert moved up to Speaker, that left open the majority leader spot. (This was in 1972 or thereabouts.) Hale Boggs was whip so he was going to run for majority leader. Hale was a very able congressman and leader. He was knowledgeable and was a powerful orator. He was from Louisiana and packed a good deal of weight in the South, even though he was considered very liberal for the South. He was respected in the North as being a liberal; he had gone along with civil rights matters, which was a bit unusual.

197

During the last term of John McCormack—Carl Albert was majority leader and Hale Boggs was whip—the pressure got to Hale. He was nearly the top ranking member on the Ways and Means Committee and was under heavy pressure on that committee. Wilbur Mills was chairman at the time. The oil companies had been very involved in Ways and Means—and always have been. There are great pressures from the oil industry in connection with tax arrangements, oil depletion allowances, and many other things. And there were other powerful forces at work in Ways and Means.

Boggs was feeling the pressure. Mills had had serious back surgery and was out of commission for a period of time. Therefore, Boggs was carrying a heavy load on that committee. (I am not trying to excuse him, but I am trying to be fair.) Anyway, he went off the deep end and became an alcoholic and totally irresponsible. I had a couple of problems with him through his aides, who were trying to cover for him. At times he didn't seem rational. He made an appearance before the Rules Committee and we felt he didn't even know where he was. Now whether this was alcohol or a combination of alcohol and drugs, I don't know.

In that summer or fall before the race, he came out to California with his wife, because she wanted to get him away from Washington. They were visiting the national parks with their grandson. Hale got lost in Sequoia National Park. There were some ugly stories. Because of all this, many people said something had to be done. Previously it had been assumed that he would automatically become majority leader.

People approached me, asking me if I would run for majority leader. At the same time, John Moss of our delegation indicated some interest in running. (I think John definitely wanted to run.) Many people said to me that there was no way John could win. John was one of the brightest, sharpest men with whom I served. He had an excellent mind, yet he had a way of getting on people's nerves; he could be very pompous in his speeches at times. He had rubbed people the wrong way to the extent that many felt he had no chance. This was the feeling within our delegation.

This matter had to be settled if California was going to be represented in the fight for the majority leadership. Our delegation had a meeting and Moss and I agreed to be bound by the vote of the delegation. The delegation, by secret ballot, nominated me. Unfortunately, I made a mistake and if I had it all to do over again, I would do it differently. I would say, "I am either going to have the full support of this delegation or I am not going to run." Originally I thought I had its full support, but some people had made other commitments, which I didn't know at the time. The fact that other commitments had been made hurt me later on. It soon became obvious I did not have the unanimous support of my own delegation, which I had assumed. I don't hold anything against people who had made other commitments. One of those who hurt my chances was

John McFall, who ultimately became Boggs' whip. (Despite the fact that my staff thought I was crazy, I later supported McFall.) My staff and some members of my delegation felt that a deal had been made. In this case, it was felt that Phil Burton and maybe one or two others had a commitment to Mo Udall, who had, in the meantime, gotten into this.

During the close of the previous session, in October, some newspaper people felt I had that race won. I remember one of our local personalities, who, according to his count, said I would win. However, several things happened. (Perhaps we got out in front too early.) A group of Hale's friends got hold of him. These were people who were interested in him because they wanted his support on Ways and Means. They brought Hale to Europe and dried him out and spent money and time. They got him back on the straight and narrow—and back into the fight.

At that point, the southerners who had strongly supported me began to say, "We absolutely must beat Udall." Udall became tinder that drew the fire. The question became, "Who can beat Udall?" They felt they could not take a chance. The people who normally supported Boggs were supporting me, so after he got back in the race, these former Boggs supporters began to wonder whether I could beat Udall if I didn't have the full support of my delegation. I didn't know enough about House politics to realize that as December approached, I was in serious trouble.

Another member who hurt me was Wayne Hays of Ohio, who got into the fight. On top of that, Jim O'Hara of Michigan got into it. Hale Boggs thought he was the rightful heir since he was dried out, and he became a powerful figure, there was no question. Udall was representing the so-called liberal bloc. He was a strong challenger whom we had not feared initially, but did later on. Divisiveness in the conservative bloc because of Hale Boggs, Wayne Hays, and my forces created a favorable situation for Mo Udall. Jim O'Hara was the strong labor candidate. It was felt that O'Hara would draw strength from Udall supporters, but that didn't happen. As it turned out, Jim O'Hara was the low man on the totem pole. (There were, all told, five people in the race.) O'Hara dropped out. Then Hays dropped out. That left three of us. I should have dropped out, but I had made commitments and decided to remain in—come what may. The southerners decided to support Boggs because he had the best chance to beat Udall. Some southerners voted for me, but not enough, and I was knocked out. Boggs beat Udall. Had Boggs not gotten himself straightened out, I think I would have become majority leader. Boggs did a good job, but his tenure was brief, just two years. After he was killed in the Alaskan airplane accident, his wife Lindy (Corinne C.) Boggs took his place in Congress. She is a person I respect, a very fine person.

AID: *May we talk about the 1977 fight for majority leader between Phil Burton and Jim Wright?*

SISK: I am perfectly willing to talk about it. I had been Burton's opponent for

199

Congressman Phil Burton, Democrat from San Francisco.

caucus chairman, yet I got into the race way too late. I was supported by the UDC group at that time, but we simply did not have enough power to take him out. Throughout Burton's reign as chairman of the caucus, the UDC acted as a moderator, trying to reduce conflicts. We worked closely with Bob Strauss, who was chairman of the Democratic National Committee. We claimed credit for having modified what we thought were wild resolutions that passed during the Miami convention, where George McGovern was nominated. That convention was pretty far off the deep end. It followed the Chicago [convention] fiasco which occurred four years before.

Getting back to the aftermath of some of these things, Burton felt it was the appropriate time for him to step up and become majority leader. Early on, I became committed to supporting McFall in that particular race. John was my next-door neighbor, representing Modesto at that time. I represented Modesto during my last four years in Congress. We had adjoining districts. McFall had been whip for several years. I felt he had done a good job. The Korean bribery scandal really blew his chances. Later, I sat down and talked frankly to John about the situation. I told him that I felt our chances of electing him were very, very thin, but since I had endorsed him, I was going to stick with him. I stayed with him and placed his name in nomination. In the background, however, I think there was a strong feeling by a substantial bloc of Democrats that Burton shouldn't win the leadership fight.

I am being completely frank without any intent to criticize Phil Burton, although we differed on political matters. Yet I respect his political knowledge. Phil knows that I opposed him very strongly on certain issues—and he opposed me. I and many other Democrats felt his attaining a position of leadership could be disastrous. I felt this country could not afford the expenditures and the kinds of budgetary considerations his leadership may have advocated. At that time we had a national debt approaching 600 or 700 billion dollars.

At any rate, Burton was very close to becoming majority leader. Except for the maneuvering of the Burton forces, Dick Bolling would have wound up, in my opinion, as the majority leader. In that race were four people: McFall, Bolling, Burton, and Wright. Jim Wright had gotten into the race rather late after some feeling Bolling couldn't swing it and real concern about what would happen if Burton got it. Dick Bolling is one of the most able legislators in the caucus, although there have been times when we have been on opposite sides and have had some bitter fights. Yet I had urged him, some years before, to run for majority leader. I would have supported him. At the time, I came to the conclusion that if McFall couldn't make it, I would support Dick Bolling, even though he was known to run roughshod over people. He was rather cold; he was not the type of person people warm up to. Other than this weakness, I think he would have been elected majority leader very easily.

Anyway, McFall dropped out; Bolling was up there with Burton and Wright. The Burton forces analyzed the situation. Under the rules of the caucus, once you start voting, you keep right on voting and don't stop. In other words, you vote and then count. (These are secret ballots.) After you count, you immediately call for the next vote so you are still maneuvering even as the voting is going on. Word got around that the Burton forces deliberately threw some votes to Wright in order to knock Bolling out of the race. This was the scuttlebutt on the floor of the House at the time. At any rate, this allegedly occurred during the second round of voting when three candidates (Wright, Burton, and Bolling) were in the race. A small group of Burton supporters cast votes for Wright to knock Bolling out because they felt they had a better chance of defeating Wright.

Sure enough, when the votes were counted Burton didn't gain, and may have lost a vote or two, which seemed to verify the story. Wright came up and Bolling, the low man of these three, was out. This was the position the Burton forces desired, because they felt they could beat Wright. The vote was very close, but Jim Wright became the majority leader by one vote. Burton was out not only as majority leader, but as chairman of the caucus.

Because we then elected Dan Rostenkowski of Chicago as chairman of the caucus, Burton always blamed a portion of the California delegation for not supporting him. I didn't vote for him and I didn't make any bones about it; he knew I wasn't supporting him. Others, I am sure, were as frank as I was. I didn't have any personal animosity toward him, but felt that the country just couldn't afford him—and I told him so.

AID: *How about Bizz Johnson and John Moss? Did they support Burton?*

SISK: It was a secret ballot, although I had an idea about how some voted.

28.
The State Delegation

AID: *We have talked about the caucus, but we haven't talked much about the state delegation. Within a state delegation, is there an attempt to gain a common ground of understanding between the Democratic and the Republican members? Do they meet?*

SISK: Yes, in California they do, but not necessarily in all states. Long ago the California delegation established a basis of interest between Republicans and Democrats because of our remoteness from Washington. You become very sensitive to this fact. The members from Pennsylvania, Maryland, Virginia, Delaware, New Jersey, and New York can go home every night; it's a different kind of a ball game.

It once took a congressman three days or more to travel by train across country to Washington—and he would stay there because he was 3,000 miles from home. In the old days, the House didn't provide a telephone allowance, so there wasn't much communication. When I first went to Washington, I didn't have enough allowance to wad a shotgun. I had only one paid trip a year to come back to California. If I made more than one trip a year, I paid for it out of my own pocket.

AID: *How often did you come home?*

SISK: I didn't come home very often because when I first went to Congress, we got paid $12,500 a year with a $2,500-a-year expense allowance, plus one paid round trip a year.

AID: *Before you retired, you got home about every three weeks?*

SISK: Now there is plenty of travel allowance, although I wouldn't consider it unlimited.

Getting back to your question—being from California, it was essential in so many cases that our interests here be bipartisan. The Democrats meet every Wednesday morning for breakfast and have for a number of years. The Republicans also have a weekly breakfast. The delegation as a whole meets at least once a month, generally. And it always meets on request. Let's say the American Legion or the VFW, or a particular group, comes to Washington in connection with docks or water, or a whole variety of problems. As long as it isn't a partisan matter, you have a delegation meeting.

We have been able to protect California because of that unity of interest; we were able to get special consideration in connection with EPA. This is the way in which we set up tougher air pollution provisions. We were able to put together enough California votes to beat back the eastern bloc on that issue. We had enough muscle with California Democrats and Republicans in unison.

AID: *Did you ever run for the chairman of the delegation?*

SISK: No, you don't run for that. When you get to be dean, you are there to stay; no one has ever been overthrown. That is part of the seniority system; although a person could be thrown out, it has never been done. Bizz Johnson, myself, Moss, and McFall were the oldest members, in that order. Bizz Johnson is the dean or the chairman of the delegation. It has always been strictly based on seniority.

AID: *Just a few more questions about the delegation. Before Viet Nam, it was a pretty united delegation—united on water, farm subsidies, highways, aerospace, military bases, and so forth. Viet Nam was the big split, the hawks versus the doves. Is this correct?*

SISK: I think that is correct. The first major split in the delegation was over Viet Nam.

AID: *Now you have growth versus ecology, energy versus environment, city versus suburb, and minorities versus majorities. Is the delegation badly split now?*

SISK: It is, unfortunately. I am sure you are aware of what the press has written about this new Congress. The California delegation is the largest in Washington—forty-three members of the House and two United States senators—for forty-five people. New York is down to about thirty-seven. The prestige and power of our delegation has fallen miserably in the last few years. I am not saying just within the last year. It is a tragic situation. There are still good people, don't misunderstand me. But unfortunately, because of petty jealousies, petty differences, and personal ambitions . . .

We didn't have this in the old days. There was a greater understanding then of the fact we were 3,000 miles from home and represented a big state with a lot of interests. We have to bury our own personal ambitions for the benefit of the state and the unity of the delegation. I really believed this and so did other members of the delegation. The delegation today has

Less than a third of the California congressional delegation is on hand for this 1976 photograph. Sisk is in bottom row at extreme left.

lost that, and a few members have been driven by personal ambition. You don't have to look very far to find them.

AID: *The delegation lost a lot of seniority. In the Ninety-fifth Congress seven California districts represented a total of 118 years of combined seniority. The present Congress has had a hundred years of California seniority wiped out.*

SISK: That's right.

AID: *I wonder if any of the present Californians in the Ninety-sixth Congress, in terms of committee assignments, have made up for the losses on Rules, Appropriations, and so forth?*

SISK: Not at the present time. I have been critical of the present delegation in my comments, but my criticism goes to the lack of unity and the unwillingness to lay aside personal ambitions for the good of the country and the delegation. I would say this if I met the delegation personally, particularly some individuals whom I blame. I don't think loss in seniority has led to that. Sure, seniority helps because as senior members you hold some key spots and wield a certain amount of political power, derived from being in a position to do some things for people who, in turn, are willing to do some things for you. Let's be cold turkey about it. That loss can be regained over a period of time if the delegation is willing to lay aside its personal animosities and ambitions, join together and help one another. For example, the delegation came up with a selection of Jerry Patterson to take my place on the Rules Committee. I was prepared to step aside, resigning from the Rules Committee early, to give an opportunity to the person selected to be assigned to Rules, which would give him seniority over other new members coming in. The Speaker vetoed that. He didn't say anything to me about it, but went to the delegation and said he wasn't going to appoint anybody—therefore, he wasn't going to accept my resignation. I stayed on the committee under that circumstance.

The Republicans, however, made a deal. Delbert Clawson from California, who was on the Republican side of the Rules Committee, stepped aside and the Republican conference appointed another man. Yet the Speaker refused to cooperate on our side. This raises questions in my mind about O'Neill, not from the standpoint of his ability as Speaker, but about his antagonism toward California and the West. Tip, in my opinion, has never been a good friend of ours in that sense. He is simply a New Englander who resents the power of the West. Ultimately we are going to clip the East's wings; there isn't any question because we have the power, the people. There is a natural movement in this direction and there isn't a thing he or anybody else can do about it. He can forestall it for the time being, which is what he has done at present. O'Neill flatly slapped the delegation in the face—a terrible blow politically—by taking another man on Rules. This is almost unheard of with a large state delegation. That shows the degree to which the delegation has fallen. This would not have been tolerated by the delegation at one time; it would have used certain powers to make a fool of him had he attempted it. Now the delegation can't turn on him as it could previously.

Unfortunately, we have almost been stripped of our appropriations power. We really took a beating on Appropriations. We lost two members on the Appropriations Committee and one of them was a chairmanship. On a number of committees we have new members, with good people like Tony Coelho. I think he will do a great job for us on Agriculture. However, these new representatives have little power to get anything done in Congress; they have no patronage to pass out. They're not in a position to do much for anybody. Whether you like it or not, that is pretty important in getting things done in the House of Representatives.

AID: *We have talked about a number of California leaders with the exception of Sam Hayakawa.*

SISK: Sam is an individual all his own who got there unexpectedly and in a rather unusual way. Yet Sam Hayakawa is not a dummy by any means; he's a pretty smart guy. They talk about how much he sleeps. All kinds of stories are told. I have seen times when Sam didn't know where he was because his staff hadn't told him. Of course, anybody brand new, going back to Washington, can get lost easily if the staff doesn't keep him guided. He got up before a California State Society party early on, at Bolling Air Force Base. Members of Congress were all introduced. Sam was late showing up. In fact, my wife and I were just on the way out and met him arriving. I said, "Sam, they are waiting for you in there." For some peculiar reason, he didn't know where he was. He got up and made a rip-roaring Republican speech to the California State Society, which is totally and very carefully bipartisan. Of course, there are more Democrats there than Republicans. It went over like a lead balloon. Sam got off on the wrong foot and got his reputation.

Sam Hayakawa has been a friend of mine. I have asked him for some help on the Senate side. He has done some things for me. Just to give you an idea, a couple of years ago I made an arrangement with the park service and concessionaires of Yosemite National Park for a Christmas party for the delegation. I put it together rather carefully. Yosemite was in my district. We had invited the entire delegation and their spouses, both Democrats and Republicans, to the Ahwahnee Hotel. It was strictly a bipartisan affair. We were expecting everybody to come home. This was arranged early in December, around the tenth; we were assuming Congress was going to get out by that time. We had a two-day program arranged so everyone could see the park and enjoy some fellowship and meet with the park service people and the concessionaires. There have been a lot of rumbles going on up there; the master plan has been very controversial in Yosemite.

As so often happens when you plan something, a real dogfight occurred in Congress. The Yosemite party was planned for Friday and Saturday and we would return to Washington on Sunday. On Friday, Congress was still fighting. Most of the Californians called me and cancelled. John Krebs and his wife came. Sam Hayakawa had accepted. He got on an airplane in Washington on Friday morning and flew to San Francisco. His wife met him with their car and they drove and arrived late in the evening. It was snowing hard in Yosemite and it was beautiful, but the snow made driving slow. I kidded the delegation afterwards: "They talk about the old man sleeping, but, by gosh, he was one of the few people who had the guts to get on an airplane and then drive his wife to Yosemite." They stayed for two days. I really like Sam. I think he says things that are misinterpreted. I don't know what his future is. He came to this job rather late in life.

AID: *What was the apparent affront to you from the Republicans in 1958 that marred a dinner?*

SISK: In Washington?

AID: *Yes.*

SISK: That I remember. I just mentioned the California State Society. The California State Society is an important part of the social functions in Washington for Californians, since we are 3,000 miles from home and isolated. This group has been active and close-knit. The society is composed of all Californians in Washington, not just the delegation. There are members of the staffs of the delegation and the executive branch agencies—like the Agriculture Department. We probably have, in Washington, about two or three thousand people from California. There are newspaper people, executives, civil servants, people in research, and others, in the society.

The delegation is the lightning rod since normally, a member of the delegation is president of the California State Society. Traditionally, it alternates back and forth between Republicans and Democrats. A board of trustees which runs the society meets about once a month. It plans a year's program, including five or six parties or receptions. A big picnic is held the first Saturday of June in Potomac Park. There may be a thousand people there, including the kids, with hot dogs and baseball. There are some formal parties at times, e.g., one big party early on every year, for the election of the society president.

The board of trustees selects a committee to nominate the officers. Members talk to people, since many don't particularly want to be officers because there are certain work obligations. Toward the end of 1957 the committee nominated me for president and I accepted. Nineteen fifty-eight was an unusual political year, the year of the trade-out between Bill Knowland and Goody Knight. Knowland was the United States senator and Knight was governor of California. The Republicans outnumbered

Above left: Rep. Sisk dispenses punch to Mrs. William Knowland, Arthur Younger, second from right, and Sen. William Knowland at a 1958 California State Society gala held in Washington. Sisk was temporarily deprived of the society presidency following a partisan prank during the 1958 affair.
Above right: Sisk and Reta, joined by Modesto Democrat John McFall, right, attend the society party in 1958.

the Democrats in those days—two-to-one when I went to Congress. Elections of officers for the society are cut and dried, so when the slate is announced by the nominating committee, it is already in.

This happened to be a big champagne party. Bill Knowland and his wife were there, also two or three bull-headed Republicans from Southern California. Edgar W. Hiestand from Orange County apparently had too much champagne. Arthur Younger, a Republican from San Mateo County, was the president concluding his term of one year. He was a good friend of mine, and was involved in my selection to succeed him. Everything was cut and dried.

What happened then was peculiar and had repercussions in Knowland's campaign. The president asked for the report of the nominating committee. After that report was given, according to the democratic process, the president asked if there were any other nominations. Someone moved to close the nominations. At that point, Edgar Hiestand jumped up and nominated a Republican member (who had no intention of serving). The group was having a good time and thought this was a gag. Nobody felt there was any partisanship, except Hiestand, probably. Anyway, this Republican was elected. At that point, poor Art Younger was caught in the middle. Bill Knowland was terribly embarrassed. He was there to get support from Democrats, because he was going to run for governor. Afterward, everybody was upset. Some Democrats resigned from the society and never again attended. It almost blew the society out the window—a kind of tragedy. I, too, thought the thing was a joke to start with. The party broke up pretty quickly. The next day Art Younger called an emergency meeting of the board of trustees.

To make a long story short (I was on the board), we agreed Art Younger would serve one more term. This was the first and only time a person had an extended term. The Republican (named Jackson from Los Angeles) whom Hiestand had nominated didn't want any part of it and apologized to me. Knowland was especially upset and wrote me a personal apology, saying it was a shame and a disgrace that the society was used as a partisan vehicle. Art Younger never ceased to apologize. It was one of those crazy things that happen when too much liquor has been consumed. I became president the following term.

29.
Impressions of National Figures

AID: *We are now getting into an area which will touch on your evaluations and impressions. You served with six presidents—Dwight Eisenhower, John Kennedy, Lyndon Johnson, Richard Nixon, Jerry Ford, and Jimmy Carter. There were also vice-presidents Hubert Humphrey, Spiro Agnew, Nelson Rockefeller, and Walter Mondale. I was wondering if you would give your impressions of each of these individuals, particularly with these facts in mind for the executives: Did he exhibit a creative approach? Did he use the prestige and potential of his position? Did he staff his key government posts effectively? I understand that you have prepared a very interesting address on this subject.*

SISK: The speech I have developed since I retired contains my own observations and appraisals of six presidents with whom I had the opportunity,, the honor and privilege of serving. These observations and appraisals are strictly *my* impressions. I was elected early in the Eisenhower Administration. Eisenhower took office on January 20, 1953. I went to Congress in January of 1955, so I served throughout the bulk of the Eisenhower years. In my opinion, Eisenhower came along during an appropriate time in the history of the country. We had been through the mill, so to speak, from the standpoint of pressure, passion and emotion, induced by all kinds of critical events. Roosevelt, a driver, had come up with broad social legislation in an attempt to meet domestic crises. There was the most profound world calamity in the form of the greatest war ever fought. The pressures continued after World War II because of existing shortages. There were the stresses of production. People wanted to get back into normal civilian life. As I see it, Americans were a tired people.

They had been kicked, shoved, and yelled at. They were waiting for a president who would let them sit back and relax and flow with the tide. Eisenhower was that type.

My impression was that Eisenhower didn't disturb anyone's sleep; he really didn't do anything much—but that is what people wanted at the time. I think that Eisenhower, himself, didn't know what he was politically; the Democrats had tried to nominate him. Eisenhower's legislative programs were of little consequence. His idea was to do as little as possible, not upset anything, and get people back to a period of peace and tranquility. But he was a stickler for protocol; he had grown up with very strict protocol. Many people (including my wife) feel Eisenhower protected the prestige and the tradition of the White House. For White House receptions, he insisted on white ties and tails. Those of us who had to wear full evening dress were not all that intrigued about it.

AID: *Will you tell the story about the White House party at which you had to wear a white tie and tails for the first time?*

SISK: I had worn a tux in college, but I have never been much for fancy dress; I had never before attempted to dress in a white tie and tails. One of the first things we attended when I went to Washington was a full-dress White House reception. What I—and practically every other member of Congress—did was rent a suit with tails and all the paraphernalia that goes with it. Fortunately, I picked these things up a couple of days ahead of time and took a look at them. I wasn't quite sure how I was going to get it all on. We decided to have a dress rehearsal the night before so I could get all the pieces together. My wife and I got pretty well tangled up and I had to call up Jackson Carle (he and his wife, Eunice, lived in the same apartment complex we did) and ask him to come over so he could straighten the situation out. We finally found all the pieces and got them together, so I was able to get dressed the next evening.

My wife and I arrived at the reception at twilight. There was one thing I still wasn't sure about. Ties are made with these clip-up corners and I was wondering whether the corners bent down and went inside or outside the tie. We were all super-conscious and sensitive about these things. I walked in and there were all my colleagues. One of them had his tie tucked in so I very carefully moved my tie inside. The next guy I saw had his tie outside and I thought it looked better that way so I slipped mine out. My wife feels this way about dressing up: There is only an occasional opportunity to go to the White House, and since the presidency is the highest office we can afford any American, it isn't all that unusual to dress formally for White House receptions. She favorably compares the formality of Eisenhower's parties with the informality of Johnson's.

At the end of Eisenhower's term in 1960, people were again ready for a challenge. We had coasted along for a number of years. Nothing much had happened. There was new pressure from the black community for civil rights legislation and pressure for federal action from other minority groups. School desegregation had been ordered by the Supreme Court in 1954 and had brought about a rather dramatic change. At the same time, little had been done in the areas of housing, jobs, and occupational training.

Kennedy came along next. I attended the Democratic convention in Los Angeles in 1960 as a Johnson delegate. I had become quite well-acquainted with Lyndon Johnson through Sam Rayburn and my Texas connections. Congressman Cecil King and I flew out to California with Johnson in the spring in order to help him launch his campaign. We worked hard at it. State Senator Hugh Burns was convinced (by me) to help us.

AID: *He was the one who got your billboards?*

SISK: Yes. In spite of the fact I was a Johnson delegate and worked very hard for Johnson, once Kennedy was nominated, I was intrigued with the possibility of the Kennedy campaign. I had no personal campaigning to do in 1960 because I won a double nomination, although cross-filing was out. (The cross-filing system used to be a disaster for Democrats.) Because the Republicans had not, for some reason, come up with a suitable candidate by the filing deadline, they dreamed up the idea of nominating a candidate by a write-in campaign. Our people thought we would take a shot at it to see what we could do on a write-in. We won the write-in and secured the Republican and Democratic nominations. The Republicans sent me the bill for the filing fee—and I paid it. Afterwards, I told them that they should have had enough respect for me to pay the filing fee.

AID: *I can just hear some Kiwanis Republican saying to his friends, "What's the matter with you Republicans? You can't even get a Republican nominated."*

SISK: I had no personal campaign so time permitted me to become active in the Kennedy campaign. I think a lot of money is wasted in national campaigns. For example, in 1960, although I had been in Congress for six years, I was certainly not a national figure. Yet the Democratic National Committee immediately grabbed me. One of the trips booked for me interfered with a dinner meeting here in Fresno. I remember it well because I had a severe head cold. They rushed in and concluded this dinner so I could get a 9:00 P.M. private flight to Los Angeles, where I would then catch an American Airlines flight to Washington at 11:30 P.M. This was so I could get to Harrisburg, Pennsylvania to make a speech the next day.

I spoke in Pennsylvania, Grant County, West Virginia, and Fairmont, West Virginia. They were double-booking—a kind of fake deal. They would get $100-a-plate dinners set up and Bobby Kennedy would be scheduled to be there. At the last minute, naturally, Bob Kennedy couldn't

With Kennedy and Johnson in 1962. This photo is a personal favorite of Sisk's.

be there. Consequently, "We are sending Congressman Sisk from California." You can imagine it was a tough deal. With travel and other costs, I wonder how much money is wasted on these national campaigns. By the time Kennedy was elected, I had become a great supporter of his.

AID: *You went from the Johnson camp to the Kennedy camp?*

SISK: Yes. An agreement had been made that Johnson would be the vice-president if Kennedy were elected, so this unified the situation.

People were willing to accept a challenge that Kennedy brought: "Ask not what your country can do for you, but what you can do for your country." People were ready to get back into the harness and be aggres-

With Kennedy at the White House, 1962.

sive. Jack Kennedy came into office as an idol to a great many people. Actually, he was quite controversial; you either loved or hated him. World wide, though, I don't think there has been an American president so idolized. This was so, whether it was Latin America, Europe, Asia, the Middle East, or wherever.

Jack Kennedy stood out in a grandiose style to the peoples of the world. He had the kind of qualities people look for in a leader. This was Camelot. He accepted full responsibility for the Bay of Pigs fiasco, and this helped, rather than hurt, him. I myself came to idolize Kennedy. This is why his death hit me as hard as it did. I couldn't speak of it even a couple of years later without having to shed tears. Kennedy had been so senselessly taken away from us. It was a traumatic thing. I have mentioned that I worked closely with the Kennedy Administration. Incidentally, after one trial with white tie and tails, Kennedy dispensed with them at White House functions, having observed the ridiculous state of the members of Congress. He went to tuxedos and it has been so ever since, at least at the White House.

I remember Jack Kennedy's dedication to civil rights. I was one of a small group of Democrats selected to work with Bob Kennedy, who was attorney general, in order to sell the administration's civil rights bill on the House floor. We have talked about this before—the presidential yachts in the evenings, etc. Yet Jack Kennedy had a very poor legislative record. We Democrats in the House were facing something new. Before Kennedy, we had dealt with a Republican administration, fighting a Republican president. All of a sudden the executive was our man, our administration. We had problems shifting gears. You will see this from time to time when opposition changes to support. Despite the fact Kennedy's legislative record was very poor, he was a very popular president. After the traumatic death, Lyndon Johnson became president.

AID: *Before you get to Johnson, you didn't mention Ted Kennedy. The newspapers, just this morning [July 1979] said Ted Kennedy's family has released him. His family is no longer opposing his candidacy for the presidency. Would you give your impressions of Ted Kennedy?*

SISK: In the early sixties, I hardly knew Ted. I had met him, but in Washington he was not yet a significant figure and not well-known. Since that time, I have come to know him, but I was never as close to him as I was to his two brothers.

My personal opinion of Ted Kennedy is that he does not match John Kennedy's ability to do the job. On the other hand, many people feel Ted is a better legislator and has a better basic knowledge of government than Jack had. Yet after the Chappaquiddick incident, many people wonder about a man who could make such a mistake. However, we all look back and see we have made a few ourselves. I have no strong feelings one way or the other about Teddy.

Getting back to Johnson, it was a unique occurrence—legislative pressures had built up for all kinds of social legislation. Civil rights was one example. There were a variety of domestic needs. All of a sudden, the Congress got into the harness. The Congress went with Johnson lock, stock, and barrel—100 percent. There was more done in the first six months of the Johnson Administration than in the three years Kennedy was in office. This is not a reflection on Jack Kennedy; it is the reflection of the times and the emotionalism of the people. The five or six years of Johnson's presidency reveal a fantastic legislative record. The personalities of Kennedy and Johnson were worlds apart. Johnson was rough-and-tumble and informal. He served chili at the White House and you went to these occasions dressed informally. My wife said Johnson was just too informal and that hurt the prestige of the White House. I am sure some of the other spouses of congressmen felt that way. It was a rare occasion when you wore a tux for a Johnson dinner. Normally, you went in your business suit, coming from the office. Johnson may have been informal, but he got things done. You have to give him credit. Johnson knew more about the legislative process than any other president with whom I served.

Johnson had his faults. He had a temper that wouldn't quit. I've seen some demonstrations. He *really* had a temper. He could use all the cuss words. But in the final analysis, he did a lot for blacks, minorities, and the poor of this country. In some cases I think he went a little too far. Don't

213

misunderstand me, I am not against helping people who need it, but some of Johnson's programs overlapped. We are still undoing some of the mistakes we made during those years.

Then, of course, Viet Nam began to expand. In a sense, the Viet Nam situation started back in the Eisenhower days and built up under Kennedy. I am not trying to be political or blame anybody because this was an outgrowth of the American people's desire to see everybody free and living in a democracy. We didn't recognize that many people in the world lack any idea of what democracy is. We were idealists, star-gazers. We were going to protect everyone in the world. Although we got bruised in Korea, we got right back into another war in Viet Nam. Johnson was one of those gung-ho boys who believed in the protection of this country, and in democracy and freedom. Unfortunately, I think he got some bad advice, but that is beside the point.

I was never critical of Johnson over Viet Nam like a lot of people were. I remember sitting in the Oval Office, next to Johnson, with others around the table. For an hour and a half we agonized over the Viet Nam policy. Nobody but nobody agonized more over Viet Nam than Lyndon Johnson. He was desirous of getting us out of there and getting our boys home. This is true in spite of all the attacks and charges. He almost shed tears over it. This is why I get a little resentful of some of the criticism directed at him. Mistakes were made, admittedly, whether he or his advisors made them. Viet Nam finally defeated him.

With Lyndon Johnson in 1966.

Congressional leaders take time out from a Viet Nam policy briefing moderated by President Lyndon B. Johnson, seated center. Sisk recalls that the session, which took place in May 1967, was marked by some two hours of "anguishing." Sisk is seated at extreme left.

In 1968, the Democrats went to Chicago and made complete fools of themselves. We got into a situation with left-wing radical groups and all kinds of terrorist activities. We nominated a good man, in my opinion, one of the most knowledgeable in the country. I think it is a tragedy that Hubert Humphrey was not elected president of the United States. I know that many people said he talked too much. He probably did, but he was one of the few people I knew who could talk intelligently on every subject under the shining stars. There was a man who was as brilliant as any I have ever met. He was an outstanding man. I believe he might have been a great president.

AID: *How was Johnson able to get civil rights legislation through despite southern caucus opposition?*

SISK: Through persuasion and some real tough arm-twisting. Johnson was the type of person who, when the chips were down and he needed a vote, didn't pull any punches. He was a good, tough negotiator.

AID: *Were you doing some of the arm-twisting?*

SISK: I supported Johnson and was of assistance wherever I could be. I was working in the group trying to pass his legislative program. I was in support of the civil rights bill.

AID: *What was the key that got civil rights through?*

SISK: I think the country changed. Even in the South, some rather liberal legislators were being elected to Congress. The word got out, "The time has come. We can no longer bury our heads in the sand and go with the [Harry F.] Byrd machine." So southerners, including Hale Boggs of Louisiana (whom I have mentioned before), and Georgians, including Carl Vinson, began to take a hard look at, and supported, civil rights. There was a new breeze blowing, so to speak.

AID: *Did rural Republicans ever change, voting in favor of civil rights?*

SISK: Yes and no. There was a very serious split in the Republican Party—as there is today—into liberal and conservative wings. With Johnson's leadership and the pressures he brought to bear, a sufficient number of Republicans went along with him on civil rights. There was also a sufficient Democratic bloc that stayed with him. Of course, the liberal bloc was with him all the way. Johnson was also able to get votes from the South. Although he wasn't a real southerner, he was the next thing to it. He put the pieces together. Johnson won passage for civil rights and voting rights legislation I don't think anyone else could have successfully pushed at that time.

AID: *Before we leave our discussion of Johnson, I'd like your impressions of a statement of how he worked as president and as majority leader. It has been said that "of every Democratic senator, he knew his strengths and his failings; where he fitted into the political spectrum; how far he could be pushed or pulled, and his hates and his loves. Moreover, he oversaw these prima donnas; he put them to work; he knitted them together; he knew when to tickle one's vanity; to inquire of that one's health; to remember this one's five o'clock nip of Scotch and that one's nagging wife. He found the legislative path between the South and the North; public power men and private power men; farmer men and union men; the bomber boys and the peace lovers; and eggheads and fatheads." [Laughter]*

SISK: I think that is a good statement. It indicates that he was a man of many seasons. Since we are commenting on him, a couple of days ago I ran across a letter. The cover letter is dated March 15, 1967 and is from the White House, Washington, D.C. "Dear Bernie: The President noted with deep appreciation your recent remarks on the floor of the House and has asked me to send you the enclosed letters. Sincerely, Henry." This was from Henry H. Wilson, Jr., administrative assistant to the president. He forwarded this letter: "The White House, Washington, D.C., March 13, 1967. Dear Bernie: I want to thank you for your kind words on the floor of the House last week. It is, as I am sure you realize, a great comfort to me to know that I have your continued support in these difficult times. The decisions we must make, the policies we must carry out are neither easily arrived at nor lightly borne. Your help and understanding have made our task less burdensome. Sincerely, Lyndon Johnson."

AID: *I interrupted you when you were talking about Humphrey.*

SISK: When 1968 came along, we nominated Humphrey in Chicago under a

President Lyndon B. Johnson greets fellow Texan Sisk at a White House reception in June 1967.

near tragic situation. People were reacting against Viet Nam. The people chose Nixon, although I am not sure why. Again, the Congress was faced with a conservative administration. Nixon wanted to be a great president, yet he had certain weak characteristics, which I felt he demonstrated back in the late 1940s during his early races in California. Unfortunately, his shortcomings came into focus later on. I sometimes wonder why Agnew was selected as Nixon's vice-president. Agnew sort of appeared without anybody knowing what he amounted to.

Considering Agnew's forced resignation, Ford's subsequent appointment, and Nixon's resignation over Watergate, we went through some unbelievable events. I hope, as I am sure everyone does, that these will never recur. It was an historic period in which to be a part of government, but the situation was tragic. Young people's faith in government was terribly damaged. We still have a long way to go to restore the confidence of the American people in our system. This is the great tragedy of Watergate. In Congress, we had our failures—and they didn't help either. The Watergate scandal and Congress's own failures created an unfortunate climate resulting in a great loss of credibility.

AID: *When the Watergate scandal began to percolate, what was the atmosphere in Congress?*

SISK: Many people felt as I did—very suspicious. We thought Nixon was more heavily involved than it appeared on the surface. But perhaps the majority of members felt that Nixon, elected by the American people to the high office of the presidency, would not descend to practicing unethical actions. However, those of us who witnessed Nixon's con-

217

gressional race and his senatorial race out here in California, and finally his "Checkers speech," had long since lost confidence in his integrity. For this reason, we were more skeptical. Most people felt he would weather the storm, despite the fact that it was a messy deal.

AID: *After the "Saturday Night Massacre" (during which Special Prosecutor Archibald Cox was fired), did you feel you were going to vote for the impeachment of Nixon?*

SISK: Yes, I did. At that point I felt he would be impeached. The firing of Cox was revealing to me. Although I didn't have prior knowledge, I felt that impeachment was going to be in order.

AID: *Tip O'Neill then placed the matter before the Judiciary Committee, headed by Peter Rodino. Did this seem to be a logical choice?*

SISK: Yes, the Judiciary Committee was the logical committee to choose, having jurisdiction over that particular area. This was true historically. There were some members who had qualms about what Pete Rodino and members of the Judiciary Committee might do; they might not be strong enough or tough enough to handle this investigation properly. Rodino was fairly new as chairman. He had recently taken over from Manny [Emanuel] Celler, who had been chairman for many years. There was some feeling this matter should be given to a special committee or a select committee rather than the Judiciary Committee. But as it turned out, the Judiciary Committee's handling of the matter justified the decision to give the panel the assignment.

AID: *This is a minor point: Nixon's most fervent supporter in the House was Earl Landgrebe.*

SISK: Yes, Landgrebe was a very staunch supporter of Nixon.

AID: *What was your impression of him?*

SISK: I knew Landgrebe as an ultra-conservative—so much so that he was never considered a heavyweight in the Congress. Many of his colleagues—even Republicans—thought of him as a lightweight, not a person with great influence.

AID: *In your opinion, would the House have voted to impeach Nixon?*

SISK: In my opinion, it would have. I firmly believe that if Nixon had attempted to sit it out and not resign, the votes would have been there to impeach him. You understand that voting to impeach meant simply putting him on trial. There were those who had reservations about every aspect of this investigation, but still would have voted for impeachment so Nixon could at least be brought to trial. All the House can do is put him on trial before the Senate.

Let me say this about Richard Nixon: With all my doubts and concerns about him—and I had many of them over the years—our relations, in a personal sense, were fairly friendly. Nixon was a Californian who visited our delegation occasionally. From time to time, we exchanged pleasantries, as you will with anyone you know, even though you don't know him well. I had no personal animosity toward Nixon. I never went out of my way to cut him to pieces. My questions concerned some of his actions. In fairness to Nixon—in spite of the bad things he did, the terrible mistakes he made, and his tragic part in destroying (to some extent) the confidence of the American people in our system—he did one thing no Democratic president could have done. He opened the door to China. There is no question that we had been living in an idealistic world. We refused to recognize the practical facts of life. This is a dangerous indulgence for a nation.

We as individuals can get away with a little more idealism. But for nations, living in the real world—and a pretty dangerous world—I don't think it is good to get too idealistic. We had been going along with the theory that Taiwan was China. We were ignoring the fact of life that the People's Republic of China does, in fact, exist. It's the largest nation on earth. Had a Democratic president attempted to open the door to China, he would have been driven out of the country on a rail.

AID: *And Nixon would have ridden him out.*

SISK: That's right, he would have been leading the pack.

I have looked at past presidents. I am a nut on history. Presidents seem to rise to meet their challenges. I don't care from what source they came, how backwoods they may have been, or how little thought of they were at the time; in most cases, once given a challenge, a president rises to meet it. There is something to the insight "the job makes the man." We have had a few presidents over the years who have had their weaknesses, for example, alcohol. In the final analysis, considering that presidents have come from every walk of life, they—and we—haven't done too badly. Peculiarly enough, certain men have come along at a time when each could do a particular job that needed doing—a job nobody else could have done.

Because of his reputation over the years as a strong anti-communist, Nixon was the only man who could have approached China. No Democrat could have gotten away with it at all—even a "normal" Republican could not have done it. You have to give the devil his due.

AID: *What was your opinion of Gerald Ford's pardon of Nixon?*

SISK: I thought it was a terrible mistake on the part of Ford—a very big political mistake.

AID: *You sat with him on the space committee?*

SISK: Yes. I have a great deal of respect for Jerry. I worked very closely with him even after he became vice-president. He was very helpful to me with my baseball activities for Washington, D.C. In fact, he and I flew to the opening game in Cincinnati when he was vice-president. (That was the year Hank Aaron broke Babe Ruth's career home run record.) If it weren't for Jerry's pardoning of Nixon there is no question in my mind Ford would have won the next election. The pardon killed him politically.

219

Members of the House Rules and Judiciary committees pause in the Rules Committee's Capitol building chambers to pay tribute to then-Minority Leader Gerald Ford following 1973 hearings on his nomination for vice-president. Rep. Sisk is seated at the main table, at right. Ford is sixth from right.

Ford was the type of person we needed as president at the time of Nixon's resignation. People had been through the agony of Watergate. Ford was like a knight in shining armor, a reputable man. He was uninvolved in scandalous events. He seemed to have a good marriage and to be of decent stature. Although not regarded as a great thinker, he was an honest man. And that is what we needed at that time—a simple, honest man. Ford—to a large extent—filled the bill. I am sad that he only served two years. Maybe he should have served six years.

Of course, this is for history to decide. Jerry, in my opinion, did a good job. As I have said, the one big mistake he made was pardoning Nixon—and it hurt him worse than anyone else. In Jerry's mind, the pardon was the quickest way to get rid of a bad situation. Here was the president of the United States, the man who held the highest office in the power of the American people to bestow, essentially under indictment. No president should have to go to trial and possibly go to prison. This was probably Jerry's opinion. Even though Jerry committed political suicide, he had the courage to do what he thought was right. I don't know how wise other alternatives might have been.

Ford's reign was brief, but I think he did as well as he could under the circumstances. His foreign policy was adequate; he was concerned with the security of this country. I have never served with a president who was not for a strong national defense. Most presidents probably want to spend more for national defense than the average American would like. Ford lost in 1976 and along came Carter.

Sisk greets President Jimmy Carter in 1977.

Let me say this about Carter: I believe he is an honest, dedicated, sincere American and the first true southerner to be elected president since the Civil War. Carter wanted to be a good president, but never in the history of this country—in my opinion—have we elected a man who was more naive and had less understanding of the relationship between the Congress and the president. Instead of getting political expertise—men who knew Congress and lived in Washington—to help him with this problem, he brought in the so-called Georgia team, which was as naive as he was. That has been the tragedy of the Carter Administration.

AID: *The only vice-president you haven't yet mentioned is Walter Mondale.*

SISK: I think it is unfortunate that the tickets weren't reversed—Mondale as president and Carter as vice-president. The country might have been in better shape.

I became fairly well-acquainted with Fritz Mondale early on, around 1975 or thereabouts. At one point, he was running as a potential Democratic [presidential] candidate. I set up a luncheon meeting for him in Turlock and Fresno in the spring of 1975. I flew to San Francisco and picked up Mondale and brought him here. Through that, I became pretty well-acquainted with him, although I had met him as a senator only briefly. Walt Mondale is an able guy. He was a devoted follower and admirer of Hubert Humphrey. He has certain attributes of Humphrey's although he isn't as vocal as Hubert was. I am sure he doesn't have the mind Hubert had, but in looking at the situation, as young as Mondale is, he could be the Democratic solution to what I think could be a rather serious situation in the 1980 election.

AID: *You mentioned Manny Celler. He was chairman of the Judiciary Committee during hearings on the question of prayer in public schools. You played a very interesting role in that.*

SISK: I was in that controversy early on, around the time the Supreme Court rendered its initial decision on prayer in public schools (there were two or three decisions, but I think this dealt with the New York case, as I recall). I read that decision to determine what the Court had said and what the various comments of the justices were. I concluded the decision of the Supreme Court of the United States was misunderstood. The Court did not say there was anything wrong with prayer. Its decision referred to a government-dictated prayer—some kind of set prayer.

I am a strong believer in separation of church and state. I think the Founding Fathers wrote this principle into the Constitution. Although I believe very strongly in prayer, am a practitioner of prayer, attend church, and have been active throughout the years in my church, I interpreted the Court as substantiating what the Founding Fathers said. Upon coming to this conclusion after reading the Court decision, I was willing to state my position—as I did on the House floor on a few occasions and in public. (I wrote my opinion in response to letters I received.)

At times I found myself in an unpopular position. Some local people here were upset. I came to Fresno and talked to ministerial groups and church organizations. Great pressure was exerted by various national groups. (In particular, there was a radio preacher in Pennsylvania who was broadcasting nationally.) Many were being misled about what the Court had said.

There was pressure on the Congress to draft a constitutional amendment. I abhorred the idea of amending the Constitution of the United States in this area because we had gotten along well for two hundred years with an accepted separation of church and state. The pressure built up so much that despite his own opposition, Manny set up hearings. One day Manny and I were at the same lunch table. After some discussion (he had read something in the record about my position), he said, "Why don't you come before my committee and testify?" I said, "I don't think what I have to say on this would be significant. Why should I take up the time of your committee? As a member of Congress, I am reluctant to go before committees when they have public witnesses to hear." He said, "Yes, but I would like you to come over." I said, "Okay. I feel strongly on this subject. I think it would be tragic for your committee to bring a constitutional amendment to the floor and I hope it never happens." I appeared before his committee. Apparently my testimony pretty much coincided with Celler's own point of view.

AID: *He called your testimony "a breath of fresh air."*

SISK: I didn't realize this at the time, but I was the first member of Congress to testify before his committee in opposition to the constitutional amendment allowing prayer in public schools. The press—especially the religious press, which was gung-ho on this issue—publicized my testimony and we were bombarded with letters by the thousands. I think I still have two or three thousand in my files. They said, for example, that I was a communist. It was a rough deal, but fortunately there wasn't much opposition to my position in my district. I got a lot of support in my district, although some people disagreed with me.

However, this is an example of what happens when you get into a very serious controversy in Congress. I think most of my constituents respected the fact that I took a position, whether or not they agreed with it. I understand there was a priest from a Catholic church on the west side who delivered a sermon against me once a month. Yet I had a lot of support from the Catholic church. I have never been an anti-Catholic, although I did take positions which didn't agree with the church; for instance, federal aid to education. The local diocese, in its regular publication, outlined in black my letter to the monsignor which stated my position. (The monsignor and I had exchanged letters on the subject of prayer in school.) I had a reputation for speaking my mind. Frankly, I think that, throughout the years, I won the respect of people for speaking out because I was at least being honest about my positions.

AID: *We have talked at some length about Speakers Sam Rayburn, John McCormack, and Carl Albert. I don't think we have talked at much length about Tip O'Neill, current Speaker.*

SISK: I will do this as quickly as possible. Of course, Sam Rayburn, to me, was the greatest Speaker who ever served in Congress. I have served with only four Speakers, so my objectivity might not be as good as it should be. Rayburn stands out as a bright and shining light. He served as Speaker of the House of Representatives more than twice as long as any other man in history.

AID: *Were you in Congress when Rayburn gave a very moving tribute to his late friend, Alben Barkley?*

SISK: Yes. I served with Alben Barkley. I couldn't quote what Rayburn said, but I recall it was a tremendously moving thing. Rayburn was not an orator in the sense of Martin Dies or some of the old-time southern politicians, but he had a very sincere way of speaking. He never spoke unless he had something to say. He had a very direct and earthy way of saying things. His tribute in this case was one of the great, outstanding tributes ever paid to a colleague in the Congress of the United States. His respect and love and admiration for Barkley came through.

Below: Speaker Thomas P. "Tip" O'Neill, Democrat from Massachusetts.

Above: Sam Rayburn, Speaker of the House and the man some say regarded Sisk as a protege, accepts a shipment of raisins from the Fresno congressman.
Below: Sisk clasps the hand of retired Speaker John McCormack during the latter's 1978 visit to Capitol Hill.

AID: *Would you like to discuss in more detail the other Speakers with whom you served?*

SISK: Okay. John McCormack came along with Rayburn's big shoes to fill. I think John McCormack made a good Speaker, and that history will record John as a much better Speaker than the media gave him credit for being, because he was in the shadow of the great man who had preceded him.

Following McCormack, Albert came along. Unfortunately, Albert was caught in the shadow of much greater men—Carl, known as "the little giant from little Dixie," was not in the same category. Carl and I served on the Agriculture Committee together. He was from Oklahoma, born just across the Red River from where I was born. We were good friends and I liked Carl, and I tried to help him. Carl had some weaknesses here and there. In light of the problems he faced, the transitions occurring with the Young Turks coming in and a total change in the complexion of the House taking place, he did the best he could. I don't know how history will record him.

O'Neill had no background in leadership other than as a member of the Committee on Rules. He and I served together on Rules, side by side, for close to fifteen years. I knew Tip O'Neill as well as any non-Massachusetts man knew him. Generally, we voted together. He was the typical "Irish Mafia" type of guy; that is just an expression used up there. I had not felt that Tip was a heavyweight. I remember the discussion about his running for majority leader when Hale Boggs passed away. I have already mentioned that I supported Dick Bolling for majority leader, even though we weren't that close, out of a desire to see a strong hand and my feeling that Carl Albert was not as strong a Speaker as we might have had.

We needed a strong hand as majority leader to give Albert help—to be his back-up—that's what the majority leader is supposed to do. I did not see that in Tip. Bolling saw fit not to run. I remember the comment he made to me: "After all, Tip is a great back-slapper and that's really about all you need and it will be all right." I didn't agree with that statement—and I still don't. Anyway, Tip became majority leader. As majority leader he didn't stay on the floor as much as he should have, and many people felt he didn't have much interest in the job. He left an awful lot of it to McFall, the whip (or assistant majority leader). Yet when Tip inherited the Speakership after Carl Albert retired, he improved.

My honest opinion is that he has done a much better job as Speaker than as majority leader. As Speaker, he has spent time and effort to do a good job. Tip and I have had serious disagreements over the years and I was frank enough to tell him when I disagreed with him. On the other hand, we have worked together at times.

AID: *Who was the strongest majority leader?*

SISK: John McCormack. There is no question about that.

AID: *We mentioned Jim Wright briefly. Is there anything special that you want to say about him?*

SISK: Jim has done a good job. Jim Wright came to Congress with me in the class of 1954, the Eighty-fourth Congress. He was from Fort Worth, not far from where I was born. I urged Jim some years before to get interested in the job of majority leader, because I didn't want to see certain others become majority leader. That's why I let myself get talked into running for it.

AID: *Where did Jim get his strength?*

SISK: He was not tied to the liberal wing, although he was a supporter of liberal programs. He had endorsed Lyndon Johnson and his whole liberal legislative program lock, stock, and barrel. Jim was known as a moderate—a middle-of-the-roader. He was a member of the UDC, the United Democrats of Congress. He had worked very closely with us. He had a lot of support from that intermediate group, those afraid Mo Udall was too liberal. The southerners thought of him as being certainly preferable to Udall or Phil Burton.

AID: *As you talk about the Congress, it seems to me as though the South has had a wealth of senators and representatives who were gifted in legislative tactics, oratory, and parliamentary procedures, more so than any other part of the country. If that is true, why?*

SISK: I think southerners take their politics more seriously than politicians in any other part of the country. They have a peculiar saying down South; they always talk about "the courthouse crowd." Everything arises around the courthouse crowd in the South. I won't attempt to prove this, but I have observed things that make this statement appear to be true. Phil Landrum of Georgia, who had been in Congress for about thirty years, is typical in length of service. Seniority is the usual case and has been for many years in the South.

The key people ("the courthouse crowd") decide, "We have Jerry Smith over here. Jerry is thirty-one years old, he is young and he has done a good job as district attorney." (You would be amazed at how many county attorneys are sent to Washington.) "Jerry is solid and has a great future. His father was so-and-so and his grandfather was so-and-so (probably a Confederate veteran)."

They talk to Jerry and he agrees to run. They get him nominated and he goes to Washington. For the first couple of years, they watch Jerry very closely. If Jerry proves to be solid and stays in line with their political philosophy and gets along up there, the decision is made to keep Jerry in Washington. On the other hand, if Jerry gets into the wrong group, in their opinion, and he votes far out on some matters, the courthouse crowd (in South Carolina in one particular case) will call him down there. The man I am thinking of had quite a set-to and blew his top and said, "Go to hell, I am going to do it my way or I'm not going to do it." So happens he was defeated in the next primary. They elected another Democrat. If he did all right, he is probably still there.

That's the way it's done. Surprisingly, they get some pretty good people. Maybe this is not the way to do it, but they pick people who have clean reputations, good courtroom style, or are adept orators who have won a few cases. Once they choose their candidate, they get behind him. They don't let anyone bother him much. They support his campaign financially. After a few years, he usually doesn't have any opposition on election day.

For the first time in years, however, southerners have been electing a few Republicans. In Florida, half the delegation is Republican. This new wrinkle is causing our southern friends some problems, so things aren't as smooth as they used to be. Under the old system, many of these people became great legislators. There is no question about it.

AID: *We haven't mentioned Estes Kefauver. You were for him back in 1956.*

SISK: Estes was one of those characters who comes along in the political life of a nation. He was a unique individual in a lot of ways. I was in his home two or three times and knew his wife, Nancy, quite well. He was the greatest hand-shaker I ever saw. I will never forget introducing him at the California Hotel back in the old days, when we had a big affair on the second floor in the ballroom area. That guy shook more hands than anybody who ever came down the pike, Estes in his coonskin cap. There were some who thought he was inclined to be a lady's man. I think he was honest. He was generally for the working people. What kind of president he would have made, I don't know.

Sisk hits the stump for vice-presidential candidate Estes Kefauver, far left, in 1956. Also on hand is Lionel Steinberg, second from left.

30.
Have a Nice Day

AID: *Please discuss a typical day for you in the House.*

SISK: I would get up in the morning around seven o'clock and go to the House to have breakfast with various groups by eight. Let's say in this case I'd have a delegation breakfast (which was every Wednesday morning). This breakfast would last about an hour and a half, then I'd run to the office because I'd have constituents waiting for me.

Hopefully, I wouldn't have any meetings for a half hour, so my secretary could bring me the most important mail; emergency-type mail is almost always waiting. I would give this mail immediate attention by making phone calls.

Then I would have a committee meeting at ten. Most legislative committees met at 9:45 or 10:00 A.M., but the Rules Committee never met until 10:30, which would give me an extra half hour. Nine times out of ten, I would also go to other meetings. It was impossible to make all the meetings. Priorities had to be set. The UDC board of directors, for example, would meet this morning. Maybe a group would be meeting about immigration and I had been deeply involved with someone from New York about the matter. But let's say I went to the Rules Committee meeting. Around 11:30 A.M. my secretary would call saying that John Smith (to use a name) had just come into the office and was very anxious to see me. I would tell her, "If he comes over to the Capitol, I will meet him downstairs at noon and bring him to the House dining room for lunch."

I would stay at Rules until noon and then rush down to get a table. (We always had a fight there because the restaurant is not nearly big enough.) I would visit with John as best I could. About fifteen or twenty minutes after I had sat down, the bell would ring for the first quorum call of the day. The House goes into session at noon, so about that time someone gets around to calling a quorum call. I would excuse myself and tell John I have to run upstairs and answer.

In the old days, I had to go there and wait until my name was called because the names of all 435 members were called twice. We switched to plastic cards and it took only fifteen minutes. I would run up and punch my card and then run down. I would return to John and get to know his problems while I was getting a bite to eat.

About one o'clock, two bells would sound for another rule. I would send John on his way, then go back upstairs and answer the call.

There may or may not be a Rules Committee meeting that afternoon. The Rules Committee had double sessions frequently. In contrast, most legislative committees meet only once in the morning unless there is something pressing. So I would run back and forth between committee

228

meetings. If there was a fight on the House floor, I would have to run there, too. The Rules Committee meets right above the House floor near the gallery. This is the only committee that has its official meeting room in the Capitol building, because it works with the leadership and is subject to call at any time within thirty minutes. The Rules Committee could meet at 2:00 A.M. There were committee meetings at all times of the day and night, particularly near the close of the session. If possible, I would get back to my office because I'd have some mail to take care of. It was important to keep up with what your constituents were saying. On a normal day on the floor, I got back to my office at 5:30 P.M. After I got done with the mail, I would get on the telephone. When it is 7:00 P.M. in Washington, it is 4:00 P.M. in California. Because of this, many people would want to talk to me when it was late in my day.

Let's say I had to get out of the office because I had promised to go to a VFW meeting and had a half dozen constituents there. I would have to go clear across the river to the old Wardman Park Hotel, now the Sheraton Park. After this dinner or reception, I would get home about ten o'clock. There were times I had half a dozen receptions on one night. I wouldn't go to all of them, but only the most important ones. When I did come by, I would shake hands and say, "Fellows, I am really glad to see you and am tickled to death, but can you come by tomorrow and see me at the office? I have to run because I have to attend a couple other receptions." So I would do the same thing at the other receptions. Then I would go home and eat dinner with Mom later that night, and thank God for the patience of a loyal wife.

That would not be an unusual day, but my days did vary.

AID: *Were weekends busy?*

SISK: They could be. I could have every weekend tied up, but I avoided it. As a freshman, you have to get acquainted since everybody wants to get to know you. Hence, you are invited all over. After a while, I said to my wife, "I am not going to be out more than two nights a week." I tried to limit breakfasts to two days a week. Otherwise, I would have gotten so worn out that I couldn't see straight. I just had to set limits. Unless I had to meet with a constituent or there was some compelling reason, I just did not go to dinners or parties on weekends. Sometimes we would go out to see friends. But weekends were the only time my wife and I had together.

I knew one fellow in Congress who wore himself out. Every weekend he would have meetings with constituents at the best nightclubs in town. He got into debt; a person can spend every dime of his salary. People don't understand the cost of entertaining at the best spots in Washington, D.C.

AID: *In what ways can a voter assess a congressman's performance? Would it be by examining the amount, type, and quality of the bills he authored or sponsored; his attendance; his voting record, and/or what else?*

SISK: There are many facets by which a congressman can be judged. Attendance is important because it shows the concern he has for the problems in his district in connection with the introduction of legislation. However, there is nothing more important than communication with his constituents: keeping them informed, answering letters and telephone calls, talking to them and making himself available. Failure here is one of the reasons new members don't get elected a second or third time. They don't keep open the lines of communication. How are you going to know what your people need or feel unless you talk to them?

We always answered our mail. It was very rare that we had a complaint about not answering a letter. I talked to people. I stressed to my staff that nothing was more important than communicating with the people we represented. Some people say you should never go home while Congress is in session. On the other hand, your constituents may think you have deserted them and that you are never there. But when you get home, some will say, "What are you doing at home? You are supposed to be in Washington." You can only try to do the right thing.

AID: *After there were jet airplanes, how often did you get back to the district?*

SISK: It wasn't unusual to make as many as three trips within one month, if important obligations existed or meetings were being held or an unusual event was going to occur. I tried to limit my trips to no more than once every three weeks—when possible, once a month. We spent about five days when we came, not just a weekend. The problems with weekends is that Saturday and Sunday are not the times to see people, generally.

AID: *Did you always fly commercial?*

SISK: Yes. I always flew United, from Dulles Airport to Denver, from Denver to Fresno, and then back to Washington via that route. However, if I had to be out here by a certain time, maybe I would come through San Francisco, arriving around noon, and then get the noon flight to Fresno. Or I would arrive at Los Angeles at three in the afternoon and get up here around four-thirty. Or I would leave Washington at night, around six, and get in here at 10:30 P.M. if I didn't have a night meeting. There were all kinds of ways. My secretary kept up with my schedule, making reservations for me.

AID: *Would you fly alone or would you be accompanied?*

SISK: I flew alone most of the time. My wife came with me if I was going to stay for an extended period of time. I had to pay her way because, naturally, there were no allowances made for families. Once in a great while, I would bring an aide with me, but normally I flew alone because I had people in my offices here, anyway. The people on my staff in Washington worked full-time there. When here, I wanted my administrative assistant in Washington to take care of things because somebody had to run the store.

31.
District Reapportionment

AID: *Following 1960 you had reapportionment and then another in 1970?*

SISK: In 1972 we had reapportionment. We had different districts three times in a row. They kept changing the lines; it was ridiculous.

AID: *How did your district change?*

SISK: Not substantially. The state Legislature couldn't agree and finally a temporary agreement was reached to do certain things, so we got through the 1972 election. In 1974, the Legislature still couldn't agree. The governor couldn't agree. Finally, for the third round, both sides selected a masters court, composed of three judges. In my opinion, it just drew lines on the map. This was the first time Fresno was separated. The entire county of Fresno had always been the principal part of this district. For the first time I wound up with Stanislaus County. I got 85 percent of the people up and down Highway 99. The court took at least two-thirds of the city of Fresno away from me. The only part left was that area west of the Santa Fe tracks and south of Shields Avenue out to about Chestnut, down Chestnut and back on Kings Canyon Road toward the west side of Fresno County. The eastern half of the county went to the other district.

John Krebs ran in 1974 against Bob Mathias and this reapportionment cost Mathias his seat because 200,000 new people came into the district and totally changed its complexion. Krebs had Fresno. He had represented it as a county supervisor. He served two terms and was defeated in 1978.

AID: *Was there a change in the complexion of your campaigning afterwards?*

SISK: No. We just did the same things in the new parts of the district that we had done in the old parts. I spent time and effort there, visiting with the people and meeting with city councils and school boards, educators, labor groups, and so forth. We had no serious problem as a result of reapportionment. I carried fairly substantially the northern part of the district, even though I was new up there.

The problem came in service to the district. After years of having my office in the federal building in the center of Fresno County, we faced this difficulty: when we received a letter with a Shields Avenue address, the first thing we had to find out was what side of Shields the writer lived on. The same was true if he lived on McKinley, Cedar, or Chestnut. For the first time, all Fresno people couldn't look on me as their congressman.

People would be resentful. I would tell them, "I will try to be of any help I can, but under congressional courtesy, I am required to turn your letter over to Mr. Krebs." I told them I would give Krebs any assistance I could, but it created a lot of problems.

231

32.
The Tony Coelho Story

AID: *We have talked only in passing about Tony Coelho. What about the Tony Coelho story?*

SISK: I didn't know Tony's family although he was born in Dos Palos, in my district, on a dairy farm there. His father was Otto Coelho, whom I had

Tony Coelho, Bernie Sisk's successor and long time staff aide.

not known; but I knew his uncle, Joe Branco, who was the head of the Western Dairymen's Association and well-known around the state. He was the lobbyist in Sacramento for Western Dairymen's. He has a dairy farm between Dos Palos and Los Banos. He is Portuguese; there are a lot of Portuguese dairymen in that area. Branco was a supporter of mine, as was the Western Dairymen's Association. About 1964, I ran into Joe one day, and he asked if I had any spots for young fellows who might be interested in politics. I said that I was interested in internship programs. I was one of the first members of Congress to have an intern program. I had started it in the late 1950s and was one of the first to support a measure paying interns enough to keep body and soul together, then about a thousand dollars a year. I believe in helping young people find out what government is about.

AID: *There is a political science organization which has about fifteen clerkships a year. It selects a member of the House or Senate, which gives them 535 choices. You were selected five times, a very high percentage, so you had these young political scientists working on your staff.*

SISK: Oh, yes. Universities and colleges have gotten interested in this, including the Stanford Political Science Association. The University of California will have around two hundred and fifty interns in Washington. We work with George Washington University, Georgetown University, and so on. I required that interns have two years of college before doing summer internships with me. It's a good program.

Getting back to Coelho, that was the sort of thing I had in mind when Joe talked to me. He said he had a nephew who was at loose ends, finishing up at Loyola University in Los Angeles. He was a political science major. I said I would be glad to talk to him.

My wife and I were going to Los Angeles on Valentine's Day. Carmen Warschaw had been state chairman of the California Democratic Council. She was a member of the Harvey Aluminum family, the daughter of Harvey, the owner of the Los Angeles-based company. She sponsored the Valentine's Day party in 1965 at the Ambassador Hotel in Los Angeles which our delegation was attending.

I called Joe Branco and asked him if he could arrange for Tony to come to the hotel. Tony came down and I introduced myself to this lonesome-looking young fellow who seemed a little out of place. After talking to him, I found out he had an excellent record at the university. He had been student body president during his senior year. I was impressed with his possibilities, so I told him that if he wanted to give it a shot, I would put him on what I called a ninety-day probation which paid a nominal amount to start. I told him that I would see him the first of April in Washington.

Tony had an old Chevrolet jalopy that he drove across the country. He started to work for me in April 1965. I turned him over to Jackson Carle, my administrative assistant, to outline the things Jackson wanted him to do. Jackson gave Tony the right kind of leadership, and Tony proved to have an excellent mind. He was about twenty-two or twenty-three and had graduated the previous June from Loyola University. Bob Hope was interested in Loyola University and was a friend of one of the bishops at the school. Hope wanted a companion for his children and one of the fathers recommended Tony, who lived with the Hope family following his graduation in June until about March of the following year.

Tony showed early on a great deal of maturity in handling problems. The first thing you notice is how mature a young intern is. When you assign a job, does he or she run back every minute and ask you questions? Tony did an excellent job and at the end of the ninety days, we were happy to consider him a permanent employee and increase his pay. He soon met Phyllis Butler, who later became his wife. She was working for a member from Indiana and was a native of Indiana herself. I announced their engagement at a party at my house, not aware she didn't know it was going to be announced—in fact, she hadn't understood they were engaged. I kind of ribbed Tony a little about that, but it worked out all right. Phyllis is a very lovely person whom my wife practically adopted. Their youngsters call us "grandma" and "grandpa," so it's almost like a family.

When Jackson retired around 1968, he had been with me for thirteen years. There was a local fellow we used in our campaigns with whom we were very much impressed: Bob Garrett of Merced. I brought Bob back to take over for Jackson.

Garrett is now head of the Las Vegas office of the Small Business Adminstration. The work in Washington was foreign to him; he had worked for a savings and loan company, and the D.C. job never quite worked out. This was no reflection on Bob, who is an able, sincere, and dedicated young man, but it was not his cup of tea. I arranged for him to go to work for the SBA. I then brought Gordon Nelson to take over when Garrett left.

Oakley Hunter, my first opponent, had become my friend. Richard Nixon and Hunter had served together in Congress and were friends. Nixon, as president, appointed Oakley to head Fanny Mae (Federal National Mortgage Association). Fanny Mae was then an agency of the federal government, although it had a lot of private money in it. Oakley had done a great job, in my opinion, for Fanny Mae.

Oakley wanted a good public relations man and he called me one day and said, "I want to hire one of your people, but want to tell you beforehand because people will say that I have stolen your help. Anyway, I have known Gordon Nelson for a long time." Gordon had been a political reporter with the McClatchy newspapers during the time that I first ran. Despite the fact Nelson was a staunch Democrat, Oakley realized his qualifications. I told Oakley I wouldn't stand in the way of a man who was trying to improve his lot and that I was only allowed to pay my A.A. so much. I thought the job Oakley had for Gordon would be challenging. After Gordon discussed it with me, he went with Oakley and became vice-president in charge of public relations for Fanny Mae at a considerably higher salary.

At that point I had to make a decision. I looked at various people— people with the McClatchy newspapers and others who had some background. But then I thought about Tony, who had been with me for about four or five years. In consultation with Jackson, although he was in California, and with Gordon and others, it was decided Tony would be my new A.A., the youngest on the hill.

Tony did an outstanding job as my administrative assistant throughout the years. He was not a "yes man," but I didn't want a yes man. On the other hand, I wanted him to understand that in the final analysis, I made the decision because I had to live with it, for good or ill. We got along superbly. He was so good that he was offered other positions. I was aware of this. The Del Monte Corporation of San Francisco tried to hire him. The Brown Administration had a spot for him; in fact, there was some discussion of his becoming director of agriculture for California.

As these things developed, I told Tony I didn't want to tell him what to do because these were decisions only he could make. "But," I said, "one of these days I am going to retire. I don't know just when, but I am not going to stay here forever—whether they take me out or I take myself out." I told him he was doing an outstanding job. I felt he understood Washington and the legislative process. Anyway, I made it known to him there might be a spot open if he wanted to seek elective office when I retired. At first, he was a little wary and had some reservations. But as time went on, he indicated interest in it.

Before I retired, I had given him the opportunity to come out to California and get acquainted. Originally, he didn't know many people out here; during his early years on the job, he spent his time in Washington. But in the last few years, I had him spend some time out here each fall. As a result, he gained much support and many friends. I think it worked out very well. However, some people probably accused me of trying to pick my successor, which I have no right to do. Yet in my own mind I felt he would do a better job than someone who had never been in Washington.

AID: *Well, the connection didn't hurt. Tony told me there were twenty-four administrative assistants who ran for office in 1978, but he was the only one elected.*

SISK: Normally, administrative assistants have not been very successful in getting elected. Had Tony stayed in Washington and not had exposure in the district, I think he would have had some problems.

AID: *Wasn't there some lobbying to get him selected U.S. assistant secretary of agriculture?*

SISK: I wasn't all that intrigued because my wife and I had decided the 1977-78 term was going to be my last. I supported Tony; it wasn't just lip service. I went all-out because I thought it could cut two ways. If Tony were appointed, it wouldn't necessarily foreclose his option to run because it would indicate a considerable amount of confidence in him by the administration. What happened was that he got clipped on this. However, I told him all along not to feel too bad because it would all work out for the best anyway.

AID: *Did a woman consumer advocate get the job?*

SISK: Yes. The sister of a congressman from Arkansas got that spot with the Department of Agriculture.

AID: *I thought there was a tradition that the assistant secretary of agriculture should be from California.*

SISK: This is the first time we haven't had more recognition. At one time there were three or four top-level people from California in the department. In my opinion, the Carter Administration has not done any favors for California.

33.
Case Work

AID: *You said one of the distinguishing characteristics of a successful congressman is keeping open the communication lines with the district. The pluralities with which you won each election indicated your lines were open. I have talked to a number of people in your various California offices. According to Mrs. Cornelius, who estimated off the top of her head, there were probably 10,000 people each year who were beneficiaries of your offices' case work. Some cases might have involved only one phone call, others might have taken years to work out. Do you think this is a fair figure?*

SISK: It sounds a little high. However, it isn't unusual to get a thousand letters a week, which means 52,000 letters a year. Twenty percent of them would represent a case, either a single contact or several contacts over a period of time. The figure sounds reasonable, if a little high. However, you are dealing with an enormous number of people and their problems. I don't think the public realizes the enormity of the task of communication, the letters that go back and forth, the telephone calls, and particularly the cost involved when you are as distant as Washington is from California. That is why we wound up with three offices in the district. We wanted to handle as much of this locally as was humanly possible.

AID: *The office staff has given me some typical cases. I thought we might put them on the record to give the readers of your memoir examples of various types of case work. Some of them you may remember. There was an American man who had married a European woman and wanted to bring her back to this country. They ran afoul of the moral turpitude law.*

SISK: I remember this well because, as I have so often said, the greatest gratification as a member of Congress is being able to help an individual who may feel totally helpless in a bureaucratic world. This is one such case. A man fell in love with a woman overseas who, because of the circumstances of the war and the difficulties of keeping body and soul together, apparently found herself in the wrong place at the wrong time. At one time a charge of moral turpitude had been made against her. If I could elaborate on this, it could be well understood what happened. The problem was, under section 212A of the immigration laws, a person found guilty of moral turpitude could not enter this country. Because of my knowledge of the case and the individuals involved, I drew up a private bill.

I remember the hearing before the Judiciary subcommittee. Tad Walters of Pennsylvania was chairman of the Immigration Subcommittee. After I gave my testimony, Walters leaned back in his chair and said, "Congressman, we have a long-standing rule around here. If, in your opinion, she is good enough for him, then she is good enough for us. Therefore, we are going to approve your bill." It went to the House and was passed. I got my friends in the Senate to carry the ball and it was signed into law by the president. The lady came to this country. The beatings you take as a member of Congress, the criticism, etc., all receded when the man brought his wife into my office. Although she could not speak a word of English at the time, her eyes were so expressive, showing her appreciation, that I will never forget the visit in all my life. It was all the satisfaction I needed.

AID: *There are more examples of case work. There was an instance in which an American couple had a daughter in Spain, who was involved in an accident and was dying. The parents had to get there in a hurry and they didn't have passports. You helped them get immediate passports.*

SISK: There were a number of cases where emergency situations had arisen. The normal bureaucratic process takes time, so we found it necessary to cut through the red tape and get to the top of the Immigration and Naturalization Service. The Department of State was generally helpful. In matters of hours, we had people on their way. I am not sure we deserve a lot of credit. It is simply a matter, as a member of Congress, of being willing to contact the right people and get all the pieces together. There is always someone who can do what you want. You just have to take enough time to pursue the matter to find out who it is.

AID: *A woman was living with a veteran and she couldn't prove she was married. He died. The question came up about her widow's pension. Do you recall this case?*

SISK: The question was whether this was a common law marriage or whether there had, in fact, been a marriage consummated under law. What we did in that case was actually draft legislation that not only affected this couple, but probably hundreds of other couples, for the benefit of women who were left in that type of situation. I well remember that case. The legislation stipulated that if cohabitation had existed for five years or more that would be, in essence, prima-facie evidence that the marriage had in fact existed.

AID: *This next case involved a refund from the IRS. It concerns two unrelated persons with exactly the same name, born two days apart in the state of Illinois. The name of each father was John; the name of each mother was Dorothy. A refund check was mailed to the wrong person. You got that refund out of the IRS.*

SISK: I remember that vaguely. It was a confused mess. We had to prove that two people with such similarities actually did exist. I recall that we finally did get the matter straightened out. Boy, I hadn't thought of that one for a long time.

AID: *Here is an unusual one. In 1962, a serviceman got meningitis. As a result of that illness, he became schizophrenic. The VA said that he was 50 percent to 75 percent disabled. Whenever he got a job, he became schizophrenic and went off the deep end. You got the VA to increase his disability pension to 100 percent. In addition, as a complication, he had also earned disability from previous employment with the post office, but had failed to apply for benefits in time because he was schizophrenic. The post office terminated him instead of putting him on disability.*

Bernie and Reta at the wedding of Alenne Pittenger, their first grandchild, August 1976.

Reta and Bernie on their fortieth anniversary, 1971.

SISK: I remember that case. I know that he got his 100 percent disability. He also got retroactive pay from the post office.

AID: *Your office worked on this next case for six years.*

SISK: The files of some of those cases are five inches thick.

AID: *A woman is in the Philippines. She, her husband and her children were incarcerated by the Japanese in 1941. Her husband died almost immediately. She was released in 1945. She filed her claim. The authorities said, "Well, too bad, there is a statute of limitations; you should have filed the claim right away." She said, "I couldn't file the claim because I was incarcerated." She was told there was legislation passed for just such cases. It turned out her husband died thirteen days before that legislation went into effect. You introduced a bill which qualified her. It passed in 1975. President Ford sent her a pin and you presented her a check in your office.*

SISK: That's right. It was a case where she was caught in a peculiar set of circumstances where she was narrowly out of luck. That is what private bills are all about, that's why they are important. Injustices happen as a result of cut-off dates, limitations, and so on. Part of the job of a congressman and his staff is to try to correct these injustices.

AID: *Congressmen may be the only ones equipped to deal with these problems.*

SISK: You almost have to be a member of Congress. Senators deal with so many people that cases can get lost there. I know I have had people write to me critical of a senator's office. A California senator is dealing with twenty-two million people, where I have only 500,000 to deal with. That is a big difference.

AID: *A Mexican woman wanted to establish derivative citizenship because her father was born in the United States, but she needed proof. You found Social Security records and Selective Service records and proved the derivative relationship to the immigration service. She was able to establish citizenship.*

SISK: I don't remember the details of that case, but it was similar to a number of situations which dealt with people who were having problems establishing their identity. The women in the local offices here and Gwen Luty in our Washington office bird-dogged hundreds of similar cases. Many dealt with this question of getting identity established for a given individual in order to prove the right of citizenship. Citizenship, of course, becomes very precious to the individual who is being horn-swaggled out of it because of the difficulties of the situation.

AID: *Here is another related one. There was a naturalized American citizen who had married an American girl. He had not been in this country five years when he was drafted.*

SISK: He went to England.

AID: *Their baby was born there. He found out that the child could enter the U.S. as the child of a citizen, but would have to be naturalized to become a citizen.*

239

SISK: We introduced legislation to correct the situation. The law provided that unless a naturalized citizen resided for five years in the U.S., his child born abroad was not a citizen. In this case, he was abroad under U.S. military orders. The law was changed to cover similar situations.

AID: *The final case I have is another interesting one. An American male went to Mexico on a cattle operation. While he was there, he adopted two Mexican boys, one of them under fourteen at the time of adoption and the other over fourteen. He left Mexico and returned home. He found out that, under our law, an adopted child over age fourteen is not an American citizen. He couldn't get him into the United States. You introduced a bill allowing him to get his own child in. Later on, when the boy reached twenty-one, he could apply for citizenship on his own.*

SISK: We permitted him to enter as an admissible alien, subject to his being able to obtain citizenship when he comes of age. Those are sample cases in my twenty-four years as congressman.

AID: *There are nearly 250,000 lives your office has touched.*

SISK: There are problems in getting some of these private bills through. The first thing the chairman of the Immigration Subcommittee asks you is, "I am sympathetic to the cause of your constituent who is caught in this trap, but what about the precedent we're setting here?" You hear that time after time. It drives you right up the wall. You say, "Yes, Mr. Chairman, it may set a precedent, but isn't it, in fact, justice and if other people fall into these kinds of situations, wouldn't it be justice if they received the kind of relief we are requesting here?" You fought the precedents they threw at you every foot of the way.

AID: *Isn't that like the typical bureaucrat? There may be some other things you want to say about your Washington and local offices. I suppose that many of your letters were written by others.*

SISK: A great deal of your correspondence is done by your staff. I have done a lot of dictating of letters, don't misunderstand me. I had an outstanding personal secretary in the person of Liz Guinn, to whom I dictated letters almost daily. She handled most of my private matters—my personal mail, for example. A great deal of your work becomes routine, so the secretary does an enormous amount of work on her own. After a time, she becomes an expert on what you are going to say or do. But in the final analysis, you sign and approve all of it. Tony wrote a lot of letters. Gwen Luty did too, in connection with her work with the military, veterans, and immigration cases. The local offices did a certain amount of their own mail. In many cases, we would authorize signatures because there were times it was literally impossible to sign personally all the letters.

I had three district offices: Modesto, Fresno, and Merced. Of course, I also had my office in Washington. I couldn't be in four places at one time. Yet the mail had to go. We once had a policy that every incoming letter had to be acknowledged in twenty-four hours. The problem didn't

Several congressional members of the Church of Christ gather outside of a Washington church. Joining Sisk are Reps. Joe Evans, right, and Omar Burleson, second from right. The minister to right of Sisk is unidentified.

necessarily have to be solved, but the letter at least had to be acknowledged. We finally extended it to forty-eight hours. There may have been a few times when we slipped on that. Those acknowledgements went out whether I was there or not. We had a dozen people on my staff who could write a decent letter; if they couldn't, they probably wouldn't have been on the staff in the first place.

Among the problems with which my staff had to deal were those of veterans. In all fairness to the veteran, he had butted his head against a brick wall to the point of becoming almost psychotic over the issue. You would be amazed at the number of veterans I contacted through the years, both by telephone and in person, who actually came to the conclusion that the world was against them. It became an obsession.

One of the things that occurred during the years was an occasional threat upon my life. Some person would call up and say, "I am coming down to Washington to shoot you." For the most part, these threats came from veterans. Lord knows I was concerned and felt sorry for them. Many were old-line veterans who needed help and maybe had not gotten it in the way they should have. If they came to the conclusion their congressman had not done what he should have, you're the one, you are the guy who is threatened.

Once, as I was getting off an airplane here, I was met by two or three agents from the F.B.I. They said, "Congressman, there apparently have been threats made against you."

Apparently, the reports had been turned in by my office while I was in the air. The F.B.I. agents decided to transfer me from my house and put me in a hotel room because it could be more easily guarded. Over the years you had threats of one kind or another. Some of them are crazy kinds of things, but some of them may be real. Of course, you never know. This is one of the conditions you go through.

34.
Retirement

AID: *Now we come to the present. What were the factors contributing to your decision to retire?*

SISK: I had always felt—and publicly stated—a concern about limiting the service of members. There have been all kinds of proposals—past and current—which would limit the service of a member of Congress, to say, three, four, or five terms, or ten years. I said I would never support such a proposal because, to some extent, it would violate the right of the people to select their representatives and make their own decisions. However, I could produce examples of why I came to the conclusion there should be an age limitation.

I well understand that chronological age doesn't mean very much. I have seen persons senile at sixty and sharp and alert at ninety. Yet on the other hand, we have numerous precedents for retirement at seventy in federal service. Therefore, in order to resolve some of the attacks on Congress, I would support a constitutional amendment to require retirement at the age of seventy. After passing the age of seventy, you could not seek re-election; in other words, it would be mandatory retirement. I'm not hung up on that, but I believe it is an alternative to some other proposals I thought were much inferior.

AID: *You would have had one more term before you were . . .*

SISK: I could have done that. Because I was barely sixty-seven, I could have had one more term. But I did not want to stay until I reached a point where I could not make a good decision.

After I had become a senior member of Congress and was well established, I made up my mind that twenty years was plenty. Twenty years is about all any man should serve in this kind of situation. That became my target. I didn't publicize it or even discuss it with my family—but in my own mind I said twenty years is going to be enough. (Twenty years would have been in 1974.)

Well, that was about the time I got tangled up in the fight for the leadership in the run for majority leader and caucus chairman. The situation started looking pretty favorable. I stayed on for another term because of it. During that term I developed an abdominal aneurism, requiring surgery. Well, I guess I had to prove to myself that I was as capable as before, so I served one term after that.

Above: Old friends reminisce about Sisk's career during his 1978 retirement dinner in Fresno. From left, Barbara Milhan, Sisk's first secretary; Phyllis Coelho, wife of Tony Coelho, Sisk's successor, back to camera; and Jackson Carle, Bernie's longtime administrative assistant and campaign advisor. Right: Bernie and Reta are greeted by Judge Kenneth Andreen and his wife at Sisk's 1978 retirement festivities.

Below: The announcement of Sisk's retirement prompted other testimonials. Here, Water Foundation chairman Jerry Cappello, left, and president Pamela Naylor greet Bernie at a September 1978 dinner in his honor. Former Westlands Water District manager Ralph Brody, far right, emceed the affair, which highlighted Sisk's role in developing federal water projects in the Central Valley.

AID: *I think you once said you felt better after that than you had before.*

SISK: That's true.

AID: *Were there any symptoms from your abdominal aneurism?*

SISK: Not that I was aware of.

AID: *Who found it?*

SISK: It was found through my annual check-up. Every year we received complete check-ups with X-rays and the whole works. That's why I'm a strong advocate of an annual physical.

AID: *X-rays of your whole body?*

SISK: Yes. They did an abdominal X-ray.

AID: *Routinely?*

SISK: Routinely. Unbeknownst to me, doctors had noticed, some years earlier, a slight enlargement of the main artery that comes out of the heart. Afterwards I got a call from the doctor, who said, "We have some news and it may not be good news, and then again it might help." The news was quite a shock, but they ran a lot more tests before making a decision.

They checked me into the naval hospital and used me as a guinea pig, as I have always said, on one of the first ultra-sonic machines. The naval hospital only had it a couple of months when I got there. It's gauged on the metric system and you lie there and look into a television screen. It's much more revealing than an X-ray machine. Of course, they are in almost all hospitals now. In fact, there's something else now—what do they call it?

AID: *A CAT scanner?*

SISK: That's it. A CAT scanner is an improvement.

After the surgery, I stayed in Washington to prove something to myself. Anyway, I thought that twenty-four years was plenty. After I ran for the twelfth term, I talked to my wife and told her what I had in mind. We discussed it, we agreed, and we kept it to ourselves for the first year. I announced my retirement late in the first session, in late January, I think.

AID: *What were the highlights of your House retirement party?*

SISK: Well, I had several retirement parties. I had one here in Fresno, which was really a lovely affair. A big turn-out; a lot of people were there. In fact, we have a big book containing communications from the president and members of the Senate and the House, and others. You do appreciate those kinds of things, no question about it.

Some people gave us a party at one of the country clubs in Washington and Bowie Kuhn, the baseball commissioner, served as the master of ceremonies. A lot of my old friends were there. George Mahon of Texas, the senior member of the House of Representatives, retiring at the same time I was; Bob Poage of Texas, who was also retiring; Mel Price from Illinois; and a lot of the old-time members and new members and friends and staff were there. It was a lovely party. We didn't know it at the time, but some months later we received a gift certificate from a local nursery in Fresno for several hundred dollars worth of garden products.

Above: Members of the Rules Committee and committee staff gather in 1978 to bid farewell to the retirees among them.

Right: Retiring members of the Rules Committee gather during the 1978 farewell party. From left, Rep. John Young, Texas; Rep. Del Clawson, California; Chairman James Delaney, New York; and Sisk.

AID: *Had you expected or wanted then to be appointed by the president to an immigration committee?*

SISK: Well, yes and no. Over the years I had been involved in immigration problems and policy and particularly the situation we're faced with here in the Southwest, because of the influx of illegal aliens. I had been critical of some of our policies and had been very strong in my contention that we need to do something to correct the situation, that we need more facts and information. I had also been interested in and concerned with population control. I had been asked to go on a committee, but refused because I had decided to retire from Congress and already had more work I was prepared to do.

I was invited to go to Singapore and visit the Far East to explore what those countries are doing to control population.

245

Meanwhile, the Judiciary Committee had passed a bill to set up a commission to study and report on the problem after a period of two years. A member of my staff, Gwen Luty, was very close to a lot of people involved and one day she said, "Mr. Sisk, I have a gentleman who would like to see you." Well, he was the head of a national organization very much concerned with getting that bill authorized and getting the commission set up; he came in to encourage me to accept the chairmanship of the commission. He was sold on the idea that my background was appropriate for this, but I had announced my retirement by that time.

It was to be a sixteen-member commission, appointed by the president, representing various departments of government and with various members of Congress on it. After considerable thought, I agreed to consider it. I would liked to have been considered, although I am not sure that had it been offered, I would have accepted. Maybe I should say I would have liked to have had an opportunity to turn it down. My questioning of it was based on the fear it represented far more work than I wanted.

Headquarters were to be in Washington and that would have required my commuting to Washington at least once a month. We were to hold hearings in various places along the border, and I would have spent a week of every month in Washington. I know the president was approached on this; my name was pushed by several groups including more than 200 members of Congress who wrote letters or signed a petition asking for my appointment. I saw the list of names. The Speaker himself, toward the end of the last session, stopped me and said the president had assured him that if I wanted to be chairman of that commission, it would be given to me.

I never discussed the matter with the president or personally asked for that spot. Frankly, I was having my problems with the Carter Administration and with some of its staff, and although I never had any personal run-in with the president, all I know is that I was not appointed. I never heard why that was the case. The truth of the matter is that it would have been too time-consuming for me to have accepted.

AID: *What are your retirement activities and hopes?*

SISK: I have enjoyed my work in Washington. I enjoyed the challenge and the friendships with my colleagues and with people whom I respected. I never caught what is called "Potomac fever." My wife and I were always ready to come to California the minute our work was completed. Here were our home, our children, our friends, our clubs, our churches, and so on. There have been no regrets. I am very happy with my retirement. My wife sometimes kids me a bit: "I don't know why you left Congress—at least you were being paid for your time there. You are busier now than you were then."

I say, "Well, I am enjoying it more."

We do keep busy. I have a breakfast meeting at seven o'clock

At Evolution Basin, 1974.

Fishing in the high country, 1974.

Around a campfire, 1974.

Wednesday morning in connection with my sports committee. We have a monthly meeting of the full board of directors of the sports committee. I am a member of the board of trustees of the [Fresno] Agricultural Museum which we are trying to set up. I am still active in the Kiwanis Club. My wife and I attend church when we can. Unfortunately, my wife's health hasn't been as good as we would have liked, but we hope it is going to get better. I have acquired some property on the coast. We are trying to get plans drawn now so we can build a home on the coast for possible use during hot weather and times of fog in the valley. But Fresno will continue to be our home. I enjoy my home here very much. I enjoy the associations and friendships.

In conclusion, my wife and I came home to retire. I, like many members of Congress, put part of my salary into a retirement fund. We are drawing a reasonably decent retirement income. This is our only income except for some small savings accounts here and there.

I made up my mind that I was not going to become a lobbyist in Washington and wasn't going to go back to twist the arms of my colleagues. That wasn't what I wanted to do. I am not critical of members who have done so, however, because it is their right.

AID: *As a former member of Congress, you can always get on the House floor, can you not?*

SISK: Once a member of Congress, you are always welcome to get on the floor. This is a lifetime right, but I don't want to take advantage of that.

AID: *Because it makes it easy to lobby?*

SISK: Yes, if you want to. On the other hand, I didn't resign from the human race and I didn't resign as a citizen or anything like that. I still participate in a committee dealing with Kings River water problems and try to be of help wherever I can. From time to time, I consult with some of our people on the west side about water problems. I had a call this morning from a member of the Westlands Water District board. I am still interested and

Sisk presides over a different sort of panel—the Greater San Joaquin Valley Sports Association, an organization assembled to establish the Harvest Bowl, a gridiron match between the top teams of the Pacific Coast Athletic Association and the Mid-American Conference.

Courtesy Fresno Bee

concerned, but I am on nobody's payroll at the present time. I may get some modified type of employment, but I don't necessarily see a need for it at the present time and do not anticipate it. As I have said, we came home to retire and to enjoy some of the fruits of life, of which there are many in California.

Unfortunately, there are many sacrifices you make as a member of Congress. You pay a price for it. The family pays a bigger price for it than you do. This is because the family often doesn't have your presence. Your kids grow up hardly knowing who their dad is. Suddenly I find my grandchildren are all grown. I have one grandchild who is a senior in high school and is still near, but all the rest are in college or married. That's what happens to you overnight. I don't know where the last twenty-five years went. But there have been a lot of satisfying moments. And there have been the trying moments. There were times when I felt we faced unjust criticism, but that is part of the price you pay as a public servant.

INDEX

251